http://www.wadsworth.com

wadsworth.com is the World Wide Web site for Wadsworth and is your direct source to dozens of online resources.

At *wadsworth.com* you can find out about supplements, demonstration software, and student resources. You can also send email to many of our authors and preview new publications and exciting new technologies.

wadsworth.com
Changing the way the world learns®

Watersheds 2
Ten Cases in Environmental Ethics

LISA H. NEWTON
Fairfield University

CATHERINE K. DILLINGHAM
Fairfield University

Wadsworth Publishing Company
I(T)P® An International Thomson Publishing Company

Belmont, CA • Albany, NY • Bonn • Boston • Cincinnati • Detroit
Johannesburg • London • Madrid • Melbourne • Mexico City • New York
Paris • San Francisco • Singapore • Tokyo • Toronto • Washington

Philosophy Editor: Peter Adams
Assistant Editor: Clay Glad
Editorial Assistant: Greg Brueck
Production: Greg Hubit Bookworks
Cover Illustration: Art Resource, NY.
  Louis Comfort Tiffany, landscape,
  stained glass window. Private collection.

Copyeditor: Molly Roth
Print Buyer: Barbara Britton
Permissions Editor: Robert Kauser
Interior Designer: Kaelin Chappell
Cover Designer: Rob Hugel
Compositor: Brandon Carson
Printer: Edwards Bros.

For more information, contact Wadsworth Publishing Company, 10 Davis Drive,
Belmont, CA 94002, or electronically at http://www.wadsworth.com

International Thomson Publishing Europe
Berkshire House 168-173
High Holborn
London, WC1V7AA, England

International Thomson Editores
Campos Eliseos 385, Piso 7
Col. Polanco
11560 México D.F. México

Thomas Nelson Australia
102 Dodds Street
South Melbourne 3205
Victoria, Australia

International Thomson Publishing Asia
221 Henderson Road
#05-10 Henderson Building
Singapore 0315

Nelson Canada
1120 Birchmount Road
Scarborough, Ontario
Canada M1K 5G4

International Thomson Publishing Japan
Hirakawacho Kyowa Building, 3F
2-2-1 Hirakawacho
Chiyoda-ku, Tokyo 102, Japan

International Thomson Publishing GmbH
Königswinterer Strasse 418
53227 Bonn, Germany

International Thomson Publishing
Southern Africa
Building 18, Constantia Park
240 Old Pretoria Road
Halfway House, 1685 South Africa

Library of Congress Cataloging-in-Publication Data

Newton, Lisa H.,
    Watersheds 2: Ten cases in environmental ethics / Lisa Newton, Catherine Dillingham.
      p.   cm.
    Includes bibliographical references.
    ISBN 0-534-51181-3
      1. Environmental ethics.   2. Environmental ethics—Case studies.
    I. Dillingham, Catherine.   II. Title
    GE42.N48   1997
    179' .1—dc20

To the land,
and to our grandchildren's future

Contents

Preface

The reason for this textbook is to bring together the scattered material of classic cases of environmental ethics—the "defining moments" when human enterprise confronts its environmental consequences. In these moments, we can focus the student's wandering attention on the real problems of environmental complexity—the biological, economic, and legal issues underscored with the damage irrevocably done to real people and the land they depend upon.

A case is just a story. We deal with theories in our classrooms, but we anchor our theories in stories, for if a theory cannot find illustration in the things that actually happen to us, the theory is bound for the dustheap. Stories are easy to remember, fun to talk about, and form the foundation of insight. With these classic stories, familiar to all, that insight is generalizable and good for the foreseeable future. Assembling them for practical use each semester has made our work as instructors considerably easier for us. We trust it will do the same for you.

We would like to thank our editor, Peter Adams, for his patience and helpful suggestions in the course of the preparation of this manuscript. We would also like to thank the reviewers for Wadsworth Publishing Company—John Ahrens, Hanover College; Susan J. Armstrong, Humboldt State University; Timothy Fahey, Cornell University; Ned Hettinger, College of Charleston; Frederik Kaufman, Ithaca College; Donald Lee, University of New Mexico; Peter List, Oregon State University; Thomas Moody, California State University, San Bernadino; Louis P. Pojman, United States Military Academy at West Point; Steven Stoll, Yale University; and Wanda Teays, Mount Saint Mary's College—who gave us encouragement and constructive criticism on the chapters as they emerged. Above all, we gratefully acknowledge the help and support of our families (especially Victor Newton and Bruce Dillingham); without their forbearance and support, the completion of this project would not have been possible.

Lisa Newton
Catherine Dillingham

THE NATURE OF
THE PROBLEM

The natural world seems to be deteriorating around us, and it seems to be our fault. We are uncertain about the extent of the deterioration, the means of reversing it, and the prospects for human life in the future if those means are undertaken. We are not sure that we have the political will to pay what this would cost, and we strongly suspect that the costs may be unthinkably high.

These have been dark days for environmental consciousness and conscience. Although the nation has never been more heavily bombarded with alarming accounts of "environmental crisis" and "disaster," although we have a Vice President of the United States who has written an excellent book (that is in itself worthy of note) on the relation between civilization and the natural environment, our nation's environmental protections have steadily eroded over the years since the first *Watersheds* came out.

All the attention directed to the environment since Earth Day 1970 has provoked its own backlash. The very passion that newly converted environmentalists—or just alarmed citizens—bring to the discussion of environmental policy can work against effective action, by antagonizing quieter sorts of citizens and by encouraging cynicism when the worst predictions do not immediately come true. Attempts to produce good scientific proofs of the state of the environment, that will make sense to the public, run into the perpetual dilemma of popular science: When the projections are accurate and responsible, they tend to be misunderstood and distorted by press and politics; when they are simplified for a mass audience, they tend not to be strictly true and often cause alarm. That alarm itself is new: It is a type of formless apprehension that could define the century to come. We are frightened, and we do not know how frightened we should be; this is not the best condition in which to formulate policy. In a typical reaction, a terrifyingly irresponsible legislative agenda, the "Contract with America," vowed to end all protection of the natural environment in the name of individual freedom and the end of big government.

In such times, the first assignment for any work on the environment is to clarify questions, sort out fact from judgment and opinion, analyze terrors into workable tasks, and focus emotion through the lens of logic into practical policy. Since the time of Socrates, that happens to be the traditional assignment of the discipline of philosophy. The question that lies before the people, not just of the United States but of the world, concerns the search for moral imperatives: What is to be done? What are our duties in this new and confusing age—to ourselves, to our children, to other nations, to all living things, to the planet? What policies should we adopt to promote the greatest happiness of the greatest number of people in the long run? Must that happiness be balanced against the welfare of the biosphere? May we give the happiness of our own countrymen some special weight in the calculation? What type of humans will we have to be to carry these new imperatives into practice? While we work to change the relationship between our own very recently evolved civilization and a natural world that has been evolving over eons of time, how will we need to change our accounts of human virtue, aspiration, and self-realization?

These are the classic questions of ethics. The crises of the environment, the headline catastrophes, and the legislative challenges have posed new ethical questions, and those questions have spawned a new literature, indeed a whole new academic discipline. Although the first effect of any environmental catastrophe, accomplished or impending, is to throw all policy and prudence into question, the second effect is to throw all philosophy into question. Let us discuss these effects one at a time.

First, disaster demands reevaluation of all policies effective at the time. Decisions that seemed prudent and cost-effective at the time they were made—the decision to build a school over an old dump, to prune excess manpower from a little-used oil-spill response team, to develop economies of scale by fishing from much larger boats, to defer maintenance on some backup safety systems at the chemical factory—these can suddenly seem terribly unwise or even criminally negligent. Our response is, appropriately, to

develop more stringent and far-reaching policies, to introduce new probability calculations into business prudence, and, in effect, to transfer some of
the costs of cleaning up a disaster to the safety preparations before it happens, hoping to avoid the majority of these costs entirely. Such shifts must
be defended with determination against the persistent efforts of the private
interests involved to transfer all costs to the taxpayer.

The debate (if so polite a word is appropriate to describe the aftermath
of an environmental catastrophe) is centrally ethical, a debate on the
appropriate balance between individual rights and the common good,
between short-term and long-term benefit, and among the interests of all
parties to the activity. We have a discipline, Applied Ethics, that encompasses all such ethical inquiries in practical issues; another new field of
inquiry, Environmental Ethics, includes these ethical issues as they extend
to take into account the interests of the biosphere itself.

Second, that last modification—the move to consider the interests of
the environment for its own sake—raises conceptual problems that go
beyond policy and prudence. The next effect of environmental catastrophe is philosophical inquiry, especially when the event is generalized to
the ongoing catastrophe of the last days of the twentieth century: an end
to all frontiers, the threat to the last wilderness, the incredible rate of consumption of nonrenewable resources, the depletion of the vast oceans, the
thinning of the ozone layer, and the extinction of species. We always
knew that we would make mistakes, that accidents would happen, and
that humans might cause isolated disasters through carelessness or venal-
ity, but only recently has it occurred to us that our entire approach to the
natural world could be a disaster in itself and a crime—not just imprudent but conceptually and morally wrong, like slavery. Perhaps humans
should not treat Nature as something to be exploited without limit.
Maybe Nature should be part of our community, like us, deserving
respect and nurture rather than mindless use. We are beginning to realize
that our resources are limited; it is even possible that they are not just
resources, in the sense of material available for the taking. Perhaps we
will need to learn to live as part of all life, subordinate to the natural
workings of the natural world that sustains us, if we are to continue to
live at all.

This philosophical doubt on the environmental front has occasioned
some genuinely original inquiry. One of the most interesting movements
in philosophy since the dawn of this newer, more acute, environmental
consciousness, has been "ecofeminism," a fusion of environmentalism
with feminism that distinguishes approaches based on *life taking* (the
exploitation of resources) from those based on *life giving* (partnership
with Nature) and argues for the superiority of the latter. Another interesting movement identifies all living matter as part of the biosphere (occasionally personalized as "Gaia"), a nurturing, life-giving superorganism,

within which we live, and which alone allows us to flourish as fully realized people. Whatever destroys this organism, destroys humanity; as long as we continue to imagine Nature as something to be commandeered to our purposes and to conceive of living organisms other than ourselves as mere objects, the destruction will continue; therefore, the human imperative for survival demands a total revision of our uses of nature and of our conception of the natural world. This organic approach is one of several that presently form the "deep ecology" movement.

The field of philosophy has expanded, very recently, to include careful treatments of the new philosophical approaches to the natural environment.[1] For this reason alone, these developments in philosophy, fascinating as they are, will receive very little attention in this book. When the thick mousse of oil is spreading toward the pristine beaches of Prince William Sound, or the last redwoods of the Pacific North Coast are falling before the corporations' greed, it matters very little whether we approach the problems created by the spill or the clearcuts from the perspective of ecofeminism or deep ecology, or (for that matter) from Kantian or utilitarian perspectives. Sound policy is needed—policy that brings the costs of predictable malfunctions forward into the making of the economic arrangements in the first place—and rigorous enforcement of that policy. It should be noted, however, that in the course of developing that policy, we will have to go deeper than the immediate surface causes of the incident that has focused our attention, to examine the political and economic practices that made it inevitable. These inquiries can be penetrating, even radical: For example, to develop a policy that will be effective in preventing oil spills, we must reexamine our entire pattern of energy use, extraction, and transport, giving special attention to our fondness for the private automobile. To develop a policy that will prevent the destruction of the ancient groves of trees in the Pacific Northwest, we might have to bring into question the whole institution of private land ownership.

Nothing should prevent either the student or instructor from going beyond the concerns of public ethics raised by these cases to fundamental considerations of the deeper philosophical issues mentioned above—the moral and metaphysical status of Nature and its relation to the humans that temporarily inhabit the Earth. Attempts to deal directly with the distortions of our national and international life caused by short-sighted energy policies will not be helped by bouncing the problem back to the conceptual level; indeed, such attempts might be significantly hindered by such redirection. Ultimately, though, we will have to engage in just such reconceptualization. As Vice President Al Gore said in his best-selling book, *Earth in the Balance,*

> The strategic nature of the threat now posed *by* human civilization to the global environment and the strategic nature of the threat *to*

human civilization now posed by changes in the global environment present us with … challenges and false hopes. Some argue that a new ultimate technology, whether nuclear power or genetic engineering, will solve the problem. Others hold that only a drastic reduction of our reliance on technology can improve the conditions of life—a simplistic notion at best. But the real solution will be found in reinventing and finally healing the relationship between civilization and the earth.[2]

THE RATIONALE OF THIS BOOK

Al Gore's formulation raises the most serious aspect of the environmental crisis. We can be very good at developing new technologies, or at least new wrinkles on existing technologies, but therein lies the problem: We have never thought of the Earth as anything but the raw materials for our technologies, and we are a total failure at reinventing and healing relationships—in our families, our communities, our nation, and between the peoples of the world. Adding the planet Earth to our list of failed relationships only takes us farther out of our depth. The question is not yet how to *solve* the problem of the environment, but how to get a handle on it, how to think about it, how to begin to comprehend its complexity.

This book begins at that point. Faced with global dilemmas of indescribable complexity that do not demand new gadgets to solve immediate problems but new ways of relating to the globe itself, we look for microcosms in which the dilemmas can be faithfully reproduced within a limited time and place and thus easier to grasp. Each one of the cases in this book is a "defining moment," in Al Gore's formulation, that "focuses media coverage and political attention, not only on the environment itself, but also on the larger problems for which it is a metaphor …"[3]

Whenever we debate environmental problems on the global level, we find we cannot agree on anything—neither on the facts nor the prospects for the future nor the ethical and political principles that should govern any solution. But with concrete cases and situations (the New England fisheries, for example, or the *Exxon Valdez*, or the gas explosion at Bhopal), we can reach certain very basic agreements—at least, that whatever happened is unfortunate and should not be allowed to happen again in the future—and we can use that agreement as the foundation for further explorations of the issues.

This book aims to be useful for a variety of purposes, academic and otherwise. It is primarily designed as a supplement to all college and graduate-level courses in Environmental Ethics, Business Ethics, Ecology, Environmental Law, Social and Legal Environment of Business, Energy and the Environment, or Environmental Economics. Five or six academic departments are represented right there: Perhaps these cases will prove sufficiently interesting to extend that range. These stories are not, after all, the private property of any academic elite or approach. They are, for better or worse, the property of us all, as unwitting and unwilling indirect agents of their occurrence and along with our children, as heirs of their consequences. We had best get to know them well.

NOTES ON THE TEXT

We have tried to keep all chapters to a length that is convenient for reading and discussing in the course of a single class assignment, prefaced by some questions to focus the student's attention as the chapter is read and concluding with questions for reflection and with a synthesis of the material, to encourage more general insights on ethics and the environment. A short list of books and articles for further reading ends each chapter. A more complete bibliography can be found after the Epilogue.

Notes

1. See Bibliography. One excellent introduction to this literature is a fine collection of essays edited by Peter List entitled *Radical Environmentalism* (Belmont, Calif.: Wadsworth, 1993).
2. Al Gore, *Earth in the Balance* (Boston: Houghton Mifflin, 1992).
3. Cited in E. J. Dionne, Jr., "Big Oil Spill Leaves Its Mark on Politics of Environment," *The New York Times* (3 April 1989): p. A12.

Watersheds 2

CHAPTER I

Dirty Bombs
The Legacy of War

PREFACE: QUESTIONS TO KEEP IN MIND

Why are the tanks at Hanford so dangerous? Why didn't anyone know about that danger until a few years ago? Why is it so difficult to find a place to store nuclear wastes? What laws and agencies are in place to get the nuclear wastes cleaned up? What are we doing about the nuclear wastes?

THE TANKS OF MENACE

Horror stories, especially on film, play on our terror of the Unknown: that which we feel to be hideously dangerous, but that lurks somewhere beyond knowing. Somehow we cannot succumb so completely to fear when we can see the danger in the daylight, analyze it, face it squarely. But then, the danger waiting in the storage places for the waste products of the nuclear warfare industry is just made for the horror film. All we need is a good screenwriter; the plot is already in place.

In this work, we set the opening scene at the "tank farm" of the Hanford Nuclear Weapons Facility near Richland in Washington State, a reservation half the size of Rhode Island, bisected by the Columbia River. In business since 1942 under a variety of caretakers (including General Electric, Rockwell International, and now Westinghouse), the Hanford plutonium finishing plant (PFP) made plutonium for atomic bombs—to keep the United States safe and secure from its enemies. The work had the terrible urgency and secrecy of all acts of war, where speed is essential and the worst danger is subversion by a foreign enemy. No one, except a very few of those who worked there, was ever told what was done either with what was made or with what remained as waste. Secrecy was the rule: Any exposure could lead to sabotage.

On Christmas Eve of 1992—three years after the last plutonium had been sent out from the PFP and three years after the plant had been put on "stand-by" status for safety concerns—Matthew Wald of the *New York Times* presented a grim report: Despite the warnings "that catastrophic explosions were possible at million-gallon waste tanks at [Hanford] the Department of Energy still does not know just what is in the tanks or how risky they are."[1] "According to internal correspondence, Energy Department reports and outside analysts, the department and Westinghouse still have not determined exactly what is in the 177 tanks, which together hold 57 million gallons." Some of the initial ingredients are known: "The tanks hold liquids left over from the production of plutonium for nuclear weapons. Complicating the problem, in the cold war years technicians added organic chemicals that were meant to make the most radioactive materials sink to the bottom of the tanks in a sludge; the remaining liquids, somewhat less dangerous, were then dumped into the dirt." In this rich stew, the chemicals began interacting: "The organic chemicals, under intense heat and radiation, are undergoing changes that produce flammable and explosive gases and solids. And because of years of transfers among the tanks, no one is sure how much of each chemical is contained in each tank."

As the reactions continue, gases, especially hydrogen, are released; when the gas pressure builds up enough inside a tank, the tank tends to leak or "burp" it into the outside air, radioactivity and all. "Energy Department reports show that 16 times since 1987, including seven times in 1991, workers have been exposed to toxic gas leaking from the tanks, and some have suffered permanent lung damage." If workers can be injured, how about the rest of us? "Experts say the question of worker safety and public safety are closely related. Although the tanks are well inside the Hanford reservation, ... the presence of uncontrolled gases that may be explosive is a bad indication for public safety, experts say."

Indeed. On more complicated matters, experts speak with less certainty: "The problem even confounds experts. For example, just last year the [Department of Energy] realized it had grossly underestimated the amount of plutonium in the tanks, and it now monitors six tanks to determine if a nuclear reaction is likely." There is a real danger of a hydrogen explosion; in the general mystery on the contents of the tanks, there is also the outside possibility that there may be enough plutonium in the waste tanks to form a critical mass and start a chain reaction. The temperature of the mix in the tank should indicate such a reaction or an impending explosion. But the scientists attempting to monitor the tanks cannot be sure of the present condition in each stew. Usually the temperature-measuring devices, where present at all, are mounted on a single pole in the center of the tank. Unless the mixture is stable and homogeneous, the plant employees have no way of knowing if the conditions away from the pole match those at the pole—or are immeasurably more dangerous. Some tanks cannot be monitored at all (it is too dangerous to insert probes).

Extremely dangerous stuff moves about in there:

> Two dozen tanks contain ferrocyanides, compounds that pound for pound, the Department of Energy said last year, have about one-quarter the explosive power of TNT....Videotapes made last year inside tank 101-SY, which has a hydrogen problem, show what looks like partly-cooled lava inside a volcano, seething and lurching as it burps noxious and explosive gases that are produced by chemical and nuclear reactions. The shifting wastes splash the walls and bend metal parts; a narrator describes "rollover events" in which the tank agitates itself.

Intensely hot and radioactive mixtures, reasonably suspected of being explosive, churn themselves forever in these tanks, far too dangerous for the workers to reach, test, analyze, and control.

In the heat of our wars—from 1950 on—the engineers at Hanford filled these tanks in order to dispose of the wastes generated by their death-dealing products. Though the wars are over, the engineers gone, these brews continue the maleficent work on their own, in the darkness of the tanks, beyond human control, churning out the stuff of death. Produced by the U.S. Department of Energy, directed by private companies, and with a cast of thousands—all the citizens in the way of the toxic plume that follows a major explosion—we need only a good screenwriter for the horror film of the century.

HOW DID THIS HAPPEN?

How could we have come to this? How, in one of the most sustained efforts our nation ever undertook to secure the safety of its citizens from the worst threats our leaders could imagine, did we manage to produce one of the worst dangers any people have ever faced since the beginning of the human race? Keith Schneider, an environmental reporter for the *New York Times*, summed up the causes of the nuclear weapons industry's waste disaster as follows:

> A cold war curtain of secrecy, coupled with inattention by Congress and a succession of administrations ... allowed poorly maintained nuclear reactors and dangerous nuclear processing plants to continue operating without any scrutiny.
>
> The industry's lethal radioactive and chemical wastes were spread across miles of open ground in the West, poured into rivers and lakes in the East, and dumped where it was most convenient and least expensive throughout the 12 states where there are nuclear weapons plants and laboratories.[2]

How could this have happened? The short answer is that no one had foreseen the problems of disposal of nuclear wastes when the industry began.

Scientists Experimenting for the Good of the Nation

In 1933 Leo Szilard, a Hungarian physicist, first contemplated the possibility of building an atomic bomb. Then, in 1939, physicists around the world learned that a uranium atom had been "split"—turning some of its matter into enormous amounts of energy—by the physicist Otto Hahn. Between 1939 and 1941 some of the world's greatest scientists, many in the United States as exiles from Hitler's Europe, plotted, pondered, researched, and worried about German research on a nuclear bomb. These giants, many of them Nobel laureates, included Szilard and Hahn, Vannevar Bush, James Conant, Ernest Lawrence, Arthur Compton, Hans Bethe, Robert Oppenheimer, Edward Teller, Niels Bohr, Enrico Fermi, and even Albert Einstein. They were associated with the country's most prestigious universities— Princeton, Harvard, Carnegie Institute, Chicago, California at Berkeley.

Letters drafted by Szilard and others and signed by Einstein finally convinced President Franklin D. Roosevelt that research on a bomb should receive top priority. Just prior to Pearl Harbor, in 1941, the "Manhattan District" (Project) was born. Construction of the famous nuclear pile in the squash court at Stagg Field of the University of Chicago began on November 16, 1941. By December 2, it had grown large enough to be considered "critical," and the world's first sustained nuclear reaction occurred. With Fermi the project leader, Compton called Conant in Washington and told him, "The Italian navigator has just landed in the new world."[3]

Then the project began in earnest, urged on by the British and fueled with fear that Germany might develop the atomic bomb first. The race to make the most destructive weapon of all time was in full throttle. The government chose to build it in the desert at Los Alamos, New Mexico, with Oppenheimer chosen to lead the scientific effort and General Leslie Groves to oversee the operation on behalf of the military. They were the oddest couple ever: General Groves was a strict, authority-oriented, disciplined military man; Oppenheimer (Oppie) was an acknowledged genius, a scientific dreamer, and a brilliant theoretician, who espoused left-wing causes.

The secrecy surrounding this project was probably the most intense this nation has ever seen. Beyond the scientists and the president, only the vice president, the secretary of war, and the Army chief of staff knew of it. The hundreds of scientists recruited by Oppenheimer found Los Alamos practically a prison. With 485 counterintelligence agents watching them, they had fake names and drivers licenses with numbers instead of names, their phone lines were tapped, and their mail went to a box number in Sante Fe. Not even their wives knew what they were doing.

The first "gadget" was tested on July 16, 1945 at the Trinity test site in Alamogordo, New Mexico, with great success—equaling the effect of 20,000 tons of TNT. On August 1, the first bomb was dropped on Hiroshima, Japan. With that bomb, and the one close on its heels at Nagasaki, that war ended—but the bomb had just got started. The Russians, who turned against the United States as soon as Germany surrendered, were well on their way to developing a bomb of their own, thanks to the effective spying of Klaus Fuchs. The Cold War, with all its nuclear secrecy, had begun.

By-products of Weaponry

The Hanford nuclear weapons complex was built in 1942. Since then, seventeen nuclear weapons facilities have been built, scattered through 13 states. They are or have been operated by private corporations such as General Electric, Rockwell International, Westinghouse, and EG&G, under contract first to the Atomic Energy Commission, and now to the Department of Energy (DOE). For 45 years, they operated in total secrecy. All of them are now polluted.

Because all activities were classified top secret, workers often had no idea what they were doing. "The Cold War atmosphere encouraged an us-versus-them mentality, and any critic of the weapon-building process could be readily dismissed as siding with the enemy." With no oversight, contractors acted in ways "that not only violated common decency, but frequently the law."[4] No one was minding the store. These operations were exempt from Occupational Safety and Health Administration (OSHA) oversight, Environmental Protection Agency (EPA) regulations, environmental laws, the Freedom of Information Act, and congressional oversight.[5] According to the Secretary of Energy, Hazel L. O'Leary, in 1994 "we were shrouded and clouded in an atmosphere of secrecy. And I would take it a step further. I would call it repression."[6] Seth Shulman in *The Threat at Home* compares our nuclear weapons facilities today to the pollution in post–Cold War Eastern Europe resulting from industry that (1) operated under one authority, (2) pressured production, and (3) maintained secrecy.[7] Though most environmental laws were passed in the early 1970s, the Atomic Energy Act at that time exempted weapons sites from compliance. Not until the late 1970s and early 1980s, when Senator John Glenn of Ohio began investigations into these facilities, did the pollution disaster details begin to trickle out.[8] Only in the last few years has the DOE become subject to the regulations and laws that govern the rest of U.S. enterprises. This means, for instance, that though worker safety remains a concern in these polluted sites, OSHA oversight is at least in place.

Every step in the process of manufacturing a nuclear weapon produces radioactive and chemical wastes, in varying amounts and deadliness. One ton of uranium ore produces only a few pounds of uranium, the remaining "tailings" being mildly radioactive. Of that ore, only 1 percent is the U-235 isotope necessary to build a bomb, so it has to be "enriched," a difficult and expensive process that took place at the Savannah River facility in South Carolina, Fernald in Ohio, Oak Ridge in Tennessee, and Paducah in Kentucky. Thousands of tons of the leftover material are stored at these plants. Because enrichment is so onerous, plutonium 239 became the preferred fuel. But we make plutonium by bombarding uranium with neutrons. After the plutonium is separated, a radioactive stew remains, which contains many highly radioactive isotopes (fission products), as well as uranium and plutonium isotopes. For every pound of plutonium produced, we are left with 170 gallons of high-level and 27,000 gallons of low-level waste.[9] This "reprocessing" procedure has resulted in 105 million gallons of radioactive and chemical waste—enough to fill a thousand-foot supertanker.[10] Most of this waste is at the Savannah River and Hanford facilities, with some in Ohio and New York. Other bomb components were manufactured in Florida, Missouri, and Ohio, the final assembly occurring at the Pantex plant in Texas (which now disassembles bombs), all contributing more waste. The grand total stands at

+ 403,000 cubic meters high-level radioactive waste (from reprocessing)
+ 2,600 metric tons spent fuel (not reprocessed)
+ 107,000 cubic meters transuranic waste (mostly uranium and plutonium)
+ 1,800,000 cubic meters low-level radioactive waste
+ 780,000 cubic meters mixed chemical and radioactive waste[11]

Three-quarters of these wastes have still not been completely identi-fied.[12] During the Cold War, workers would frequently dispose of waste without sampling, labeling, or recording; as a result many storage tanks hold unknown contents.[13] Between 1943 and 1970, billions of gallons of radioactive wastes were simply poured on the ground and leached into ground water. The Columbia River at Hanford, the Clinch River at Oak Ridge, and the Savannah River at that complex are all radioactively con-taminated. Spent fuel rods are stored in rusting containers, some of which are 50 years old, in unlined pools. The worst-case scenario is a "critical-ity" event during which enough fissile material accumulates to spark a nuclear chain reaction.[14]

THE EXTENT OF THE PROBLEM

Hanford

The Hanford PFP, the oldest and largest of the facilities, presents the worst case for any cleanup. According to Seth Shulman, "All of the government's nuclear facilities are polluted—possibly beyond repair.... But none matches the scale of the problems at Hanford [which] ... represents one of the most daunting environmental catastrophes the world has ever known."[15] The Hanford site contains enough radioactive waste to cover 15 football fields 3 feet deep.[16] Between 1944 and 1947, 400,000 curies of radioactive iodine 131 (a thyroid-cancer threat) was knowingly released into the air, expos-ing 10,000 people to radioactive fumes. For comparison, during the Three Mile Island accident, the public was exposed to 30 curies of I-131. This information was suppressed for 40 years. Over the years, 200 billion gal-lons of radioactive waste water has been poured onto the ground. Con-centrations of radioactive Strontium 90 (a bone-cancer threat) at 500 times the federal standard have been measured in the Columbia River.

Hanford is probably most notorious for its "tank farm," with which this account began: 177 leaking tanks, some with a million-gallon capac-ity, containing a total of 61 million gallons of mixed high-level radioactive and chemical waste. The earlier tanks were designed with a single lining, to last 25 years, since their designers were sure that some permanent solu-tion to the problem of nuclear waste would be found by then. By now, some of them are 50 years old, and the lining has eroded. Sixty-seven of them are either known or suspected to have leaked up to a millon gallons of waste that includes nitrates, nitrites, chromium, mercury, cyanide, cesium 137, strontium 90, and iodine 129. Twenty-four of them have been considered in danger of exploding. As described previously, one has been burping hydrogen, causing workers to fear even probing it to determine its contents. (A mixer has been installed to lessen the threat.)[17]

The Rocky Flats Trial

The public's first real exposure to the problems of nuclear waste came after armed FBI agents invaded the Rocky Flats facility in June of 1989. The Rocky Flats plant, located 16 miles northwest of Denver, Colorado, manufactured the "triggers" for nuclear bombs from 1952 until its closure in January 1990. Rockwell International, the company managing the plant when the FBI arrived, had run the facility since 1975, before which Dow Chemical Company had run it.

The FBI agents carried a search warrant including accusations that Rockwell had dumped toxic wastes into drinking-water sources and that they had illegally operated an incinerator closed for safety reasons. The FBI seized thousands of documents. After hearing some 100 witnesses, the grand jury had evidently reached a number of conclusions by March 1992, when a settlement between the U.S. Department of Justice (DOJ) and Rockwell was announced. By that settlement, Rockwell pleaded guilty to ten crimes and agreed to pay an $18.5 million fine—but the case would be closed, and none of the executives who made the decisions would be charged with a crime or brought to trial.[18] This was one of the conditions for the plea agreement.[19]

Given the evidence of public danger covered up by its caretakers, this "deal" provoked public outrage. The members of the jury hit the ceiling at the self-serving cynicism of such an agreement. Though federal grand jury deliberations are, by law, sealed, some jurors leaked a part of their report, in which they accused DOE of conspiring with Rockwell to violate environmental regulations. Not only that, the grand jury believed that violations continued, in the collusion of the DOE, even as they were deliberating the case.[20] They would have recommended criminal indictment of Rockwell and DOE officials. Later, one FBI investigator testified to a House of Representatives subcommittee that when he heard that no individuals in the case would be charged, "I physically got sick." The jurors, and the citizens who joined them, even wrote President-elect Clinton asking for a special prosecutor.

The plea agreement not only insured that no individuals would go to jail, but also lacked any admission of guilt regarding release of toxic materials into the environment. That charge, of toxic release, had been a part of the original search warrant. Such an admission, given the plant's proximity to Denver, would have opened the door to civil lawsuits.[21] Despite juror and congressional pressure, the Bush administration's Department of Justice resisted requests to pursue the matter further. One DOJ official offered, "Environmental crimes are not like organized crime or drugs. There you have bad people doing bad things. With environmental crimes, you have decent people doing bad things."[22] However, in a memorandum that accompanied the Rockwell plea, the DOJ did chastise the DOE, saying that it "established a 'prevailing culture' that put production of plutonium triggers for nuclear weapons above any other concern, including care for the environment and public safety."[23]

How badly polluted was Rocky Flats when the deal went down? Testimony contained allegations that in 1957, a fire resulted in radioactive emissions equal to 16,000 times the level considered safe. No state or local officials were notified.[24] Sludge containing cadmium, chromium, barium, lead, and silver had been mixed with cement after it started to leak from the solar pond where it had been discarded. The resulting slabs were placed in a parking lot, but not having solidified, started to leak again. Workers had disposed of waste water by simply spraying it onto the ground—some 80 million gallons per year. When a 2,760,000-gallon chromic acid spill occurred and leaked to the sewage treatment plant, that too was sprayed around.[25] Meanwhile, plutonium, unused because of the virtual halt of bomb manufacture, contaminates the plant and is a serious threat to the clean-up workers. Containers of that plutonium have ruptured, contaminating workers.[26]

The legal settlement took care of the problems of the executives facing indictment. But what did it do for Rocky Flats? Nothing—Rocky Flats was and still is a polluted "plutonium dump."[27]

Savannah River and Others

Hanford and Rocky Flats are by no means the only problems facing the Department of Energy. The Savannah River complex is considered second only to Hanford in concentration of contamination. Indeed, the two account for 96 percent of all of the DOE's high-level radioactive wastes. Savannah River was also a plutonium producer. Its tanks leak into groundwater. It also produced tritium, a bomb component, some of which has leaked into the Savannah River.[28] Among other wastes, one can find ammonium nitrate, the stuff of which the World Trade Center bomb was made.[29]

The other contaminated sites also pose threats. At the Oak Ridge, Tennessee, laboratory, for instance, which saw early work on the first bomb, 68 pounds of weapons-grade uranium remains, 4.4 pounds of which has leaked, and fear of a nuclear chain reaction has been reported. According to the Oak Ridge Environmental Peace Alliance, "They've got a nuclear pipe bomb in their backyard there."[30] The remainder of sites have similar problems, but on a smaller scale.

WHAT DO WE DO NOW?

There is broad agreement on the general direction the nation must take in order to remedy this appalling situation:

1. We must do whatever we can to prevent explosions that would spew toxic waste over the regions near the obsolete plants and cause other sorts of deterioration and damage. We must keep these situations from getting worse.

2. We must find a way to neutralize and store all those wastes in a setting that will keep them out of harm's way until they are safe.

3. We must arrange to pay for the security, the neutralization, and the evacuation of the wastes; we must carry out and pay for their transportation and storage, however long it takes.

Just *how* we can take these directions, given the extent and novelty of the problems and the astronomical costs, is a separate question. Let's take the problems in order of priority.

Security

The Department of Energy must secure all these facilities to prevent further leaks, explosions, terrorist attacks, theft, and radiation exposure to workers.[31] Only after security is established, by no means an easy task, can we consider the work of cleaning up these sites. As we know, the situation is so dangerous now that the engineers in charge of the plants dare not even place monitors in the accumulated sludge. Secretary O'Leary has given worker safety top priority in the operation of these plants.[32] Additionally, O'Leary has promised, and delivered, openness regarding DOE's present and past activities. These developments seem to foretell a better future than the past, but that may not be saying much. At least the law of the land applies to these operations now.

Storage

Finding a safe place for plutonium will also be difficult. Some consider this element the most toxic substance known—minuscule amounts inhaled can cause lung cancer. Because it ignites spontaneously, storing it as part of spent fuel presents a problem—just a few kilograms can constitute a critical mass and cause a nuclear reaction.[33] Compounding the problem is its half-life (the time during which one-half the amount becomes nonradioactive) of 24,000 years.

We're working on it. A $2 billion vitrification plant is being built at the Savannah River plant; already it is rife with cost overruns and missed deadlines.[34] The plant is designed to mix glass with high-level radioactive waste to solidify it, after which it would be stored in impermeable casks that eventually would be transferred to a permanent geologic repository.

Potential sites. After extensive surveys of geological stability, Congress selected Yucca Mountain in Nevada as a permanent disposal site for high-level radioactive waste of commercial origin. Opponents, however, have successfully blocked implementation of the idea, claiming that the mountain may not be safe for the thousands of years required.[35] Plutonium wastes, while halving their radioactivity each 24,000 years, remain significantly radioactive for 250,000 years, over four times as long as the time since the last glacier. Because one can hardly conceive of that number of years, the government set the criterion for permanence of any site at 10,000 years; that's only as long as it's been since the origin of agriculture. There are worries that Yucca Mountain may not make it.

Another site, much further developed, is the Waste Isolation Pilot Plant (WIPP) in New Mexico, designed to absorb the wastes of weapons plants. This site too has encountered problems, such as pressurized brine reservoirs distressingly close to where the waste is to be stored, raising the possibility of unpredictable leaks. Worst-case scenarios show nuclear waste, in the form of liquid slurry, oozing out through the cracks and invading the water supply. For the moment, by federal injunction, the site is not used for storage; the remaining geological problems have to be solved before permission to store wastes will be granted. However, it still costs us $160 million a year to maintain it.

Keep out! When it opens, the site may absorb a significant percentage of the wastes. But if they're going to be dangerous for tens of thousands of years, how can we ever make sure that people stay away from it? Clearly, what we need is some ultimately monumental "Keep Out" sign. But how shall we write it? To design the sign, the EPA assembled a blue-ribbon panel who met in 1991 and 1992 to design the monument that would unequivocally warn the future. The problems that they encountered, while insurmountable, come almost as a relief after the horror scenes of Hanford and Savannah. For instance, "Who knows whether humans will speak English ten millennia hence—or whether the term "human" will still apply?"[36] We cannot assume the political ascendancy of our present government—dynasties thousands of times greater than ours have waxed, waned, and faded—nor the persistence of our language, or any language now spoken. To last an enormous timespan,

> what architectural model should the markers panel follow? Of the original Seven Wonders of the World, only one—Khufu's pyramid in Egypt—still stands, a mere 4,500 years old; Stonehenge is a thousand years its junior. The marker, too, must compete for uniqueness with all the monuments yet to rise and fall; the millennia of liberty and civil war statuary, the carcasses of shopping malls, the innumerable legs of stone both vast and trunkless.[37]

The physicists and astronomers of the panel suggested a "black hole" approach: a covering of black asphalt that, in the desert sun, would get too hot for anyone to approach. The artists suggested a design called *Forbidding Blocks,* "one square mile of massive, irregularly carved boulders, laid out in a tight grid like some Flintstonian Manhattan."[38] Others included the Landscape of Thorns, the Rubble Landscape, the Spike Field, and the team favorite, "Menacing Earthworks: an expansive empty square, surrounded by 50-foot-high earthen berms jolting outward like jagged bolts of lightning. And at the center of the square, a 2000 foot-long walk-on map displaying all the world's nuclear dumps, including this one."[39] Before now, we have never really taken on the need to communicate with future generations on matters of urgent importance. How might it, in the end, be done?

Cost

The costs of dealing with nuclear wastes simply boggle the mind. For starters, we must pay the companies that now run these sites, and they charge very high rates. The price tag charged to the U.S. taxpayer continues to grow. The DOE spends about one-third more on contractors than industry does.[40] Secretary of Energy Hazel O'Leary, who is nominally in charge of these contracts, appears to be "getting tough." For example, Westinghouse was denied a bonus after a steam pipe rupture killed a worker at Hanford. Nevertheless, Westinghouse was paid $5.4 million from April to September 1993.[41] Although the DOE refused to pay the court costs to Rockwell for the case previously described, documents reveal that the U.S. has reimbursed Rockwell for other civil cases brought by nearby residents and employees.[42] EG&G, the contractor that followed Rockwell as plant manager, did not meet contract obligations, according to the *Rocky Mountain News.* Therefore, it lost its $9 million *bonus* for the second time![43] EG&G and the DOE have since parted company. The company also lost a contract with the DOE's Idaho Engineering Laboratory that had been netting them $5 billion every 5 years for 18 years.[44] The cost to establish real security—to render those tanks harmless at least to the region—will be much higher.

Then there are the costs of the cleanup. All those deadly substances have to be vitrified or otherwise rendered inert, packed in trucks, and taken to that place that by then, we will have decided is safe to keep them for 250,000 years, or at least 10,000 years. How much is this going to cost? Estimates in 1989 put it at $92 billion; even so, Senator John Glenn attacked the figures as a serious underestimation.[45] Since then, cost estimates have gone through the roof; estimates vary, but DOE documents predict the cleanup will cost somewhere between $230 to $500 billion over the next 75 years just to "stabilize" the sites.[46] Hazel O'Leary, who has done more than anyone else to bring these waste sites to public attention, despairs of actually cleaning up all of them. As she says, "Are we going to clean-up each one of these sites so they become greenfields where young children can picnic with their families? There's not enough money in the country to do that. There's probably not enough money in the world to do that. So we will go after the worst messes first."[47]

With perhaps not enough money in the world to clean up even the worst ones, the remainder pose intractable problems. DOE says that *after* the cleanup job is completed the sites will need "continued guarding and monitoring" and that in some contamination cases "no effective technology is yet available [for remediation]."[48] During the 1980s, the military and the DOE suggested that the Hanford facility might become a "national sacrifice zone"—that is, just fenced off and abandoned forever, an area too contaminated to clean up.[49] Have we come to this? How will we ever explain this to our children?

The only certainty is that we will have to muster a steady national will to engage this cleanup. To quote a DOE publication, "The Cold War is over, but its legacy remains. Solving the waste management and contamination problems of this legacy will take decades and enormous resources.... One thing is clear: the challenges before us will require a similar—if not greater—level of commitment, intelligence, and ingenuity that was required by the Manhattan Project."[50] Are we still capable of achieving such a level? The nuclear waste problem will surely answer that question.

QUESTIONS FOR DISCUSSION AND REFLECTION

+ One source points out that beyond being a toxic and radioactive waste disaster, Savannah River happens to be located in a "heavily African-American area of South Carolina."[51] Was this fact part of the planning? What is the significance of the choice of sites for "bad neighbors" such as nuclear weapons plants?

+ "Security" has traditionally been interpreted as a matter of weapons directed at foreign powers. Yet nuclear wastes pose a threat to our security that has nothing to do with either—ironically, in this case, generated by efforts to provide for national "security." What other areas of environmental degradation might pose large-scale national safety hazards or threats to security?

+ How would you structure a debate on whether or not to clean up Hanford? Try to frame a solid argument that we should spend not one penny on that site, but should just fence it off and abandon it until those chemicals run out of energy, nuclear or otherwise. What are the drawbacks to that solution?

✦ Was there any human wrongdoing, as far as you can tell, in the generation of this embarrassing and dangerous situation? Should the companies in charge of operations have foreseen the end and taken steps to avert it? Is the fact that the private corporations who administered this site for the government were public corporations responsible to their shareholders to make a profit—or at least, not to incur losses—relevant to our judgment of their oversight?

✦ Is the problem of waste disposal sufficient proof that we ought not to use nuclear energy? Why or why not?

✦ For fun: Try your hand at scripting the horror movie. How will the legacy of the Cold War figure in your script?

Notes

1. Matthew L. Wald, "Hazards at Nuclear Plant Fester Eight Years After Warnings: Little Has Been Done to Ease Fears of Catastrophic Explosions," *New York Times* (24 December 1992): p. A11. The remainder of this section comes from this article.

2. Keith Schneider. "Wasting Away," *The New York Times Magazine* (30 August 1992): p. 45.

3. Most of the material on the history of the bomb is taken from Peter Wyden, *Day One: Before Hiroshima and After* (New York: Simon & Schuster, 1984); and corroborated by Arjun Makhijani, "Always the Target?" *Bulletin of Atomic Scientists* (May/June 1995): p. 23.

4. Linda Rothstein, "Nothing Clean About the Clean-up," *Bulletin of Atomic Scientists* (May/June 1995): p. 15

5. Pamela Murphy, "Coming Clean," *The National Voter* (4 March 1994): p. 14. See also Seth Shulman, *The Threat at Home: Confronting the Toxic Legacy of the U.S. Military* (Boston: Beacon Press, 1992): p. 95.

6. Murphy, "Coming Clean," p. 14

7. Shulman, "The Threat at Home," p. 94

8. John F. Ahearne, "Fixing the Nation's Nuclear Weapons Plants," *Technology Review* (July 1989): p. 24.

9. Murphy, "Coming Clean," p. 14.

10. United States Department of Energy (DOE) Office of Environmental Management, *Closing the Circle on the Splitting of the Atom* (January 1995): p. 18.

11. Rothstein, "Nothing Clean About the Clean-up," p. 34

12. Ibid.

13. DOE, *Closing the Circle,* p. 31

14. Rothstein, "Nothing Clean About the Clean-up," p. 34.

15. Shulman, "The Threat at Home," p. 94.

16. Murphy, "Coming Clean," p. 14.

17. The numbers of tanks, gallons, etc. vary from source to source; the major sources used are DOE, "Closing the Circle," p. 7; Rothstein, "Nothing Clean About the Clean-up," p. 34; Schulman, *The Threat at Home,* p. 97; Wald, "Hazards at Nuclear Plant Fester," and Matthew L. Wald, "Uranium Rusting in Storage Pools Is Troubling U.S.," *New York Times* (8 December 1993): p. A1.

18. Keith Schneider, "U.S. Takes Blame in Atom Plant Abuses," *New York Times* (27 March 1992): p. A12.

19. Matthew L. Wald, "Bomb Plant Draws More Fire," *New York Times* (2 November 1993): p. A18.

20. Matthew L. Wald, "New Disclosures over Bomb Plant," *New York Times* (22 November 1992).

21. Matthew L. Wald, "Justice Department Called Too Lenient in Bomb Plant Case," *New York Times* (5 January 1993).

22. "Let's Hear the Rocky Flats Jurors," Editorial, *New York Times* (1 November 1993).

23. Schneider, "Wasting Away."

24. World Resources Institute, *The 1993 Information Please Almanac* (New York: Houghton Mifflin, 1993): p. 141.

25. Rothstein, "Nothing Clean About the Clean-up," p. 34

26. Len Ackland, "A Dump Called Rocky Flats," *Bulletin of Atomic Scientists* (Nov./Dec., 1994): p. 12.

27. Ibid.

28. World Resources Institute, *Information Please Environmental Almanac,* p. 141.

29. Matthew L. Wald, "At an Atomic Waste Site, the Only Sure Thing Is Peril," *New York Times* (21 June 1993): p. A1.

30. Matthew L. Wald, "Uranium Leak at Tennessee Laboratory Brings Fears of an Accidental Chain Reaction," *New York Times* (25 November 1994): p. A18.

31. DOE, *Closing the Circle,* p. 6.

32. Matthew L. Wald, "Worker Peril Seen in Waste Clean-up," *New York Times*: (10 March 1993).

33. DOE, *Closing the Circle,* p. 40.

34. Rothstein, "Nothing Clean About the Clean-up," p. 34.

35. John F. Ahearne, "The Future of Nuclear Power," *American Scientist* (Jan.–Feb., 1993): pp. 24–35.

36. Alan Burdick, "The Last Cold-War Monument: Designing the "Keep-Out" Sign for a Nuclear-Waste Site," *Harper's Magazine* (August 1992): p. 66.

37. Ibid., p. 63.

38. Ibid., p. 64.

39. Ibid.

40. John H. Cushman, Jr., "U.S. Pays More than Industry for Atomic Clean-up," *New York Times* (30 November 1993): p. A30.

41. Matthew L. Wald, "Manager of No. 1 Nuclear Site is Rebuked by U.S.," *New York Times* (9 December 1993).

42. "DOE Picks up Court Cost Tab for Rockwell," *Denver Post* (20 September 1993).

43. Katie Kerwin, "Rocky Flats Contractor Gets Second Bad Review," *Rocky Mountain News* (3 April 1994).

44. Steve Bailey, "Saying So Long to Uncle Sam: Veteran Cold War Contractor EG&G Marches into the Commercial Market After Turning Its Back on the Energy Department," *Boston Globe* (11 September 1994): Business Section, p. AB5.

45. Philip Shenon, "Atomic Cleanup Is Seen Costing U.S. $92 Billion; Some Say Energy Department Still Underestimates," *New York Times* (5 January 1989): p. A16.

46. Rothstein, "Nothing Clean About the Clean-up," p. 34.

47. Anthony Lawler, "As O'Leary Struggles to Preserve Energy Department," *Science* (19 May 1995): p. 965.

48. DOE, *Closing the Circle*, p. 9.

49. Shulman, *The Threat at Home*, p. 94.

50. Ibid., p. 9.

51. Karl Grossman, "Environmental Racism," in *People, Penguins, and Plastic Trees* (Belmont, CA: Wadsworth, 1995): p. 39.

Suggestions for Further Reading

Burdick, Alan. "The Last Cold War Monument: Designing the `Keep-Out' Sign for a Nuclear Waste Site." *Harper's Magazine* (August 1992): p. 62.

Lenssen, Nicholas. *"Nuclear Waste: The Problem That Won't Go Away."* Worldwatch Paper 106. Washington, DC: Worldwatch Institute, 1991.

Rothstein, Linda. "Nothing Clean About the Clean-up." *Bulletin of the Atomic Scientists* (May/June 1995): p. 34.

Schulman, Seth. *The Threat at Home: Confronting the Toxic Legacy of the U.S. Military.* Boston: Beacon Press, 1992.

The United States Department of Energy, Office of Environmental Management. *Closing the Circle on the Splitting of the Atom.* January 1995.

CHAPTER 2

Too Much of a Good Thing

The Population Problem

PREFACE: QUESTIONS TO KEEP IN MIND

Why do we talk about the population "explosion" in the last few centuries? Why did the human population start to rise so quickly during that time?

How many people can the earth support? How do we know (or do we)? Can we manage our resources in such a way as to support more people, more comfortably? How?

We generally acknowledge our ethical obligations not to take human life (Thou shalt not kill) and to make efforts to save, sustain, and extend human life. If people are our problem, what happens to these duties? Can we thread a moral path through the maze of conflicting directives?

INTRODUCTION

In 1968 Paul Ehrlich warned, "In the 1970's and 1980's hundreds of millions of people will starve to death in spite of any crash programs embarked upon now"[1] unless certain solutions were adopted. "One is a 'birthrate solution' in which we find ways to lower the birthrate. The

TABLE *2-1*   Human Population Growth

Year (A.D.)	Population	Doubling time
1650	500 million ⎫	
1850	1 billion ⎬ ⎫	200 years
1930	2 billion ⎭ ⎪	80 years
1950	2.5 billion ⎫	
1985	5 billion ⎬	35 years
1996	5.7 billion	

other is a 'deathrate solution' in which [a way] to raise the deathrate—war, famine, pestilence—FINDS US."[2] Though his timing may have been a bit off, Ehrlich's deathrate solution seems to have come to pass, given the famines and spasmodic genocidal warfare in Somalia, Rwanda, the Sudan, and Bosnia; given the worldwide outbreaks of AIDS, the Ebola and Marburg viruses, and the increases in yellow fever, malaria, dengue fever, and cholera. Indeed, in 1990, Anne and Paul Ehrlich wrote that "since 1968 at least 200 million people—mostly children—have perished needlessly of hunger and hunger related diseases."[3] In sum, to quote Ehrlich again, "As the old saying goes, whatever your cause, it's a lost cause without population control."[4]

Paul Ehrlich's *Population Bomb* was to human population growth what Rachael Carson's *Silent Spring* was to the problem of indiscriminate pesticide use. Ehrlich was certainly not the first to warn us of the problems inherent in continued human population growth—Malthus is undoubtedly his most famous predecessor—but just as they did for Carson in 1962, the American people paid attention to Ehrlich in 1968.

POPULATION PRIMER

In the year 8000 B.C., there were about five million people on the planet, with human population doubling every 10,000 years. By A.D. 1650 there were 500 million, and the doubling times started to become shorter and shorter, as you can see in Table 2-1.[5]

By now, those of you who are mathematically inclined have recognized the distinct characteristics of exponential growth—a long period of slow growth followed by increasingly rapid growth over a very short period. Here are two problems that illustrate exponential growth.

1. I'll either give you a dollar a day for a month, or a penny on the first day and double it each day of the month (two cents on the second day, four cents on the third day, etc). Which do you want? On second thought, I'll give you a thousand dollars every day for a month, or a penny on the first, two cents on the second, etc. Now which do you want? (Figure it out.)

2. A farmer's pond had a tiny patch of lily pads that was doubling in size every day. He was warned that it would kill everything else in the pond if he let it grow over the whole surface. He didn't start to worry about it until it had grown to cover one-eighth of the pond. How many days did he have to find a solution?

Population growth is usually described by two statistics:

1. *The growth rate*—the difference between the birthrate and the deathrate, that is between those born per thousand population and those who have died per thousand. This is usually expressed as a percentage. For example, if 80 people were born to a population of 1,000, and 60 people died, in one year the growth rate would be 20 per 1000 or 2 percent.

2. *The fertility rate*—the average number of children born per woman over her lifetime.

Nigeria has a 3.1 percent growth rate, which translates to a doubling time of 22 years. If that rate continued for 140 years, Nigeria's population would exceed the 1989 world population.[6] Further statistics show the projected growth in population from 1990 to 2030, in selected countries at the 1990 growth rate for each,

+ India: 800 million to 1.8 billion (exceeding projections for China)
+ Bangladesh: 104 million to 342 million (Bangladesh is about the size of Wisconsin)
+ Ethiopia: 46 million to 185 million (quadruple)
+ Mexico: 80 million to 160 million (double)
+ African continent: population would increase tenfold to 2.3 billion[7]

We must be careful to distinguish *overpopulation* from *population density*. If population density were the criterion for concern, the Netherlands, Japan, and Taiwan—to say nothing of Hong Kong—would be in big trouble, and there would be no problem at all in Africa. Overpopulation implies that the number of people (whatever that number may be) exceeds the carrying capacity of the given environment; that is, the water, arable land, forests and other resources cannot sustain the people without becoming depleted.[8]

To predict the future growth of a population, it helps to represent it as a *population pyramid*. These diagrams, usually in the shape of a triangle, illustrate the ages of a given population. The key factors shown by the pyramid are the number of women in the reproductive age group (15-45 years) and the number of children yet to enter that group; secondary factors include the number of people in the youngest and oldest groups who must be supported by the middle. Third-World pyramids tend to be large at the base (children) and small at the top (old folks), whereas the industrialized

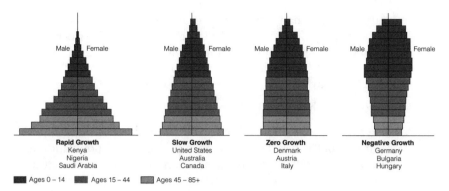

Figure 2-1 Population age structure diagrams for countries with rapid, slow, zero and negative population growth rates. (Data from Population Reference Bureau)

nations tend to be more consistent in all ages, with a "pyramid" that looks like the Empire State Building.

India's diagram illustrates the meaning of these pyramids (Fig. 2-1). It shows a population of 850 million in 1990 heavily skewed toward the youngsters. If India's fertility rate should drop tomorrow, from 4.3 children per woman to the replacement rate of 2.4 (the number of children needed just to replace their parents), with no change in the death rate, the population would continue to grow for about 100 years and would reach two billion.[9]

Here is the problem: It took *10,000* generations to reach 2.5 billion humans on the planet, but only *ONE (1)* more generation to reach 5.7 billion.[10] There are too many of us, and we are multiplying much too fast.

WHAT HAPPENED? THE DEMOGRAPHIC TRANSITION

Why did our population grow at such a rapid rate over such a short period of time? As we've seen, the doubling time has grown shorter and shorter, consistent with exponential growth. The generally accepted explanation centers on the industrial revolution: the move to the factory in the developed countries, resulting in a reduced need for many children and the subsequent stabilizing of the birth rate; countered by the world-wide health/sanitation/medical revolution, resulting in a precipitous decline in the death rate; and the characteristic time lag known as the demographic transition.

As we proceed we will be using the term *North* to represent the world's less populated, industrialized, rich, countries, generally located north of the equator—the United States, Canada, Western Europe, Japan, Australia, etc. ("the First World," or the "developed nations"). *South* will represent the more populated, less industrialized, poorer countries, generally located south of the equator—much of South America, Asia, and Africa ("the Third World," or the "developing nations").

Until the last part of the eighteenth century, human society was based almost entirely on agriculture; that is, most of the labor was needed to grow food, and most people lived on the land. In that setting, children are needed to work the land—the more the better—but people suffer from poor sanitation and primitive medicine. The birthrate is high, the deathrate is high, and the population grows very slowly. Then, in the early 1800s, the developed nations (the "North") began to industrialize, beginning a major and drastic change in demographic structure known as the industrial revolution. By the end of that century, this change resulted in a significant increase in per capita income and an improved life expectancy (decline in the deathrate). Safer factory jobs, better sanitation—above all, better drinking water and treatment of body wastes—and better health care all contributed. Doctors learned to wash their hands before surgery or childbirth, and they were more available in the cities. Meanwhile, Pasteur, Jenner, and other giants of medicine gave us vaccines and generally better management of disease, freeing us from some of the plagues that had destroyed families, especially infants, since the dawn of the human race. Meanwhile, urban industry usually presented less need for many children, and women became (a bit) more independent. As industrialized families realized that many children no longer implied free labor and care in old age, the birthrate dropped. When a new pattern emerged, it again reflected a slowly growing population, this time with birthrate and deathrate low.

Years later, essentially the same thing happened in the nonindustrialized, less-developed nations (the "South") but more slowly. In health care as in all matters, the rural, less affluent, and less educated populations took longer to accept the technical miracles of hypodermic needles and scrubbed bathrooms.

The catch is the demographic transition, the time interval between the fall in the deathrate and the fall in the birthrate. It takes at least a generation after the deathrate falls for the birthrate to decline. A common example is the Third-World peasant couple who need many children to work the fields and take care of them in their old age, and who know that of six to eight pregnancies at least one or two will result in babies who are stillborn or die in their first year, with two more likely to die before adulthood. But with improved health care and falling infant mortality rates, these children live. With all those infants surviving, the population grows exponentially. Not until these children have children is the increase in life expectancy realized. For instance, in East Asia, before living conditions improved, less than half the children born lived to become adults. In the 1930s, Chinese women by the age of 45 had birthed an average of five children, of whom only three survived.[11] The demographic portrait of this enormous transition, from high birthrates and deathrates to low ones, is the famous *S-Curve* of population. This curve predicts that when an agrarian society industrializes, its population will grow very rapidly during the process but will stabilize at a higher level. That prediction has been the basis of optimism that the population explosion would cure itself—when all nations are developed and interested in extended education and women's careers, the birthrate will fall all by itself. The other side of this optimistic coin, of course, is that right now the population is doubling every 35 years, and it isn't obvious that we can wait until the demographic transition is over before the population crashes under its own weight, taking all of us with it.

Given the dramatic statistics, why hasn't the world paid more attention to human population growth as a threat to the survival not only of our own species, but perhaps of all life? The answer probably lies in a number of reasons, including a puritanical taboo on the public discussion of sex, birth control, contraception, and abortion; a lack of understanding of the implications of the demographic transition and exponential growth; the opposition of some religions to birth control and/or abortion; and general cultural mores. Interestingly, in the United States, shortly after the publication of *The Population Bomb*, considerable interest in population issues arose, and population growth became an integral part of most environmental studies courses. The controversy caused by *Roe* v. *Wade* may have steered mainstream academics and policymakers away from the topic. Now, however, with the U.N. Conferences on Population in Cairo, and on Women in Beijing, the topic has again been put on the stove, if not the front burner.

ENVIRONMENTAL IMPACTS OF HUMAN POPULATION GROWTH

The environmental effect of the growing human population is related not only to numbers, but also to how people live—what resources they use, how much energy they expend, how much pollution they produce. To determine the environmental impact of humans, John Holdren and Anne and Paul Ehrlich have proposed the equation, $I = PAT$, where I = impact, P = population, A = affluence per capita, and T = the damage caused by the technology that supports that affluence. By these measurements, obviously, one U.S. American with energy intensive and consumptive ways causes much more degradation than a Masai herder in Kenya does. In fact, using this equation, one U.S. American has the impact of: 70 Ugandans and Laotians, 50 Bangladeshis, 20 Indians, 10 Chinese, or 2 Japanese, British citizens, French persons, Swedes, or Australians.

"Viewed in this light, the United States is the world's most overpopulated nation."[12]

PEOPLE AS A PROBLEM

Population growth creates a number of evils for human beings. The most obvious is simply the danger that we will use up our resources. As the impact calculation shows, we use our resources inefficiently as it is. For example, in 1990 one billion people were hungry and 400 million people's health and growth were threatened by lack of food, while *one-third* of the world's grain went to feed livestock to satisfy the increasing human demand for meat.[13] As a rule of thumb, we grow ten pounds of grain to produce one pound of steak. If we would eat the grain instead of the steak, we could feed ten people for every one we feed now.

Overpopulation not only consumes the product of the land, but also degrades the land, water, and air—by erosion, deforestation, water pollution from poor sanitation, and air pollution from emerging industries. As it does so, the land is less able to produce food, and even with the same or smaller population, we will be less able to feed the next generation than we are this one.

Another effect of population pressure, less well known, is the emergence of damaging viruses. As people venture into areas uninhabited by humans, and disrupt or destroy them by farming, burning, logging, or ranching, they come in contact with viruses from insect vectors, animal excretion, or rodent "reservoirs." Some of these emerging viruses may be a million years old, but with changing conditions may mutate, multiply, and spread among new hosts.[14] The AIDS virus is certainly the best known of these, but the recent appearances of hemorrhagic fever viruses, such as Ebola, have intensified concerns that AIDS may be just the tip of the iceberg. Increased human presence in tropical rain forests, which house at least half of all known species, pose a special concern, given that all organisms host myriad viruses. It may well be that "the wild beasts of this century and the next are microbial, not carnivorous."[15]

While the impact of human population growth is far reaching and, at least to some, profoundly disturbing, the impact itself is growing faster than the population. Using a common indicator of environmental impact, energy use, we see that while the human population quadrupled from 1860 to 1991, energy use by humans grew 93 times, from 1 to 93 billion megawatt-hours per year.[16] Obviously our *per capita* environmental impact is also growing, not only in the industrialized North but the rapidly industrializing South.[17] And the source of this impact is not equally distributed, no more than are the resources the consumption of which causes it. The more people who share the planetary pie, the smaller the piece per person. But the North, with 25 percent of the world's population, uses 80 percent of the world's resources; the United States alone, with 5 percent of the world's population, uses 30 percent of its resources.[18] In 1992, 15 percent of the world's population controlled 79 percent of the world's wealth.[19]

From an ethical standpoint, a further problem is posed by the fact that overpopulation's hardships are not equitably distributed. Arguably, the women in the developing world suffer the most from these inequities, though some would say the children do. A majority of women in Africa, Asia, and Latin America produce the food as well as cook it. They work longer than men, and in some instances will spend eight hours a day collecting fuel and water, but are denied education, health care, land ownership, monetary credit, and outside employment.[20]

RESPONSES

These issues and inequities received a thorough airing at two U.N. conferences: on population (Cairo, September 1994) and on women (Beijing, September 1995). A complete discussion of these events is beyond the scope of this chapter; however, the role of women as an absolute necessity in solving global problems was made apparent in both conferences, arguably for the first time in the history of international conferences.

At the first UN conference on population, held in Bucharest in 1974, the North pressed the South to control their population while the South argued for equitable distribution of resources. It was here that the North came up with the slogan, "Development is the best contraceptive," which became a mantra for policymakers from industrialized countries in following years. At the Mexico City conference ten years later, the United States, embroiled in abortion controversy at home, declared that population was a "neutral issue," that market forces would solve our problems. But at Cairo, the Clinton administration reversed the U.S. stand, supporting women's and environmental advocates. From this conference came support for improved women's education, improved health care for women and children, improved prenatal care, access to reproductive services, empowerment of women, support for adolescent needs, and support for sustainable development.[21] There was a general consensus that family planning programs by themselves would not solve the problem of population growth, that addressing underlying social problems, such as illiteracy and women's status, was an essential element of the solution.[22]

Women in general and women's advocacy nongovernmental organizations (NGOs) have been given much deserved credit for the successes of both the Cairo and Beijing conferences. Because of experience at the U.N. Conference on Environment and Development held in Rio in 1992, they were fully aware of agendas being pursued by such varied groups as the Vatican, radical environmental groups, Islamic and other fundamentalists, and even the accepted family planners who believed that "development is the best contraceptive"—agendas that would draw attention away from their women-centered agenda. As a result, they lobbied tirelessly and, in Cairo, it was those women from both North and South who wrote much of the final document, the "World Programme of Action," which recognized "the realities of women's lives in terms of lack of power, economic insecurity, abuse, violence and coercion, unrecognized and unmet health needs, and poor quality or no services."[23]

Among the many individual contributions made at these conferences, the speeches of Gro Harlem Brundtland and Hillary Rodham Clinton stand out. Dr. Brundtland, as well known for her global environmental advocacy as for holding the post of Prime Minister in Norway, delivered the keynote address in Cairo. Here are a few excerpts:

> Women will not become more empowered merely because we want them to be, but through legislative change, increased information, and redirection of resources.

> For too long women have had restricted access to equal rights.

> Women's education is the single most important path to higher productivity, lower infant mortality, and lower fertility.[24]

Hillary Rodham Clinton made it very clear that she wanted to attend the Beijing Conference despite a rather heated, and political, debate over whether or not she should, and if she did, what she should say, or would say, given U.S. policy toward China, especially Chinese human rights abuses. The day of her address to the NGOs, hundreds of women stood in a driving rain for over two hours hoping to get a chance to hear her.[25] Her address to the full conference, in which she forcefully promoted human rights and deplored atrocities such as female infanticide, women sold into slavery and prostitution, and women being burned to death because of insufficient dowries, electrified the audience. She proposed that "If there is one message that echoes forth from this conference, let it be that human rights are women's rights and women's rights are human rights, for once and for all" to an applauding, cheering, table-thumping response.[26]

Denial

Not everyone is worried. In a collection of comments on population as an environmental issue in *The Amicus Journal*, Francesca Lyman posits that "lack of progress in population control is a result of the perception that the threat of world overpopulation is an elitist, racist, myth." In the same issue of the journal, Frances Moore Lappé states that population is not the problem, poverty is; Barry Commoner repeats his long-held conviction that our problems stem from technology gone awry; Julian Simon says that "more people mean more brains—to think up more solutions"; while Paul Harrison points out that Malthus was wrong in predicting that food production would not keep up with population (though he acknowledges we have not maintained our natural resources in a manner commensurate with the growth in population).[27]

While many biologists fear that 10 billion people by 2050 will produce a total environmental disaster, many economists and others predict that technology will solve problems of scarcity, environmental degradation, and such.[28] In *A Moment on the Earth,* Gregg Easterbrook suggests that, in the long run, population growth will be desirable,[29] and he discusses UN projections that, although predicting a population of 14 billion for the twenty-first century, also predict that, if the entire world reached Scandinavian fertility rates by mid-twenty-second century, the population would decline to 4.3 billion. He points out that, should population recede over a few centuries, its threat to the planet would be shorter than that of historical natural events, such as ice ages.[30]

The denials have a hollow ring. For starters, the effects of overpopulation are nothing like the effects of an ice age. Further, when Easterbrook asserts that "orthodox environmentalism considers the preservation of Bengal tigers a priority, the death of a peasant a distraction better left unmentioned,"[31] one must wonder just how much he knows about the mainstream proponents of environmental protection and about the issues they deal with. Interestingly, Rush Limbaugh, in *See I Told You So,* doesn't comment on population control, other than to deplore the distribution of condoms in schools.[32]

The United States' Position

Where does the United States stand on population control? It's probably fair to say that most U.S. policymakers and a majority of the American electorate do not know much about the issue or have chosen to ignore it. As we have seen, the United States' 5 percent of the world population uses 30 percent of the world's resources, but it is "the only *industrialized* nation in the world that doesn't have a federal population policy."[33] However, in 1970 (shortly after *The Population Bomb* appeared), Congress enacted the Family Planning Services and Population Act, which includes the Title X provision for aid to family-planning agencies. In 1972 a Nixon population commission recommended that "the nation welcome and plan for a stabilized population." President Carter's Global 2000 Report included an admonition that we should be more aware of future issues such as population and environmental control and consider them in decision making.[34]

At the U.N. Population Conference in Mexico City in 1984, though, the Reagan Administration called population growth a "neutral issue," and both the Reagan and Bush administrations denied funding to the U.N. Fund for Population Activities and the International Planned Parenthood Federation, major funders for family planning, population education, and services to developing countries, because of any possible aid or advice concerning abortions.[35] Still true today, conventional wisdom then was that the politicians retreated from even the slightest action related to population control because of the controversy surrounding the *Roe* v. *Wade* decision.

President Clinton reinstated the funding of these agencies, albeit at the lowest rate of all developed nations except Ireland, as a percent of GNP/capita.[36] At this writing, though, Congress has passed, and the president signed, legislation that will cut the population and family planning budget of the Agency for International Development (AID) by 35 percent. This agency is the largest provider of these services in the world. (The legislation was part of the Foreign Appropriations Bill, which in turn was part of the legislation passed to prevent another government shutdown.)

Agency experts say that the cuts "will be crippling, not only to birth control programs but also to related activities like maternal health care and AIDS prevention." Senator Mark Hatfield (R, OR), in a press release said, "What we did is bar access to family planning services to approximately 17 million couples, most of them living in unimaginable poverty."[37]

PROJECTIONS

The trends are not reassuring. In a study on the social implications of population growth, Matthew Connelly and Paul Kennedy describe the future:

> In broad figures the future pattern of global population increases is not in dispute. At present the earth contains approximately 5.7 billion people and is adding to that total by approximately 93 million a year....

> By 2025 the planet will contain approximately 8.5 billion people. The pace of growth is expected to taper off, so the total population may stabilize at around 10 or 11 billion people by perhaps 2050, although some estimates are much larger.

After a short roster of those slated to gain the most in population, the authors point out that "95 percent of the twofold increase in the world's population expected before the middle of the next century will occur in poor countries, especially those least equipped to take the strain."[38]

There are no immediate indications that the fertility rate worldwide will fall, or that the population will stabilize. China, with one-fifth of the world's population, has a fertility rate of only 1.5, but as Lester Brown points out, that rate is over a population of 1.2 billion. Even a low rate puts China "on track for adding some 490 million people between 1990 and 2030—the equivalent of four Japans—swelling its population to more than 1.6 billion."[39] And China's the worst example of a nation changing its tastes toward the more expensive: In their new prosperity, the Chinese want larger houses, lots of roads, and good beef to eat, all of which means much less agricultural land to grow food for its people. "China could thus become such a massive importer of grain that the United States and all the rest of the exporting countries combined will not be able to meet the need."[40] So much for drawing hope of population control from China's famous (or infamous) "one-child contracts": To the extent that they ever worked at all (Robert Kaplan calls that a "misconception"),[41] as soon as a signatory family becomes moderately prosperous in China, it tends to buy out of the contract.

China remains orderly, however; in the new economy, it is probable that its fertility rate will probably rise only slightly. The real population explosions take place in the poverty-stricken developing nations. In the Arab world, the birthrate is more than 3.2 percent. "Seventy percent of the Arab population has been born since 1970"[42] and is just entering reproductive life. Population growth is even greater in areas that have lost social order and all expectation of prosperity. Thus the highest birthrates in the developing nations come from areas where the traditional limitations of village life have been destroyed by urbanization. In agrarian villages, the population adjusted to available resources over centuries— that's how the villages survived. The move to the city shantytown, after leaving the land, takes away previous limits, so that the birthrate goes up.[43] For example, the Rwandan Hutu in the refugee camps in Zaire have had every status in life shattered by war and exile; in the fear and boredom of the camps, the birthrate has soared to almost 6 percent. About 2,800 babies are born every month in one camp in Goma, more than the number of Hutu who choose to leave the camp and return to Rwanda. Contraceptives and shots of Depo-Provera are freely available in the camp, but in general, the Hutu do not choose to use them.[44]

How far can this increase go before we crush the crust of the earth? Predictions of how many people the planet can hold range from less than three billion (obviously wrong) to 44 billion.[45] From Malthus forward,

TABLE 2-2   Declines in Fertility Rate, 1960–1995

	1960	*1995*
South Korea	6.0	1.6
Singapore	6.3	1.8
Taiwan	6.5	1.8
China	5.5	1.9
Brazil	6.2	2.9
Costa Rica	7.4	3.1
Mexico	7.2	3.1

the major factor considered in predictions is, of course, food production. But more sophisticated studies have included other variables, such as distribution of wealth, technology, politics, economics, values, tastes, and fashion.[46] For instance, a society that insists on beef in the diet will need vastly more food than one that does not; a society that insists on fur coats will have to grow predators, at the top of the food chain, consuming even more of the available food.

SOLUTIONS

For years, the generally accepted solution to population problems in the Third World, at least among policymakers in the North, has simply been access to contraception and other modes of family planning.[47] They have also insisted that "development is the best contraceptive," the phrase bandied about at the 1974 population conference, because the more developed nations have a consistently lower birthrate. Since then, numerous studies have demonstrated declining fertility rates in countries that have not necessarily had economic growth, but have had improved population planning programs and increased services to women. As the authors of one article on fertility decline conclude, "Contraceptives are the best contraceptive."[48]

Recently, some dramatic drops in fertility rates have been recorded. Once again, the *fertility rate* is the average number of children born to a woman in her lifetime in a given country. You can see a sampling of these declines in Table 2-2.

You can see that, with one-fifth of the world's population, and an extremely aggressive population policy, China has a fertility rate that has declined from 5.5 in 1960 to 1.9 in 1995.[49] Evidence mounts that economic development may be a less important factor in reducing population than societal factors such as better women's and prenatal health care, better access to reproductive information, better education for women, and an increase in the status of women. Countries with minimal economic growth, such as Costa Rica, Cuba, and Sri Lanka, have shown declines in fertility. Additionally, countries with high fertility rates also have high mortality rates, low per capita income, low literacy, and a high percentage of rural population.[50]

A study reported by the Worldwatch Institute surveyed the effect of various social and economic factors on fertility rates in 80 countries between 1960 and 1980. Among the indicators looked at were literacy rate, health care, life expectancy, family planning programs, urbanization, per capita income, and energy use. They found that "fertility levels were much more closely related to the social indicators—literacy, life expectancy, and family planning effort, than to any measure of economic development."[51]

Nevertheless, it appears that social advancements alone cannot provide the cure. Countries that have strong birth-control programs, such as China, Indonesia, Thailand, and South Korea, have also seen dramatic drops in birthrates. In Indonesia, for example, one family-planning program includes 40,000 village centers that distribute free contraceptives and provide reproductive information and services. The slogan "Families should be small, happy, and prosperous" is promulgated. Religious leaders favor contraception, family-planning jingles are broadcast, and at 5:00 P.M. sirens go off to remind women to take their pills. The fertility rate is down from 5.6 in 1972 to 3.5 in 1989; contraceptive use is up from 400,000 couples in 1972 to 18,600,000 couples in 1989. Abortion is illegal.[52] Similarly, in Zimbabwe, a family-planning worker goes from hut to hut carrying "a log book, blood pressure gauge, pills, condoms, and a seven inch wooden penis for demonstration purposes."[53] The fertility rate is down and contraceptive use is up. Success does not require high technology.

SUMMARY CONCLUSION

Some contend that there is no population problem. The evidence appears to deny that. Some still believe that "industrialization is the best contraceptive." The evidence appears to deny that as well. Even if it were so, given the mathematics, we don't have time to let industrialization do its contraceptive work. Emphasis on social programs as well as the availability of reproductive services appears to be the best hope for maintaining the human population at numbers commensurate with the survival of our species at a reasonable standard of living, not to mention the rest of the living planet. To quote Henry Kendall of MIT, "If we don't control the population with justice, humanity, and mercy, it will be done for us by nature—brutally."[54]

QUESTIONS FOR DISCUSSION AND REFLECTION:

✦ What options are open to us for controlling population? Which are feasible as suggested for voluntary adoption? Which are acceptable as coercive measures? (For instance, would it ever be justifiable to condition a woman's freedom on her acceptance of Norplant contraceptives?)

✦ Can we make a case that population simply is not the problem—that work on something else (food production, education for women, for example) will solve the problems that we now identify with "overpopulation"?

✦ From your familiarity with world history, construct a probable scenario for the next 100 years. How will the population problem *probably* be dealt with *in fact*?

Notes

1. Paul Ehrlich, *The Population Bomb* (New York: Ballantine Books, 1971): p. xi.

2. Ibid., p. 17.

3. Paul R. Ehrlich and Anne H. Ehrlich, *The Population Explosion* (New York: Simon & Schuster, 1990): p. 9.

4. Ibid., p. 23.

5. Resources on population figures abound, but check the Ehrlichs' works, any number of resources at the Population Reference Bureau (Washington, D.C.), and Joel E. Cohen, "Population Growth and Earth's Human Carrying Capacity," *Science* (21 July 1995): p. 341.

6. Nathan Keyfitz, "The Growing Human Population," *Scientific American* (September 1989). From *Managing Planet Earth: Readings from Scientific American Magazine* (New York: Freeman, 1990): p. 64.

7. George Mitchell, Jr., *World on Fire* (New York: Scribner, 1991): pp. 88–89.

8. Ehrlich and Ehrlich, *The Population Explosion,* p. 2.

9. Ibid., pp. 59–60. India's fertility rate in 1995 was 3.4, according to the Population Reference Bureau's "World Population Data Sheet."

10. Editorial, "Birthrates and Earth's Fate," *Boston Sunday Globe* (10 July 1994).

11. Griffith Feeney, "Fertility Decline in East Asia," *Science* (2 December 1994): p. 1518.

12. Paul R. Ehrlich and Anne H. Ehrlich, *Healing the Planet* (New York: Addison-Wesley 1991): pp. 7ff.

13. Ehrlich and Ehrlich, *The Population Explosion,* pp. 67ff.

14. Bernard LeGuenno, "Emerging Viruses," *Scientific American* (October 1995): p. 56.

15. Cohen, "Population Growth," p. 341.

16. Ibid.

17. "How Much for How Many," *Environmental Action* (Summer 1994): p. 17.

18. Brian Donahue, "Putting Population in Perspective," *Friends of the Earth* (Sept./Oct. 1994): p. 7.

19. Cohen, "Population Growth," p. 341.

20. Donahue, "Putting Population in Perspective," p. 7.

21. Lincoln C. Cen, Winifred M. Fitzgerald, and Lisa Bates, "Women, Politics and Global Management," *Environment* (Jan./Feb. 1995): p. 4.

22. Worldwatch Institute, *State of the World 1995* (New York: Norton, 1995): p. 177.

23. Gita Sen, "The World Programme of Action: A New Paradigm for Population Policy," *Environment* (Jan./Feb. 1995): p. 10.

24. Gro Harlem Brundtland, "Empowering Women" [edited version of Gro Harlem Brundtland's address to the U.N. Cairo Conference on Women], *Environment* (December 1994).

25. Bobbie Hill, et al., "A Beijing Diary," *National Voter* (Dec./Jan. 1996): p. 11.

26. Patrick E. Tyler, "Hillary Clinton in China, Details Abuse of Women," *New York Times* (6 September 1995): p. A1.

27. "Our Earth, Ourselves: Population, Consumption and the Planet," *The Amicus Journal* (Winter 1994): pp. 15ff.

28. Sharon Begley, "Can More = Better?" *Newsweek* (12 September 1994): p. 27.

29. Gregg Easterbrook, *A Moment on Earth* (New York: Viking Press, 1995): p. 475.

30. Ibid., p. 490.

31. Ibid., p. 483.

32. Rush Limbaugh, *See I Told You So* (New York: Pocket Books, 1993).

33. "How Much for How Many?" p. 16.

34. Ibid.

35. Population Institute, "Overpopulation Is Escalating Poverty," *Popline* (March/April, 1995).

36. Editorial, "Birthrates and Earth's Fate."

37. Barbara Crossette, "U.S. Aid Cutbacks Endangering Population Programs, UN Agencies Say," *New York Times* (16 February 1996): p. A14.

38. Matthew Connelly and Paul Kennedy, "Must It Be the Rest Against the West?" *Atlantic Monthly* (December 1994), pp. 61–91; 72.

39. Lester Brown, "Averting a Global Food Crisis," *Technology Review* (Nov./Dec. 1995): pp. 44–53.

40. Ibid., p. 46.

41. Robert D. Kaplan, "The Coming Anarchy," *Atlantic Monthly* (February 1994): p. 60

42. Ibid., p. 70.

43. Virginia Abernethy, "Second Opinion: Optimism and Overpopulation," *Atlantic Monthly* (December 1994): pp. 84–91.

44. James C. McKinley, Jr., "Anguish of Rwanda Echoed in a Baby's Cry," *New York Times* (21 February 1996): pp. A1, A8. Depo-Provera is a hormone application that hinders ovulation.

45. Cohen, "Population Growth," p. 341.

46. See Cohen, "Population Growth," and Francesca Bray, "Agriculture for Developing Nations," *Scientific American* (July 1994): pp. 30–37.

47. Donahue, "Putting Population in Perspective."

48. Bryant Robey, et al., "The Fertility Decline in Developing Countries," *Scientific American* (December 1993): p. 60.

49. *Planning the Global Family*, Worldwatch Paper No. 80 (Washington, DC: Worldwatch Institute, December 1987); "World Population Data Sheet" (Washington, DC: Population Reference Bureau, 1995).

50. Brown, "Averting a Global Food Crisis," p. 6.

51. Worldwatch, *State of the World*, p. 42.

52. Keyfitz, "Growing Human Population," pp. 66–67.

53. Bill Keller, "Zimbabwe Taking a Lead in Promoting Birth Control," *New York Times* (4 September 1994).

54. Editorial, "Birthrates and Earth's Fate."

Suggestions for Further Reading

Brown, Lester. *Who Will Feed China? Wake-up Call for a Small Planet.* Worldwatch Environmental Alert Series. New York: Norton, 1995. See also his "Averting a Global Food Crisis," *Technology Review* (Nov./Dec. 1995).

Connelly, Matthew, and Kennedy, Paul. "Must It Be the Rest Against the West?" *Atlantic Monthly* (December 1994): pp. 61ff.

Ehrlich, Paul. *The Population Bomb.* New York: Ballantine, 1968.

Ehrlich, Paul R., and Ehrlich, Anne H., *The Population Explosion,* New York: Simon & Schuster, 1990.

Kaplan, Robert D. "The Coming Anarchy." *Atlantic Monthly* (February 1994): pp. 44ff.

CHAPTER 3

The Legacy of
an Explosion

Bhopal and Responsible Care

PREFACE: QUESTIONS
TO KEEP IN MIND

1. According to a *Scientific American* report in June of 1995, after more than ten years, the toxic effects of the accident at Bhopal persist in the environment—and the victims.[1] What characteristics of pesticides make them so dangerous for such a long time?

2. How did the tragedy of Bhopal come about? What were the factors contributing to the explosion itself and the extensive damage that followed?

3. Besides the explosion at Bhopal, what other considerations led the Chemical Manufacturers Association (CMA) to conclude that proactive measures had to be taken for public health and safety?

4. Had the Bhopal plant been in the United States, would safety standards and work practices have been different? What makes you think so—or not?

5. How did the origin and culture of the company—from the United States—influence the press and the lawyers? Is responsible care fundamentally an American or an international initiative?

6. Review the section on ethical reasoning in the introduction. How do the provisions of Responsible Care match the general imperatives of ethics?

PROLOGUE

We are long on stories of environmental disasters and the inadequate attempts made, by public and private authorities, to clean them up. We are short on stories of disaster responses that not only further the cause of the cleanup but also proactively insure that such disasters will be less likely in the future; as a rule, no such responses occur. The Chemical Manufacturers Association's institution of Responsible Care, a program designed to protect the health and safety of its workers, customers, and host communities, is a refreshing exception to this rule. Arising largely in response to industry disasters such as Love Canal and Bhopal, Responsible Care serves as a hopeful example of private sector initiatives to save the world, at least from certain kinds of disaster.

THE INCIDENT AT BHOPAL

The Night of Death

On December 2, 1984, about 11:00 P.M., a discontented employee (who is known, but has not been named) removed the pressure gauge from MIC Storage Tank 610 on the grounds of a pesticide plant run by Union Carbide India Limited (UCIL). He knew, or had very good reason to know, that the tank contained *Methyl Isocyanite (MIC)*, about 41 metric tons of it, and that water must never get into it. He almost certainly did not know why contact with water should be prevented; his home and family were most likely nearby, and injury to the people of the area was surely the furthest thing from his mind. But he knew that water would ruin the batch of pesticide being prepared from that MIC. This is apparently what he intended when he attached a hose, already connected to a faucet in the corner of the yard, to the hole left where the pressure gauge had been, and turned on the water.[2] Within hours, the ensuing chemical reaction had blown the safety valve in the tank[3] and allowed poisonous gas to spread over 25 square miles of the area downwind of the plant, killing about 4,000 people[4] and causing an undetermined number of injuries.[5]

The Significance

The aftermath of this simple-minded act of destruction engraved the name *Bhopal* on the international scene as a synonym for the senseless, unexpected, disastrous injury that can follow industrial accidents—and for the economics, law, and politics of compensation for that injury. The drama attracted a disproportionate amount of public interest and acrimony; within a few years of the incident, even as lawsuits continued, at least three books had been written about it, none of them friendly to Union Carbide or chemicals generally. Two of them—Dan Kurzman's *A Killing Wind* and David Weir's *The Bhopal Syndrome*, have been consulted extensively, along with materials from Union Carbide, as primary sources in the account of the incident; the CMA has supplied the material on Responsible Care.

The Company in India

Despite its American name, the company whose gas exploded into that lethal cloud was largely Indian-owned and completely Indian-operated. It was founded as a branch of Union Carbide Corporation, a U.S. company, almost 50 years ago to provide pesticides for India's agricultural "green revolution"; the plant at Bhopal dated from 1969.[6] There was nothing exotic or extraordinarily dangerous in the operation of its plants; the most common kind of pesticide produced in them is *carbaryl*, an ester of carbamic acid, a reliable and relatively safe product, marketed in the United States under the brand name *SEVIN.*[7]

Chemistry of disaster. There is no doubt that the chemicals employed in making the pesticide are dangerous. *Phosgene*, the deadly gas briefly used in World War I on the battlefield (and also in the gas chambers of the Third Reich) is a precursor of SEVIN. The UCIL process for its manufacture uses phosgene ($COCl_2$) and a methyl amine (CH_3NH_2) to produce the intermediate compound methylcarbamoyl chloride ($CH_3NHCOCl$). This last compound breaks down with heat into *Methyl Isocyanate* (CH_3NCO) and hydrochloric acid (HCl).

MIC is a variation of the cyanide group NCN_2, of which the highly poisonous hydrogen cyanide (HCN) is probably the most famous. Extremely unstable and dangerous, MIC is not ordinarily studied in a laboratory situation. Its boiling point is 39°C (102.4°F). Lighter than water in liquid form but heavier than air in gaseous form, it hugs the ground when released. Its breakdown products include carbon dioxide and stable amines (organic compounds of carbon, hydrogen, and nitrogen), but the process releases a vast quantity of heat (exothermic). It reacts violently with water (producing breakdown products and high temperatures) whether it be the water that entered the MIC storage tanks or the water in human tissue. Therefore, it is an extremely dangerous human poison, with no known antidote.[8] OSHA regulations allow human exposure at 0.02 parts per million (ppm) over an eight-hour period; irritation is felt at 2 ppm and becomes unbearable at 21 ppm.[9] Half an experimental rat population (LD_{50}) is killed by 5 ppm.[10] Of course, no one measured the concentration of the escaped gas at Bhopal, but as 50,000 pounds of it escaped,[11] the heart of the cloud must have greatly exceeded those limits.

The MIC is used as an intermediate in the production of SEVIN, considerably less poisonous than its chemical precursors.[12] Incidentally, the MIC route is not the only way to SEVIN, which can be produced by adding methylamine to a reaction of phosgene and napthol. MIC can also be produced without using phosgene. In Germany, Bayer makes MIC by combining dimethyl urea and diphenyl carbonate. What considerations led to the choice of this particular method of making SEVIN? Are either of the others preferable?[13]

When the CMA faced the problems raised by Bhopal, one of the first questions asked concerned the safety of this and all processes in their plants. Were there safer ways for them to operate?

Capitalists abroad. Why make the pesticide in India, in the middle of a dense colony of people, instead of some remote area in the United States, whence the relatively safe finished product could be exported? For one, transportation costs (and dangers) were eliminated and labor costs were a good deal lower in India, making the whole operation safer and more profitable as far as Union Carbide (UCC) was concerned. It also provided tax revenues and good jobs in a chronically depressed economy, in consideration for which the Indian governments sought, welcomed, and catered to those American companies willing to locate plants in their country. Bhopal is the capital of Madhya Pradesh, the largest and one of the poorest states in the nation. As part of the plan to bring industry into the area, the Indian government leased land in Bhopal for $40 an acre per year to Union Carbide.

As in most such enterprises, the host nation soon insisted on assuming a large share of the ownership of the "foreign" plants; however, in the case of Union Carbide's subsidiary, UCIL, India did not insist on a majority holding, because the plant was "high-technology" enterprise.[14] The Indian government held about 25 percent of the stock and the rest, up to 49 percent, was held by Indian citizens.[15]

The management of the plant was wholly Indian; the last American employee had left the Bhopal plant in 1982. This meant that American safety procedures could not be assumed. Union Carbide was very well aware of the instability of MIC, as well as the potential for any of a wide variety of contaminants, including water, to set off an explosive and lethal reaction. To prevent that reaction, UCC had left UCIL with a meticulous series of systems and rules all "aimed at preventing MIC from escaping, getting overheated, or being contaminated."[16] In general, the procedures work; similar plants in the United States maintain excellent safety records. Also, there had been only one fatal accident at the Bhopal plant—a worker had died of phosgene inhalation after cleaning out a pipe without a mask.

Investigations after the incident, though, revealed a litany of collapsed systems. Weir gives us a partial list:

> Gauges measuring temperature and pressure in the various parts of the unit, including the crucial MIC storage tanks, were so notoriously unreliable that workers ignored early signs of trouble. The refrigeration unit for keeping MIC at low temperatures (and therefore less likely to undergo overheating and expansion should a contaminant enter the tank) had been shut off for some time. The gas scrubber, designed to neutralize any escaping MIC, had been shut off for maintenance. Even had it been operative, post-disaster inquiries revealed, the maximum pressure it could handle was only one-quarter that which was actually reached in the accident.... The flare tower, designed to burn off MIC escaping from the scrubber, was also turned off, waiting for replacement of a corroded piece of pipe. The tower, however, was inadequately designed for its task, as it was capable of handling only a quarter of the volume of gas released. The water curtain [high-pressure spray], designed to neutralize any remaining gas, was too short to reach the top of the flare tower, from where the MIC was billowing.[17]

What had gone wrong? One of the main problems affecting decision making before the incident was the slim budget for maintenance. The Bhopal plant had never made very much money; its projected market never materialized. Designed to produce 5,000 tons of pesticides a year, it had produced 2,308 tons in 1982 and 1,647 in 1983; in 1984, it dropped below 1,000 tons.[18] Cost-saving measures were mandated, such as shutting down the refrigeration unit. As in many cases of cash-flow problems, routine maintenance was deferred. Suggested remodelings (to increase the height at which the "water curtain" could work, for instance) or movings (to the "obnoxious industry" zone outside of town) were impossible.

Other warnings were readily available. A Union Carbide investigative team had visited the site two years prior to the incident. Discovering many flaws in the safety arrangements, they had recommended changes, which had not been implemented. An enterprising journalist, Raj Kumar Keswani (who uncovered the UCC report), had written a series of exposés in the local newspaper on the safety problems at the plant. "Why didn't the insurance companies covering Union Carbide in the event of a chemical disaster require that the Bhopal plant fortify its safety systems? Why didn't the Indian authorities heed the repeated warnings sounded by [Keswani] of the impending danger posed by the Bhopal plant?"[19] Where, in short, were the others supposedly watching the store?

The problem underlined by Bhopal, from UCC's point of view, is one of proximity and control. For instance, before the accident, there was no reason to believe that Indian managers could not maintain the same safety standards maintained in similar plants in the United States; the plants were built to the same specifications. Nevertheless, when the accident happened, the managers on that shift were taking a tea break together, contrary to company rules and explicit instructions.[20] Was that foreseeable? In retrospect, should Union Carbide have terminated the operation as soon as it lost effective control—despite the loss of jobs for the areas and the financial interests of its shareholders? Again, when the CMA faced the problems posed by Bhopal, they examined accountability for safety procedures.

People in harm's way. Why were all those people in the way of the gas? The plant had been built in a small city, with perhaps a million souls in it before the establishment of the pesticide operation. It soon found itself surrounded by people. Employees who found housing near the plant brought their extended families with them. Meanwhile, a veritable army of India's homeless constructed shantytowns near the plant, occasionally against the plant walls themselves. These clusters of shacks, amounting to villages with names of their own (*J. P. Nagar, Kazi Camp, Chola Kenchi, Railroad Colony*) had grown into crowded slums since the plant arrived, and largely because of it.[21] These were the people so horribly gassed when the tank exploded. What were those people doing there, where they did not "belong"? Presumably it makes no moral difference that the people were poor and uneducated. But does it make any difference that the people had no "right" to be there? Is it appropriate to introduce the notion that people squatting on land that is not theirs (government land, in this case) are there somehow "at their own risk"?

The fact remains that the people were there, and the company knew it. Regardless of property rights, the company had a moral obligation to carry on operations safely—which, as we have seen, they were unable or unwilling to do.

Pain and ignorance. There were more victims than there had to be. Many of the citizens of Bhopal apparently ran toward the plant when they heard all the noise—to see what was happening. The suffering of the victims was intense and terrifying. MIC reacts furiously with moisture in exposed tissues, burning everything it touches.[22] The moisture in the lungs was first and most affected, although burns also occured in the eyes; cardiovascular, gastrointestinal, neuromuscular, reproductive, and immune tissues were also affected.[23] Respiratory symptoms were the most common (choking and shortness of breath) in the survivors, and may have lasted a long time in some of the victims. Good data may be hard to come by, though. Clinical studies done on the medical sequelae of the incident apparently lacked controls, impugning their validity, and show evidence of bias in design and conclusion.[24]

The damage caused by the disaster was compounded by the inability of the medical community to offer any real help. No one had ever talked to them about the possibility of injury from this gas. MIC poisoning was all but nonexistent; indeed, the gas was widely believed to be harmless, as Union Carbide's medical director continued to claim for some time after the gas had escaped.[25] When the injured began to turn up at hospitals, no one knew what to do for them. Drops for the eyes, oxygen for the ravaged lungs, was about all anyone could come up with.

This inexcusable ignorance became the first concern of the CMA group studying Bhopal. The most obvious flaw in the safety provisions at Bhopal was the total lack of communication with the community. All the safety provisions, operable or not, stopped at the factory gate. No one had ever tried to make the people in the crowded town around the factory aware of what to do should an accident occur at the plant.

It seemed obvious to the CMA group that injuries could have been prevented by more attention to public warnings. Had the people in the path of the gas known even to put a wet cloth over their noses and mouths, hundreds of lives might have been saved; but no one had thought to tell them. Their had been neither drills nor information. Should there have been? The probability was that there would never be any need at all to know what to do in the case of a massive gas leak, and attempts to "educate" the people might just cause panic. How do you balance, the industry had wondered, the known and certain disadvantages of fearful warnings with the unknown and unproved disadvantages of chancing a disaster without the warnings? As far as the CMA was concerned, Bhopal landed with the weight of 4,000 corpses on the side of public awareness and education.

The Industry That Night

As soon as the explosion hit the front pages, the Chemical Manufacturers Association, realizing that the welfare of the entire industry was at stake, entered the picture. Edward Holmer, then the president of the CMA, took the position that the crisis was not Union Carbide's alone—it affected every one of the CMA's members. So he assembled a committee, a special-purpose study group, and embarked on the task of responding to Bhopal. Eventually the CMA study group devised a series of codes for plant safety, requiring constant monitoring, self-assessment, reporting—and a third-party audit. All of these would become part of Responsible Care.

One reason that the CMA reacted as positively, and vigorously, as it did to the Bhopal explosion is that the ground had been prepared several years before. For that reason, some background on this organization may be helpful. The CMA is a trade or industry association. Like most such associations, it was formed for specific purposes—as a mutual support group among the companies that manufacture chemicals, to serve its members by providing technical support and advice, and most important, to protect its members from unwelcome government attention. By nature, an industrial association is a booster, a cheerleader for its members; the CMA was no exception. Founded as the Manufacturing Chemists Association in 1872, an industry club and forum for information and opinion, it became the Chemical Manufacturers Association (CMA) in 1978, with the express purposes of lobbying and technical support for its member companies. But by the early 1980s, the industry faced problems that went deeper than the next round of lunches with legislators.

Love Canal and Bill Simeral's speech. By this time *Love Canal* was a household word. As most people know, Love Canal was an abandoned ditch, dug in solid clay, in Niagara Falls, New York, that Hooker Chemical had used as a chemical dump. Disposal had been strictly in accord with the law of the day; the dump was covered with an impermeable clay cap. When Hooker deeded that land to the city school board in the 1950s, the deed had specifically warned the city not to pierce that cap—not to put any structures on the land or dig below the surface.[26]

But elective memories are short. By the time the trouble began, there were a school, a playground, and numerous houses on the old landfill. What Hooker had warned against came to pass: Whenever it rained, water coursed into the chemical wastes through the holes in the clay cap and, finding nowhere to go, filled the canal like a well-plugged bathtub, carrying who knows what witches' brew of chemicals floating on its surface up to ground level, to run out over the land.[27] Dogs came home with burnt paws, probably from lindane; children had odd burns on their hands and unusual illnesses. In June 1978, the *Niagara Gazette* began chronicles of sickened individuals who attributed their illnesses to exposure to the leaking chemicals of the abandoned dump; national media attention followed.[28]

In August 1978, the New York State Commissioner of Health declared a health emergency at Love Canal, ordering the first of several relocations of families from the area. In 1980, the U.S. Congress passed a bill called the Comprehensive Environmental Response Compensation and Liability Act (CERCLA, or "Superfund") to empower the EPA to make sure that hazardous substances were not released into air, water, or earth, and above all to clean up the old toxic waste disposal dumps. The chemical industry had opposed it, but given the headlines from Love Canal, opposition was unlikely to succeed. By the terms of that legislation, all toxic dump sites had to be cleaned up—and the chemical companies had to pay for it.

In July 1982, Attorney General Abrams had said that two studies showed that the levels of dioxin in homes next to the canal were among the highest that had been found in residential areas. So in June 1983, when the outgoing chairman of the CMA, Bill Simeral of Du Pont, stood up to give his valedictory address to this band of cheerleaders, he had a somber message to append to the upbeat figures and promise of profitable years to come.

> In recent years we have witnessed one sensational media story after another in which our products have been depicted as direct threats to the safety of people and the environment: PCB's, saccharine, fluorocarbons, formaldehyde—the list goes on. The problems of hazardous wastes and abandoned dumps have almost become syndicated features in many newspapers.[29]

The result has been a veritable phobia in the public mind—a near-universal fear of chemicals.

> In a sense, we have a one-item agenda: all the major issues facing us flow from the fear of chemicals, their presumed toxicity, and their potential impact on human health. Unless we can get the issue of chemical toxicity into proper perspective in the public's mind, we will never make genuine progress in the public policy arena.[30]

It is not unusual for a trade association to feel itself, and its industry, to be misunderstood by the public and maligned by a spiteful press. The usual proposed solution is a massive public relations campaign, but Simeral departed from the script:

> Let's begin by recognizing that we'll never do it with words alone. Public relations and advertising campaigns have their place, but what the public really wants is concrete action.

> What should we do? *To start, we can clean up the dumps.* It doesn't matter whether your company or mine has anything to do with a specific site. We are all being tarred with the same brush....

> What the public needs to understand—and what we have to continue to remind ourselves—is that the chemical industry represents the major resource of technical capability that the country has for dealing with this problem. I'm convinced that the best way to get the job done is for us, wherever feasible, to organize the cleanup ourselves and execute it ourselves.... The bottom line is that doing

something about abandoned dump sites doesn't mean talking about the problem; it doesn't mean holding press conferences; it doesn't mean conducting studies. *What it means is rolling up our sleeves, assigning project managers and going to work.*[31]

He recognized that the effort would be expensive, time consuming, and worst of all, from the company officers' perspective, a legal mine field. Granted; but to succeed, these expenses and risks had to be accepted.

The work was to be accompanied by attempts to correct misinformation wherever it showed up and by attempts to change the process by which sites were declared "hazardous" by the EPA. But the core of the effort to change public perception was to be undertaken not by the CMA but by individual companies, and was to be addressed not to public opinion but to the reality of toxic chemicals in unsafe dumps. This startling challenge from the podium that day woke the conscience of an industry and launched concrete measures to improve the land and protect the public.

Initial reflections. There are two oddities in that speech by Simeral in 1983. First, he criticized the industry he was supposed to be cheering. Second, he asked for an immediate commitment to action with no indication that any profit would result. Consider the implications of the latter point.

We recall how the business system is supposed to work, the finely constructed box, the outlines of which we traced briefly in the introduction. Within that box, the only motive is that of the deliberate and rational implementation of the company's long-term interests. Publicly held business corporations have no choice but to put profits first: The managers who make the decisions are no more than agents of the owners, the shareholders. They have a fiduciary obligation to serve their owners' economic interests; indeed, they have no right, as corporate officers, to put any other interests first. (Wall Street quietly reminds them of this every quarter.) Of course, Simeral's problems with public image and the danger of punitive legislation were real enough, oriented to the bottom line, and entirely acceptable. All companies have public relations departments. But if that was a public relations problem, why did he not treat it that way? If you have a problem with public perception, you adjust corporate communications, advertising, neighborhood sloganeering—whatever it takes —to create a positive public image. That's worth paying for, and we have many firms that make their living creating images. But Simeral had not gone that route. Besides worrying, inevitably, about the public image of the industry, he seemed to be thinking about the reality of the dumps, thinking outside that box, making a genuinely moral critique of his industry's practices.

He also asked for action that had no apparent positive link to the bottom line, but reflected genuine responsibility for the effects of chemical storage in the old dumps. But no one had *ever* suggested, save in the heat of a lawsuit, that the industry should in some individual and collective way take responsibility for chemicals discarded after their manufacturing cycles were completed. A utopian's dream and a lawyer's nightmare, such a voluntary extension of responsibility—hence of liability—seemed way out of proportion to the problem of public perception that he had mentioned. Yet the suggestion of cradle-to-grave responsibility for chemical products, as envisioned by the Resource Conservation and Recovery Act of 1976, far outside the box as that must have seemed for a private industry at the time, became incorporated in the ultimate Responsible Care provisions.

Bhopal came to the CMA as a piece of very bad news: Once again, the industry was all over the front pages as unsafe, badly run, a deadly threat to anyone who might be in the area. Industries have a variety of responses to pieces of bad news, most of them wrong or counterproductive or both: denial, lies, secrecy, cover-ups, and other forms of damage control; promoting and firing all the wrong people; public relations campaigns—anything but dealing with the problem. The CMA members' positive response to Simeral's challenge, however, had prepared the association well for rapid and useful responses to very bad news, and within the limits of the situation, it responded very well indeed.

LAWYERS AND POLITICIANS

Union Carbide Corporation's response to the explosion was instantaneous: Warren B. Anderson, the chairman of the board and chief executive officer of the company, announced that the company took full moral responsibility for the disaster, and that the victims would be compensated. He then left immediately for Bhopal, authorized by his board of directors to offer anywhere from $1 million to $5 million in aid on the spot, and pledged to find out how the company could best help the victims. But Anderson was arrested by the Indian authorities when he stepped off the plane at Bhopal and detained in a company guest house for a few days. He never got to interview the victims or his managers from the plant, never got to offer help. Promised interviews with the governor and the prime minister never materialized; not even the environmental minister would talk to him. As is now widely known, that official reaction to Anderson was symptomatic of the Indian response as a whole: The incident was played for political advantage by Indian officials in that election year until the lawyers arrived from the United States to take up the cause of the victims.

Litigation was initiated by teams of lawyers who wanted to represent the victims in damage suits against UCC, before U.S. District Court Judge John Keenan, with the object of having the cause tried in the United

States. Judge Keenan accepted on behalf of the victims $5 million from UCC, the first money actually to be routed toward the sufferers. More significantly, he ordered the cases back to India, on grounds that the accident had occurrd there and so the victims, witnesses, documents, and applicable laws were there also. The government of India promptly invalidated the lawyers' claims, taking on itself the right and duty to speak for the victims. After more litigation, dragging on for three more years, Chief Justice R. S. Pathak of India's Supreme Court directed a final settlement of all Bhopal litigation in the amount of $470 million, to be paid by March 31, 1989; full payment was made by the end of February.[32] In January 1993 another legal challenge was brought, attempting to reopen the case in U.S. courts; that challenge was rebuffed.[33] At that time, very little of the money set aside to pay compensation to victims (by that time totaling over $700 million) had been distributed to the "tens of thousands" of actual sufferers, with no end to the distribution process in sight.[34]

Why did it take so long to get money to the victims? The answer seems to be a combination of politics and calculation. On the political side, much advantage seemed to flow from portraying Union Carbide as "murderers" who had knowingly foisted a terribly dangerous operation on an unsuspecting community. The political players were soon competing with each other in hyperbolic condemnation of the company, in scornful rejection of any proposed settlement as a tiny fraction of what was really owed, and in posturing as saviors from the unimaginable dangers of anything the company might ever again do with regard to Bhopal. In what may have been the supreme act of cynicism in the entire Bhopal affair, Arjun Singh, the governor of Madhya Pradesh, created a full-blown panic in Bhopal when UCC Vice President Van Mynen led a technical team in on December 18, 1984, to convert the remaining MIC to SEVIN (the safest way to dispose of it). Singh urged residents to evacuate the town if they could, but pledged that he personally would guarantee that these "murderers" would do no harm during this routine operation. He would personally order the appropriate safeguards—which included shutting all the schools and colleges, which were in the middle of examinations. He then announced that wet cloths would be draped over all the fences, a tent of wet cloths would be erected over the MIC tank and continually sprayed with water, and, just to make sure, "Indian Air Force helicopters would hover overhead and periodically spray the plant with water."[35] The conversion operation was perfectly safe, but the panic caused even more lives and much more property to be lost. In such an atmosphere, who would dare sit down at a negotiating table with Union Carbide and presume to talk about a "fair" settlement?

Nor was that the only time that political frustration resulted in real damage to the residents. Union Carbide funded a Vocational Training School to relieve the poverty of the area, but the government closed it.

Thwarted in their attempts to go through the government to reach the victims, UCC provided over $2 million to Arizona State University to build and operate a rehabilitation center for the injured. "The center was built, and operating well, but when the state government learned that Carbide money had funded it, bulldozers were sent in to knock the building down."[36] UCC and UCIL together offered to fund a hospital to treat the victims over the long term and provide more jobs and better medical care for the area; at last accounting, they had not obtained permission to start it up. On the one hand, in the light of the political situation, these actions are not surprising, and they were expected to produce a larger compensation in the long run. On the other hand, the victim of the killer cloud, the impoverished Indian sickened by the gas, might have been helped by the vocational school and hospital, but could not possibly benefit from merely symbolic acts.

Liability

Efforts to attribute fair liability and determine compensation, in the aftermath of the leak, rapidly drowned in exaggerated estimates of the amount of money available from the company. In a poor country, the amounts demanded in "compensation" were not at all in line with the experience of the justice system. First, the estimates of damages payable were high by any standards. Within a year after the incident, Alfred de Grazia, writing on behalf of the India-America Committee for Bhopal Victims, concluded that UCC owed the victims and their survivors $1,318,650,000 (American dollars).[37] And he did not know that more were to die. Families and individuals discovered or invented reasons for thinking that they were owed particularly large amounts. Depending on political advantage, Indian officials alternately dangled and withdrew promises of much more money for the victims.[38]

Further, because records of deaths and injuries were woefully inadequate, it was impossible to verify who had actually suffered from the gas and who had suffered "only" from poverty, malnutrition, and disease.[39] Because emergency measures that were supposed to save lives, at the hospitals and in the town, were impossible to coordinate in the heat of the incident itself, one could not attribute blame for injury and death with any reasonable certainty. After the incident, attempts to register who deserved compensation were shot through with bureaucratic inefficiency and blatant corruption; with UCC money looming in the background to repay all debts, there seemed no reason why every official and secretary—and even the occasional doctor or policeman—should not seek maximum financial reimbursement for performance of duty.[40] Swamped with bills and documents of dubious reliability, the government officials simply could not determine who should get how much;

most of the money remains in the banks. Between the lawyers and the politicians, the victims were promised millions. They have received next to nothing.

THE CHEMICAL INDUSTRY AND RESPONSIBLE CARE

For the victims and industry alike, life went on in the shadow of the explosion. It went very unpleasantly for UCC for some time. There was the trauma of the explosion, the waves of guilt (deserved or not), and the frustration of not getting real help to the victims. Then GAF, noting the depressed stock and sensing weakness, made a run at the company to take it over; though the attempt was thwarted, it drained UCC's energies and coffers. Then there was a recession; then, nine years after the explosion, an Indian court ordered Union Carbide officials to stand trial for culpable homicide.[41] In 1994, just about ten years after the explosion, UCC sold its stake in the Indian plant for "about $90 million," donating the proceeds for eventual help for the victims. That ended the incident for the company; by the following summer, UCC was reporting higher demand for its products, higher earnings, and tripled sales.[42] Indeed, the whole chemical industry seemed to be doing better. One likely reason for this recovery was the industry response to Bhopal.

CAER: The First Step

Bhopal showed that the industry must always deal with the safety of the community. How could the industry assure people of such safety in towns that hosted chemical plants, given proof that these plants were terribly dangerous? In 1985, the CMA was given a draft of a set of requirements, for voluntary adoption by the membership. Called the Community Awareness and Emergency Response program (CAER), it reflected a solid commitment on the part of the study participants to cooperation with localities for the protection of the public. The CAER code required members to communicate with the public outside the plant—not just to answer questions truthfully, but to reach out to the community to begin the dialogue. They had to tell the public what sort of safety provisions the plant had made against various possible accidents. Above all, they had to discuss with the local police and fire departments just what sorts of disasters might occur, how to cope with them, and how the chemical company might help. In a radical development, they were required to work out with local governments some means of conducting a disaster drill once a year. The essence of the program was communication: within each plant, to make sure all emergency procedures were known to all employees; with all local authorities, especially police and fire; and with the public at large, to make sure that the community was aware of the overall plan.[43]

Meanwhile, the Canadian Chemical Producers Association had concluded that it required radical changes in all aspects of its operations in order to regain the trust of the public. Two aspects of CAER made it particularly attractive as a model. First, it was specific as well as general, mandating certain practices and reporting procedures on those practices. Second, the industry had voluntarily accepted it and was already actively implementing it. After adopting CAER, the Canadians went beyond it in three significant ways:

1. They generalized CAER to encompass all activities of the chemical industry, projecting management codes for research, transportation, distribution, health and safety, manufacturing processes, and disposing of hazardous wastes, as well as emergency response to accidents. They called this comprehensive program Responsible Care, the name that survives to the present.

2. They derived a set of "guiding principles" from these practices, a short list of imperatives that would govern the whole enterprise of manufacturing principles (see the next section).

3. They made adherence to this plan mandatory for all members of the association. There is no misreading the last sentence of the "Statement of Commitment": "The most senior executive responsible for chemical operations in each member company of CCPA has formally accepted these principles and endorsement is a condition of membership."[44]

The Adoption of Responsible Care

When the CMA conducted surveys among its members in 1986 and 1987 to see how it might be more useful to them, it found that the first item of concern was the public image of the chemicals industry. So it launched a public perception committee (PPC), led by Paul Oreffice of Dow, which had had its own experiences with public perceptions over the manufacture of napalm during the U.S. engagement in Vietnam. Possibly the membership hoped that a truly effective public relations campaign would emerge from the PPC. The PPC, though, took a totally different route, following the path blazed by Bill Simeral; the "public perception" problem was not one of public impressions but of industry performance. To change those perceptions they would have to change their performance—radically, permanently, and visibly.[45]

The Canadian program provided a viable model. Anything that worked in Canada would likely work in the United States; for the most part, Canadian companies are branches of U.S. companies or of European companies that also have plants in the United States. The CMA executive committee looked over the Responsible Care provisions, liked what they saw, and decided to import it wholesale. In the summer of 1988, the officers of the CMA built consensus in the industry through a series of meetings with chemical company executives. All of their objections were addressed during those meetings, so that when the CMA Board (composed of 45 executives of member corporations) took a vote in September, the decision was unanimous in favor of adopting Responsible Care as mandatory.

Members were required to sign a statement of principles, "known as the 'Guiding Principles,' and they had to agree to implement any requirements, or Codes of Management Practice, that the organization might develop in the future."[46] No guarantees were available except that CAER seemed to work, the CEOs of many companies had bought into the idea, and every firm would have to participate or be forced out of the association.[47] What they had, in short, was trust. On the strength of the same trust, the entire membership voted to change the CMA bylaws to make Responsible Care a condition of membership. Despite lingering doubts about everything from legal liability to equity for smaller firms, the corporations that make up the chemical industry in the United States had handed their trade association a mandate to write rules to promote safety, health, the natural environment, community involvement, and fairness in allotment of burdens, especially where hazardous wastes were concerned. The CEO of each company promised in advance to adopt, publicize, sell to his employees, and adhere to these rules as well as be judged on them by his company, his peers in the CMA, and the public at large. On the whole, this is an extraordinary commitment within a market system.

Experimental Structures

Two emerging experimental structures of Responsible Care should, if successful, further challenge the standard business mindset. First, the third-party audit means that, in the standard understandings of American business, the company must have outsiders determine that Responsible Care's management procedures are in place. Though it goes against business traditions, the industry has agreed to give it a try. As of November 1994, the CMA was set to test a model management verification system that it has worked out with the help of the nonprofit group Clean Sites, Inc. (of Arlington, Virginia); DuPont and Haltermann Ltd. have agreed to be the guinea pigs. Already, code performance audits have been carried out in OxyChem, which employed four community advisory groups for the purpose, and Ashland, which invited the nonprofit group Ethics in Economics to evaluate its progress in the implementation of Responsible Care.[48]

The second challenge is the practice of mutual assistance: The larger companies have pledged to help the smaller ones with implementation. There have been instances of such assistance already; it is foreseen that the practice will grow.[49] Recall, however, that these companies are competitors. In the understanding of competition and the free market presented in the introduction, they should *want* each other to incur extra costs achieving compliance, or better yet, fail to comply, and be expelled from the CMA. The provision requires managers to move easily between a competitive and a cooperative mode, which is not supposed to be part of the job for a person employed in the business system.

PERSISTENT PROBLEMS

We are left with some persistent problems, or more appropriately, problems of persistence, in the chemicals industry. The MIC continues to cause damage at Bhopal because it is a deadly poison that persists in all environments. That, after all, is why it was made: to be deadly and to persist in the environment. That is why chlorine is useful in purifying water: It kills things, and it persists. Much too much in our lives depends on killing the little things that compete with us for our crops, lawns, shade trees, even the wood of our houses, and the lethal substances we use are ineffective if they break down and disappear from the environment too quickly. The final question we will have to answer is deadly simple and deadly serious: Are we willing to take the risks of continuing deaths by lethal chemicals for the sake of the usefulness of the final product? Have we, as some have suggested, made a pact with the devil by accepting the danger for the sake of convenience? What alternatives do we have?

QUESTIONS FOR DISCUSSION AND REFLECTION

✦ How do we strike a balance, in a crowded society, between the convenience of products and the risks associated with manufacturing them? Should the balance be different for a developing nation such as India than for a developed nation such as the United States?

✦ Are there alternatives to pesticide use and other uses of the products of dangerous processes? How might we work out such alternatives?

✦ Is Responsible Care a viable model for other industry associations? Can we discover a model for communications to promote public safety?

Notes

1. Madhusree Mukerjee, "Persistently Toxic: The Union Carbide Accident in Bhopal Continues to Harm," *Scientific American* (June 1995), pp. 16-18.

2. Ashok S. Kalelkar, "Investigation of Large-Magnitude Incidents: Bhopal as a Case Study," Paper presented at the Institution of Chemical Engineers' Conference on Preventing Major Chemical Accidents, London, England, May 1988.

3. Alfred de Grazia, *A Cloud over Bhopal* (Bombay, India: Kalos Foundation, 1985): p. 12.

4. Denise Lavoie, "Bhopal Still Haunts Former Carbide Chief," *Hartford Courant* (5 April 1992), pp. D1, D7. Union Carbide estimates 3,800. "Union Carbide Corporation Bhopal Fact Sheet," available from Union Carbide Corporation, Corporate Communications Department, Section C-2, Danbury, CT 06817-0001. Hereafter, documents obtained from that source will be identified as "UCC." Dan Kurzman, in *A Killing Wind*, estimates 8,000 "at least," and suggests that bodies were dumped anonymously in the river to account for the lack of evidence for more. See Dan Kurzman, *A Killing Wind: Inside Union Carbide and the Bhopal Catastrophe* (New York: McGraw-Hill, 1987): p. 77. de Grazia estimates 3,000 killed (*A Cloud over Bhopal*, p. 15), but he wrote before the toll of indirect death was complete.

5. Lavoie ("Bhopal Haunts") estimates 20,000 injuries; Union Carbide estimates closer to 3,000 with measurable injury after the fact (Ibid; UCC). Kurzman (*A Killing Wind*) estimates 300,000; de Grazia (*A Cloud over Bhopal*) has 30,000 disabled and 180,000 "affected to minor degrees." Such discrepancies are the rule in this issue.

6. Warren M. Anderson (former Chairman, Union Carbide Corporation), "Bhopal: What We Learned," distributed by Union Carbide Corporation (Danbury, CN 06817-0001; UCC Document #158). Kurzman, *A Killing Wind*, p. 21.

7. Kalelkar, "Investigation," p. 11.

8. "India's Tragedy: A Warning Heard Round the World," *U.S. News and World Report* (17 December 1984), p. 25; Pushpa S. Mehta et al., "Bhopal Tragedy's Health Effects: A Review of Methyl Isocyanate Toxicity," *Journal of the American Medical Association*, Vol. 264, no. 21 (5 December 1990): p. 2781.

9. Mehta et al., "Health Effects."

10. Kurzman, *A Killing Wind*, p. 41.

11. Union Carbide Corporation, *Bhopal Methyl Isocyanate Incident Investigation Team Report*, Danbury, CT (March 1985).

12. Union Carbide Corporation, *Team Report*; Paul Ehrlich et al., *Ecoscience* (San Francisco: Freeman, 1977); Kurzman, *A Killing Wind*, p. 22; David Weir, *The Bhopal Syndrome: Pesticides, Environment and Health* (San Francisco: Sierra Club Books, 1987), p. 31.

13. Kurzman, *A Killing Wind*, p. 22.

14. Weir, *Bhopal Syndrome*, pp. 30–31.

15. Anderson, "Bhopal: What We Learned;" UCC, "Bhopal Fact Sheet," p. 1.

16. Weir, *Bhopal Syndrome*, p. 33.

17. Ibid., pp. 41–42.

18. Ibid., p. 35.

19. Ibid., p. 49. See also de Grazia, p. 44.

20. Kalelkar, *Investigation*, p. 21.

21. de Grazia, *Cloud over Bhopal*, p. 12. Weir relates a personal interview with M. N. Buch, a former planning director for the state of Madhya Pradesh, in which Buch claims that old maps of the city showed the existence of these slums prior to the arrival of the plant; Union Carbide claims that the squatters arrived after it did. The two accounts are not incompatible. Weir, *Bhopal Syndrome*, pp. 36–37.

22. John Rennie, "Trojan Horse: Did a Protective Peptide Exacerbate Bhopal Injuries?" *Scientific American* (March 1992); p. 27.

23. Ibid.

24. Mehta et al., *Health Effects*.

25. Kurzman, *A Killing Wind*. pp. 81–82.

26. Deed of Love Canal Property Transfer, Niagara Falls, New York (28 April 1953).

27. When analyses were finally made, the mess included 43.6 million pounds of 82 different chemical substances, including benzene, chloroform, lindane, and other substances known to be harmful. See Ralph Nader, Ronald Brownstein, and John Richard, eds., *Who's Poisoning America? Corporate Polluters and Their Victims in the Chemical Age* (San Francisco: Sierra Club Books, 1981).

28. See Michael Brown, *Laying Waste: The Poisoning of America by Toxic Chemicals* (New York: Parthenon, 1980).

29. "Clean up Old Hazardous Waste Dumps to Allay Public Fear, Simeral Urges," *CMA News* (Summer 1983), pp. 6–8.

30. Ibid.

31. Ibid. All emphasis in original.

32. Union Carbide Corporation, Bhopal Chronology.

33. Sanjoy Hazarika, "Settlement Slow in India Gas Disaster Claims", *New York Times* (25 March 1993).

34. Ibid., p. A6.

35. Kurzman, *A Killing Wind*, p. 142.

36. Anderson, "Bhopal: What We Learned."

37. de Grazia, *Cloud Over Bhopal*, p. 116.

38. Kurzman, *A Killing Wind*, p. 157.

39. Ibid., p. 159.

40. Ibid., pp. 161ff.

41. News item, *New York Times* (12 April 1993), p. A17.

42. *Connecticut Post* (25 July 1995), p. C1.

43. Christopher Cathcart, "CAER Means Educating Communities," *CMA News* (April 1985).

44. Canadian Chemical Producers Association (Ottawa), "Responsible Care."

45. Interview with Jonathan Holtzman, cited in "Process Safety: Underscore Safety from Start to Finish: The Chemical Industry Responds with CAER and the Responsible Care Initiative," *1992 Safety Manager's Guide*, Bureau of Business Practice, pp. 320–332; also, interview with Clyde H. Greenert, director of Public Issues and Contributions, Union Carbide Corporation, Danbury, CT (3 May 1990), cited in Jeffrey F. Rayport and George C. Lodge, "Responsible Care," Harvard Business School Case Study #N9-391-135: 15 January 1991: p. 9.

46. Interview with Holtzman, "Process Safety," p. 324.

47. Rayport and Lodge, "Responsible Care," p. 10.

48. "CMA Gives Green Light to Third-Party Audits: 'One of the More Difficult Issues,'" *ChemicalWeek* Special Double Issue on Responsible Care (6 and 13 July 1994): p. 38.

49. "Refining the Role and Obligations of an Industry: Mutual Aid and Outreach Are Moving Forward," *ChemicalWeek* Special Double Issue on Responsible Care (6 and 13 July 1994). p. 32.

Suggestions for Further Reading

Brown, Michael. *Laying Waste: The Poisoning of America by Toxic Chemicals.* New York: Parthenon, 1980.

Carson, Rachel. *Silent Spring.* Boston: Houghton Mifflin, 1962.

Chemical Manufacturers' Association. *Responsible Care: A Public Commitment.* Available from the CMA, Washington, D.C.

De Grazia, Alfred. *A Cloud over Bhopal.* Bombay, India: Kalos Foundation, 1985.

Kurzman, Dan. *A Killing Wind: Inside Union Carbide and the Bhopal Catastrophe.* New York: McGraw-Hill, 1987.

Nader, Ralph, Brownstein, Ronald, and Richard, John, eds. *Who's Poisoning America? Corporate Polluters and Their Victims in the Chemical Age.* San Francisco: Sierra Club Books, 1981.

Weir, David. *The Bhopal Syndrome: Pesticides, Environment and Health.* San Francisco: Sierra Club Books, 1987.

CHAPTER 4

Diversity and the Trees

The Tropical Rainforest

PREFACE: QUESTIONS TO KEEP IN MIND

What, in general, do we mean by *life*? How do we define *diversity* so that diversity of life is desirable? By *life* we must mean at least biological life or lives, the community of all living things. The drive to preserve biodiversity—the diversity of life among the myriad species of the world— eventually entails an imperative to preserve species of insects that live on only one tree in the Amazonian Rainforest. Why do we want to save the lives of distant insects? What is the role of biodiversity in survival, for humans and other species?

What constitutes sustainable use, or sustainable development, of land? We say that ecosystems are being treated *sustainably* when we can continue to do whatever we are doing in that ecosystem indefinitely without hurting or using up the living environment around us. Sustainability entails limiting our intrusions into nature to those that the environment can repair in the normal processes of its life. Should we, ideally, be able to live on the land as the hunter-gatherers did before us, so that after hundreds of years of human activity, the nonhuman life would still flourish?

There are isolated and unique tribes of humans living in the rainforests whose existence is threatened, as are those of the insects. If their forest is felled, these people will die. Why? What sort of life do they lead that makes them so vulnerable to change?

These tribal groups are not biologically unique (all humans belong to the same species, *Homo sapiens*), but their culture is. What kind of culture do they have that we should value it? Is cultural diversity desirable in itself?

Sometimes, when we use the word *life,* we simply mean lifestyle, occupation, our way of getting on in the world. Are rubber tappers worth preserving, simply as an occupational subset not known elsewhere in the world? We do not protect steelworkers in their lifestyle, but we do protect family farms. What relation do the rubber tappers have with the forest that makes it possible for them to live compatibly with it?

Still, most people consider individual human life to be of infinite value. We shall start our story with one such human life.

CHICO MENDES: THE MAN AND HIS HERITAGE

Francisco Alves Mendes Filho (Chico Mendes), the president of the Xapuri Rural Workers Union, was murdered on December 22, 1988, as he walked out the back door of his house toward the outbuilding that contained his only source of fresh water.[1] The suspected murderers are the agents of a local cattle rancher who despised the rural rubber tappers, their union, and its president.

Chico Mendes "was to the ranchers of the Amazon what Cesar Chavez was to the citrus kings of California, what Lech Walesa was to the shipyard managers of Gdansk."[2] His funeral was held on Christmas Day and attended by thousands from around the world: labor leaders, academics, celebrities, reporters, environmentalists, and politicians.

The year 1988 had been the hottest year on record; it had seen massive (deliberate) burning in the Amazonian Rainforest and massive (natural) burning in Yellowstone Park in the United States. Also in 1988, Jim Hansen had warned of global warming known to be associated with deforestation (see Chapter 7). In that year, too, this simple worker, Chico Mendes, had attained world recognition for singlehandedly confronting the powerful cattle barons who were slashing and burning the forests of the Amazon.

In 1925, Chico Mendes' grandfather had moved from the coast of Brazil to Acre in the Amazonian interior, near the borders of Peru and Bolivia. He had moved to escape a lethal drought and to pursue his trade tapping the rubber trees. Mendes' father, Francisco, was 12 years old when his father moved to Acre, and he grew up in the rubber-tapping community, enduring its cycles of booms and busts, cycles controlled by the global supply of cheaper Asian rubber. The employment situation was terribly exploitive, one of classic servitude; the tappers were almost always in debt to the bosses who had virtually complete control over their lives. World War II brought a boom to the region; the rubber desperately needed by the Allies was no longer available from Singapore. The boom, however, did not mean prosperity for the imported and local labor, including Chico's father, whose rewards for their patriotic efforts were malaria and more exploitation.

Mendes was born in 1944 as a child of the Amazon. He developed an intimate knowledge of the forest, helped with the rubber work by the age of 9, and became a full-time tapper by 11. Shortly thereafter, he met Euclides Fernandez Tavora, a communist-trained tapper who introduced him to the radio, taught him to read and write, and incidentally instilled him with Marxist ideology by regaling him with tales of coups, dictators, class struggles, Brazilian history, and the enormous gap between Brazil's rich and its poor. By 1966, at age 22, Mendes was agitating for better conditions for the tappers, for schools for their children, and for the right to sell the fruits of their labors.

SOME BACKGROUND ON BRAZIL

During the 1960s, Brazil was saddled with a terrible burden of foreign debt and a population of 70 million. Only 3.5 percent of the population lived on 50 percent of the land, the Amazon basin; the rest of the population, mostly landless, crowded the coastal cities. The settlement of the Amazon seemed a logical solution to the debt and urban poverty, following the precedent set by Indonesia's "Transmigration," which called for the relocation of 140 million people from densely populated islands to less-populated ones, from 1950 to 1985.[3] Also, to reduce the debt, Brazil could log the rainforest and sell the logs to Japan, always a ready market for raw wood. So the government developed an elaborate plan to build roads into the Amazon for some 30 million people to travel to the interior and lay claim to practically free land. The authors of the plan expected the land to be not only a source of lumber for foreign exchange but also a useful social safety valve: land reform that would cause no distress whatsoever to the few but wealthy and powerful owners of most of Brazil's arable land.

By 1970, the Trans-Amazon Highway was underway, aiming at the sparsely populated areas such as Rondonia in the northeast, built by malaria-ridden work crews as exploited as the rubber tappers, directed by the usual bosses. The death toll during this construction is unknown; there were no roadside graves.[4] By 1972, a 1,200-kilometer section of road was open, with about 70,000 families on their way from cities and rural areas. One million kilometers were open by 1980 and, eventually, some 100,000 families took advantage of the government's offer of 250-acre wooded lots, free to those who would claim and clear them.

Besides the free land, the people had been lured by promises of schools, churches, and other amenities that never materialized. Most of these would-be homesteaders shortly abandoned their claims, defeated by malaria, poor soil, and the decrease in the price of coffee, but the government's terms, which included tax breaks and subsidized loans and credits, encouraged wealthier ranchers, who could clear the land surely and efficiently, to invest in a no-risk situation: The government paid their expenses and they were allowed to keep all profits. The agents of these ranchers followed the hopeful settlers down the highway with every intention of displacing them, along with any Indians or rubber tappers who might be in their way.

The settlers or the cattlemen's crews cut the forest, burned it during the dry season, and used the ash to fertilize crops and fodder. Here, the limitations of rainforest soil became crucial: The clearing, burning, and planting could provide useful grazing or crops for a few years (estimates range from 2–3 years to 10–12 years, depending on the estimator and the area in question), but then the settlers would be forced to move on to do more slashing and burning elsewhere; because there is no topsoil in the rainforests, agricultural use is nonsustainable.

One outstanding characteristic of the soil is its nutrient paucity. The rainforests are like "wet deserts," to use Edward Wilson's term, considered to be as fragile as any biome on the planet. The soil is naturally nutrient-poor, partially because of runoff from the drenching rains of the tropics; any topsoil or organic materials added to the soil would not stay and decay but would wash away. Additionally, any available nutrients are locked in the immense biomass of the trees. So when the trees are cut and carted away, the nutrients go with them; when the trees are cut down and burned, the remaining ashes serve as a one-shot-only fertilization. Even when the land is selectively cleared and fertilized by decaying litter, it quickly becomes almost sterile. The decay rate is so fast in the hot, humid conditions of the tropics, decaying soil quickly reverts to *laterite*, a hardpan of inorganic minerals with no supporting organic humus. Consider this: In temperate latitudes, a leaf takes about a year to decompose, and the combination of the decomposing organisms, the products of their metabolism, the partially decomposed organic material, and the soil minerals all form the humus that builds up topsoil. None of this happens in the tropics; after a few years of farming, the soil is lost forever.

Knowing this then, why do the ranchers slash and burn the rainforests? One or two experiences of watching their ranches turn to desert should teach them the futility of ranching on the rainforests. The answer seems to be that they do not care if the land is wrecked as long as they own the wreckage. All the ranchers want is more land, free of complications such as the rights of native Indians and rubber tappers. As Shoumatoff states in *The World Is Burning*, "The cattle are a smokescreen for land speculation. The forest is not even being converted to hamburgers. Most of it is going up in smoke to augment the holdings of the 1 percent of Brazilians who own most of the country's arable land, the majority of which is not in use."

So the ranchers are engaged, indirectly, in a form of *ecotage*, sabotaging the environment for some unrelated purpose. All attempts to convert this magnificent ecosystem to agricultural uses are doomed to failure because of the lack of topsoil. Allowing land to be ruined, so that no one else can use it and you can then buy it inexpensively and hold on to it, is perfectly legal in most places in the world—but is it right? If not, why not? Who is being hurt by these practices?

Most of us are being hurt, as it happens. A tropical rainforest is good for only what it is: a genetic gold mine; a biological wonder of the world; a source of fruit, nuts, rubber, and sometimes rare woods; a carbon storehouse; a defense against global warming; a climate maker; and an artist's delight—a farm or ranch it will never be. Chico Mendes died attempting to stop an activity that had no purpose beyond turning forest into desert; like the ranchers, he knew ranches would not work in the rainforest but, unlike them, he knew the value of the forest.

TROPICAL RAINFORESTS

The Amazon system encompasses about 2.7 million square miles—approximately 90 percent of the area of the contiguous United States—and touches areas of eight South American countries besides Brazil. This system is a 2,000-mile-long, continuous, 200-foot-high canopy of growth that has been called a "green cathedral."[5] The Amazon River is 4,000 miles long and dumps 170 billion gallons of water every hour into the Atlantic Ocean. The forest stores seven billion tons of carbon in its biomass; in an area of four square meters (about six square feet) have been found 750 species of trees, 125 species of mammals, 400 species of birds, 100 species of reptiles, and 60 species of amphibians—and, in one tree alone, 400 species of insects. According to Thomas Lovejoy of the Smithsonian Institution, "The Amazon is a library for life sciences, the world's greatest pharmaceutical library and a flywheel of climate. It's a matter of global destiny."[6] The world is at stake here; the wealth of the world is tied up in that enormous mass of life.

The world's tropical rainforests have been evolving for the last 350 million years, and natural selection has been acting on the species within them for 150 million years. Flowering plants began to dominate the land some 100 million years ago, taking over from the conifers, ferns, mosses, and other more primitive plants. Around the time the dinosaurs departed, 60 million years ago, began the immense increase in the biodiversity of the tropical forest. Although only about 1.5 million species have been identified and catalogued worldwide, it is generally agreed that somewhere between 10 and 100 million different species exist on this planet, *half* of them in tropical rainforests: 30 percent of all the world's birds are in the Amazon; another 16 percent in Indonesia. One entomologist saw 429 butterfly species in 12 hours in Brazil; there are 440 butterfly species in the entire eastern United States. In Peru, one hectare (2.5 acres) of land supports 300 species of trees, whereas all of Canada and the United States support 700 tree species.

In a landmark experiment, Terry Erwin of the National Museum of Natural History counted the species of insects in one small section of the rainforest canopy. An estimated two-thirds of all the forest's species live in the canopy, where there is abundant sunlight and thus photosynthesis, as opposed to the lower levels where less light is available—but reaching the canopy poses obvious logistical problems. So, Erwin devised a bug bomb that reached the treetops, set the bomb off, and then methodically collected and analyzed the thousands of insects that fell out of the canopy. Extrapolating from his data, Erwin estimated that there were 8,150,000 species of beetles living in the tropical canopy and a total of 30 million species of tropical arthropods.[7]

What makes this forest (a mere 6 percent of the world's landmass) the richest ecosystem on the Earth? Some factors that clearly contribute to this biodiversity are the heat of the tropical sun, the large contiguous area of living trees, the stability of the climate, and the humidity. (Interestingly, the greatest marine biodiversity is found at the same latitude, occupying the coral reefs.) Some marshes might be even more productive than the rainforests in terms of total mass of life, but certainly not in terms of the number of species, presumably because of the impact of seasonal changes. Within the stability of the tropical rainforests, one small piece of the system can provide a large habitat; for instance, the pools of water found in *epiphytes* ("air plants," plants that anchor to trees but get all their nutrients and water from the air) are the habitat for the damselfly nymphs that would be found in ponds in more temperate latitudes.[8]

The Threat to the Forest

The diversity of species is severely threatened because the rainforests are threatened, which is the very problem that brought these Brazilian provinces to our attention. Extinction is now proceeding at an increasingly rapid rate: "A fifth or more of the species of plants and animals could vanish or be doomed to early extinction by the year 2020 unless better efforts are made to save them."[9] As Wilson points out, we cannot afford to lose these plants and animals:

Why should we care? What difference does it make if some species are extinguished, if even half of all the species on earth disappear? Let me count the ways. New sources of scientific information will be lost. Vast potential biological wealth will be destroyed. Still undeveloped medicines, crops, pharmaceuticals, timber, fibers, pulp, soil-restoring vegetation, petroleum substitutes, and other products and amenities will never come to light. It is fashionable in some quarters to wave aside the small and obscure, the bugs and weeds, forgetting that an obscure moth from Latin America saved Australia's pastureland from overgrowth by cactus, that the rosy periwinkle provided the cure for Hodgkin's disease and childhood lymphocytic leukemia, that the bark of the Pacific yew offers hope for victims of ovarian and breast cancer, that a chemical from the saliva of leeches dissolves blood clots during surgery, and so on down a roster already grown long and illustrious despite the limited research addressed to it.[10]

The highly specialized evolution of the tropical rainforest, the product of millions of years of climatic stability and ecological integrity, adds to the problem of regeneration. After human assault, not only is the topsoil gone, but the seeds of the forest's plants have trouble germinating in the new conditions. These tropical species evolved in a stable environment, so they tend to be less adaptable to changing conditions. The seeds have a short germination time that precludes their being spread by wind or animals to a more suitable location or remaining dormant until favorable conditions return. All this bodes ill for the recovery or regeneration of the rainforest, once we have cut it down.

Without exception, every scheme to develop tropical rainforests has been a disaster—if not an immediate disaster, certainly a disaster for the well-being of the forests and all species, including our own, that depend on them. When farming and ranching fail (as discussed before), the ranchers simply add the resulting desert to their landholdings. When the settlers left Rondonia, the miners also moved in; seeking iron, tin, and gold, they slashed and burned as they went, destroying one-fourth of the trees in the state of Rondonia and causing intolerable water pollution. One immediate result of this assault on the environment was the decline in the area's Indian population from 35,000 in 1965 to 6,000 in 1985, because of disease and the stress of resettlement. These indigenous tribes, like the plants, evolved in conditions of stability unthinkable further north and are just as specialized as the damselflies. As Linden pointed out, "Move a hunter-gatherer tribe 50 miles and they'll starve to death."[11] The dislocations caused by the miners' assaults were beyond endurance and impossible to hide; finally, in an atmosphere of anarchy, the government closed the area to mining.[12]

The Role of International Agencies

The World Bank must take some of the responsibility for this series of debacles. The Grand Carajas Mining Project had been supported by a $3.5 million loan from the World Bank, as an alternative to cutting down the forests, but the project backfired: The miners required loggers to produce the wood for charcoal necessary to store the iron smelters, resulting in extensive deforestation and serious pollution of the air and water. Yet the mining continues, yielding 30 million tons of iron per year and aiming at 50. The Polonoroeste resettlement project, also backed by the World Bank, was equally disastrous; the settlers who survived the malaria epidemic left the unproductive land for the ranchers to exploit, as we have already described.[13]

The debate over deforestation of the Amazon region soon became global. Environmentalists started to take on the multilateral development banks, in response to loans that they had apparently made without any environmental or human considerations whatsoever. Even the dams these banks supported resulted in little power but lots of breeding areas for malaria-carrying mosquitos. Brazilians, stung by international criticism of Amazonian destruction through road building, became defensive and chauvinistic, pointing out that Americans would certainly not have appreciated outside objections to a road being built from New York to San Francisco.

It is sadly ironic that, as Edward Wilson points out, the poorest countries of the world have the responsibility of caring for its richest resources.[14] Yet one Brazilian environmentalist, Jose Lutzenberger, comments that, "This talk of 'we can do with our land what we want' is not true. If you set your house on fire it will threaten the homes of your neighbors."[15]

World pressure on Brazilian President Collar (exacerbated by pressure from U.S. environmentalists during his visit to the United States) contributed to the eventual creation of a 36,000-square-mile reserve for the Yanomami tribe, who had suffered a 15-percent population decline, primarily because of epidemics introduced by the settlers and ranchers.[16]

Other Amazonian tribes suffered equally: The Yuqui of the Bolivian Amazon were resettled to a missionary outpost as a means of resolving the battles between them and the loggers and settlers attracted by land grants. Totally uninitiated in modern ways, the Yuqui were suddenly forced to cope with a ten-thousand-year culture shock. The missionaries, dedicated to the material and spiritual welfare of those they served, were prepared to offer food, shelter, medical care, and education in Western ways to the disoriented Yuqui but tended to be insensitive to efforts to preserve their culture. Meanwhile, another road-building project was funded by the Inter-American Development Bank to train the Yuqui to farm, but the project's road builders conflicted with the missionaries over the treatment of the tribe. Finally, the government intervened (by now, there are *three* groups of outsiders telling the natives how to live); this discouraged the missionaries' evangelical approach but allowed them to provide education and medical care to the tribe. The Yuqui were torn from their land, normal occupations, traditional learning, rituals, and recreations and lost virtually all contact with their past.[17]

This loss of Amazonian culture as a result of development is a major concern for anthropology, beyond the human concern for the suffering of the individual uprooted tribespeople. Since 1900, 90 of Brazil's 270 indian tribes have disappeared. In cultural extinction, the Yuqui will join a growing roster of human groups who maintained an independent and unique culture but have now succumbed to the restless forces of modernization. Of the world's approximately 6,000 languages, for instance, it is estimated that 3,000 are "doomed."[18]

A GLOBAL RECAPITULATION

Stepping back from the Amazon for a moment, we note that the problem of tropical deforestation is terribly serious worldwide. Not all of it is happening in Brazil, and not all of it is the result of human inequality, national and individual poverty, or simple shortsightedness. The Sarawak Forest in Borneo, Malaysia, the oldest rainforest on earth, is being depleted solely for profit; it houses the last remaining stands of Philippine mahogany, highly valued by the Japanese, who are involved not only in purchasing the lumber but also in the actual logging operation.

In Borneo, the Japanese and the local politicians and lumber merchants are becoming millionaires at the expense of a forest the size of New York State that houses 20,000 plant, thousands of tree, and hundreds of butterfly species. Once again, the natives (in this case, the Penang, comprising half the local population) are the big losers. One tribe of hunter-gatherers, isolated from and ignorant of any other cultures, were driven from their home and habitat by government officials who tagged them as communists. It is estimated that Malaysia, now responsible for two-thirds of the world's export of raw logs, will become a net importer in ten years even though two-thirds of its remaining forest is licensed for logging.[19]

Tropical rainforests once covered 14 percent of the planet's landmass. Less than half remain, and most of the loss has occurred since World War II; an area about the size of Germany is lost every year. The Indian teak forests have become deserts; the Philippines have lost 90 percent of their forests over the last 50 years; and Thailand, which was once 53-percent forested, now has only 14 percent of its land as forest.[20] Rainforests are disappearing at a rate of 2 percent per year, or one football field per second. The world's tropical rainforests roughly equal the contiguous United States in area; the annual loss is equivalent to the size of Florida.[21]

ALTERNATIVES

It doesn't have to be like this. Alternative development strategies are working in Costa Rica, which has become the paradigm country for tropical rainforest advocates. Costa Rica's stable and historically democratic government has a cultural reverence for its ecological treasures; its three million people have managed to preserve 85 percent of their original rainforests. The movers and shakers in Costa Rica have discovered and tapped the international appeal of conservation and, with the financial help of First-World foundations, have managed to create enough national parks and protected reserves to give guarded assurance to the future of the 5 percent of the world's animal and plant species they house. These reserves also feed the national treasury by attracting crowds of "ecotourists." The nation also has an agreement with the Merck pharmaceutical company to share the profits from any medically useful discoveries that occur within their boundaries.[22]

Similarly, the Ranomafana Forest in Madagascar, which houses some endangered species and others unique to the island, has become a national park and has thus been saved from the logging that would have destroyed it by 2025. Once again, First-World money was involved: In this case, the U.S. Agency for International Development donated $3.2 million to provide schooling and health care to the peasants affected by the changes and also to train the peasants to become "ecotourist guides."[23]

Other than ecotourism and the gathering and harvesting we have discussed, the highest and most sustainable use of the resources of the rainforest is as a source of medically and industrially useful chemicals from its magnificent array of flora and fauna, including all those yet to be identified. Some 80 percent of the world's population uses *traditional* (folk) medicine to tend to their ills. (Given the growth in world population, these must be fairly successful.) Research done in Belize for the New York Botanical Garden and Yale University revealed that the dollars made from medicines gathered on two test plots (0.7 and 0.6 acre) equalled $294 and $1,346, respectively, versus the profit of $137 per acre in Brazilian Amazonian agriculture.[24] The potential profits are thus beyond belief—even setting aside the benefit of acquiring better medicines for the world's health—if we can keep the rainforest alive.

THE PEOPLE AND THE FOREST

Chico Mendes became the symbol of the fight to save the forest, although that had not been his first concern. He was a rubber tapper fighting for his people and their livelihood. Mendes himself was not comfortable being labeled an environmentalist. At one point when he heard himself so described, he said, "I'm not protecting the forest because I'm worried that in 20 years the world will be affected. I'm worried about it because there are thousands of people living here who depend on the forest—and their lives are in danger every day."[25] The unique feature of this environmental conflict is the unity of interest between the indigenous (aboriginal) hunter-gatherers and those who live off the natural bounty of the forest, such as the rubber tappers. This means that the forests have a real human voice pleading for them, as long as that voice is allowed to live and to be heard.

Chico Mendes' first marriage collapsed for the same reason that his second was being threatened at the time of his death: He was spending most of his time away from home, roaming the forest, and organizing the tappers to fight the incursion of the ranchers. Because Acre was the poorest state in Brazil in 1970, its governor followed the national policy of promoting road building and ranching, and the battle lines were quickly drawn between the newly arrived ranchers and the tappers who had been there for generations. In 1975, the union of rubber tappers was formed, and Mendes was elected secretary-general. In 1977, Mendes was elected to the local town council. By 1978, there was a statewide association of unions, real political power, and the beginnings of a political strategy, largely due to Mendes' leadership.

The unions' primary tactical weapon was the *empate*, a species of non-violent confrontation developed at the beginning of the battle to save the Amazonian Rainforest. An *empate* is conducted like this: Once the location of future logging was determined, the union leaders would enlist tappers who then marched to the site. There, after a civil conversation with the loggers, which might include an assessment of the loggers' future after the trees were cut, the loggers usually gave up their chain saws peacefully and went home while the tappers destroyed their camp. (The loggers and tappers had a lot in common as victims of bosses.) Each *empate* set back the ranchers' progress and absolutely infuriated them. The rubber tappers actually managed to drive two of Brazil's largest ranchers out of the area.[26]

The Amazon was Brazil's "Wild West," where might (and only might) made right and where there was (in fact if not in theory) no enforceable law or justice. In the late 1970s, there was a slight increase in political freedom and, therefore, more union activity; the rancher-sponsored killings then increased from under 25 deaths per year in the early 1970s to 39 deaths in 1975, 44 in 1976, and 51 in 1977.[27] Since 1980, one thousand people have been killed in arguments over land.[28] In July 1980, Wilson Pinheiro, the president of the local union, was murdered. The tappers, too incensed to attend to Mendes' pleas for nonviolence, retaliated by killing the rancher (de Oliverea) known to have hired the killers. Thus the cycle of increased violence began.

In 1981, Mendes replaced Pinheiro as the president of the Xapuri Rural Workers Union; he then organized schools, promoted educational projects, and participated in regional and nationwide rural workers' meetings and demonstrations. In 1984, while 4,000 delegates, including Mendes, attended a national meeting of rural workers, the government was still backing (slash-and-burn) "agrarian reform," and the confrontations between the tappers and ranchers continued. The *empates* continued to be successful and continued to enrage the ranchers. By 1985, Mendes' life was being openly threatened. From January 1985 to June 1987, 458 activist rubber tappers (rural workers, priests, union workers, lawyers, and so on) were killed, with 114 of those murders proven to have been committed by hired killers.[29]

A WORLDWIDE CAUSE

Meanwhile, Mendes was discovered and lionized by international academe; ecologists, anthropologists, and the media began to pay attention to him. The Brazilian anthropologist Mary Helene Allogretti signed on for the cause in 1976 and remained for the duration. She helped Mendes plan a national meeting of rubber tappers in 1985. At the meeting, Allogretti, Steve Schwartzman (former free-lance anthropologist currently with the Environmental Defense Fund), and the English photographer Adrian Crowell promoted Mendes as a spokesperson for the Amazon and backed his idea of creating extractive reserves—areas to be protected from chain saws and to be used only sustainably. The group was joined by Bruce Rich, an attorney with the Natural Resources Defense Council (and later with the Environmental Defense Fund) and an expert on the workings of the multilateral development banks (such as the World Bank and the Inter-American Development Bank) that were funding various destructive projects in the Amazon. This team believed that the outside world would never rally around such a narrow issue as freedom for rubber tappers in Brazil, and so they set out to convince Mendes that the only way he could gain international support was to be seen as a savior of the Amazon.

Meanwhile, they rallied support from other constituencies, especially by demonstrating the value of the intact rainforest. Schwartzman published articles appealing for the protection of the Amazon as no mere "elitist environmentalist" idea but as a means of saving a way of life and a threatened economy. Studies of forest and agricultural output showed that an acre in the jungle, used to raise cattle, would earn $15.05 per year over a 20-year-period; whereas the same land, used to extract rubber, nuts, and other products, would earn $72.79 in the same period. Another study showed that tappers, when freed from the rule of the bosses, earned twice as much as those living in Brazil's slums, while enjoying a much better standard of living.[30]

In 1987, this group arranged for Mendes to visit the United States and attend a meeting of the Inter-American Development Bank. (Mendes procured the first suit he had ever worn through a friendly nun whose order had received a charitable shipment of clothes from Italy.) The group arranged visits with members of Congress who influenced the development banks, and they promoted Mendes' nomination for several environmental awards, including the United Nations Environment Program's prestigious Global 500 award, one of those he did receive.

So behind the "greening" of Chico Mendes was a conscious strategy by environmentalists to save the world's tropical rainforests. By publicizing Mendes' legitimate status as a folk hero, the group focused attention on the forests and the plight of their indigenous citizens and rallied public support for their cause. At the same time, it became apparent that one of the best ways to stop the ecological and human devastation wrought by poorly conceived development projects was to attack their funding, which meant taking on the international development banks. The route to the banks was via those members of Congress responsible for determining the U.S. contribution to the banks' assets. So it was that the Marxist-educated, rural Brazilian rubber tapper, Chico Mendes, who was fighting cattle ranchers, met with Robert W. Kasten, the conservative Republican Senator from Wisconsin, a state dependent on dairy products. Impressed by Mendes' recitation of the effects of the loans on the Brazilian environment and the peasants, rural workers, and natives, Kasten threatened to withdraw U.S. funding if the banks involved did not start to factor ecological concerns into their loans.[31]

DEATH SENTENCES

With Mendes' considerable notoriety abroad came, predictably, opposition at home. He was blamed for blocking progress in Brazil and even called a "tool of the CIA."[32] Nevertheless, he continued his true life's work, recruiting and organizing tappers. His principal enemy, the Alves da Silva family, owned a 10,000-acre ranch that they planned to expand to take advantage of the government's generous conditions. This family had a history of violence and killings; its members were known to have killed anyone who dared cross them. When their attempts to buy out the tappers failed, the inevitable *empate* occurred and brought tensions to a fever pitch.

By now, the government was more sensitive to the potential violence, so they settled the issue, for a time, by buying the land from the Alves da Silva family—land that the family may very well not have legally owned in the first place—and converting it to an extractive reserve. Although, on the surface, this solution was a compromise, the Alves da Silva family members considered it a defeat; their gunmen now openly roamed the streets of Xapuri, brandishing their weapons. By early 1988, the violence was out of control; one friend of Mendes' was shot in cold blood. Although Mendes was enraged by the harassment of his family and friends and had taken to carrying a gun, he continued to counsel nonviolence. In May of that year, some demonstrators were shot by hired guns and, in June, one of Mendes' fellow councilmen was killed. The death *threats* that Mendes had been receiving, implying a probability of death, were replaced by *pronouncements,* implying certainty.

The incident that most likely led to Mendes' death was the discovery of an old indictment against the Alves da Silva family. Mendes and his supporters pursued the issue to the point that family members were forced into hiding. The most prominent son, Darly, was furious, saying, "Chico won't live out the year. No one has ever bested me. And Chico wants to do that."[33] Mendes' friends and family accepted that his death was inevitable, but a local priest, Otavio Destro, said, "Chico had the wisdom of the Indian and the guile of the Indian so it was difficult for a rancher to catch him in the forest."[34] His murderers did find him at home, however, and killed him.

In December 1990, Darly Alves da Silva and his son, Darci Alves Pereira, were convicted of the murder and jailed in a "maximum-security" prison that actually had no security—no searchlights, towers, or high walls. On February 15, 1993, the two escaped, to no one's surprise. Mendes' widow said that warnings about the jail's lax security had been ignored, and the acting security secretary admitted that "the only people who don't escape from our jail are those who don't want to."[35]

The senior Alves da Silva's conviction had actually been overturned in March 1992. Evidently, an impending trial in another Brazilian locale for a 20-year murder charge[36] had prompted the escape: The prison to which he would have been moved was *truly* a maximum-security facility.

Nevertheless, Chico Mendes' legacy lives on. Forest reserves, parks, and streets have been named after him, and his U.S. environmentalist friends continue to exert pressure on the Brazilian government to mete out justice.[37]

PRESERVING BIODIVERSITY

We must start to save the forest by at least attempting to map the biosphere—to find out what species are out there before they disappear forever. We know that, in the tremendous undiscovered chemistry of the tropical rainforests, we will find benefits for our species; we can learn from the plants of the forest. As Diane Ackerman pointed out in her *New Yorker* article on the golden monkeys of the rainforest, those jungle plants are no wimps. The survival mechanisms that have evolved over geologic time include all sorts of strategies to attract the proper pollinating insects and to turn away possible predators. Colors, fragrances, and poisons abound in the rainforest, and all of these could contain formulas useful to us. This is the currency of *coevolution,* the development of unique relationships among specific species (for example, plants and pollinators).[38] Wilson has mentioned one example out of thousands, the rosy periwinkle of Madagascar; it has given us two alkaloids involved in curing Hodgkin's disease (a once-lethal cancer of the lymph nodes) and acute lymphocytic leukemia, formerly a notorious child killer. From an economic viewpoint, these drugs net their manufacturers $188 million per year.[39] As Wilson says, though, "useful products cannot be harvested from an extinct species."

The results of the loss of our tropical rainforests are probably well beyond estimation. In fact, it has to be, because we have only an inkling of what we are losing. Beyond the rainforest's biodiversity and its roles as carbon storehouse and thus shield from global warming, as the home of ancient human cultures, and as global climate maker, there are other, perhaps more subtle, considerations worth our attention. For instance, the part of the Brazilian Amazon that has suffered the most deforestation lies in western Brazil, away from the coast. We know that the Amazon system produces at least half its own rain through transpiration and evaporation, but if the forest becomes denuded and lies away from coastal humidity, some predict it will start to destroy itself by drying out—another example of positive feedback with very negative results.[40]

There are so many unknowns here. We know that symbiotic relationships exist, for example, between plants and insects, as we have mentioned. What we do *not* know is what happens to a whole food web when an integral part of it, a relationship developed over thousands of years, falls apart. Does the whole web and all the life that depends on it then fall apart as well?

A less esoteric and more topical consideration, perhaps, is one described by Richard Preston in *The New Yorker*: "The emergence of AIDS appears a natural consequence of the ruin of the tropical biosphere." He continues to explain that, because these tropical ecosystems contain the most species, they contain the most viruses, given that each species hosts viruses. As humans intrude, destroy, and stress these ecosystems, adaptable viruses that lose indigenous hosts might happily jump to *Homo sapiens.* Many viruses have already done this. Perhaps the most frightening pronouncement in Preston's article (which, after all, was written about viruses, not tropical rainforests) is that HIV is considered "an emerger...since its penetration of the human race is incomplete and is still happening explosively with no end in sight."[41]

It stands to reason that this one small area of the planet, which houses half its treasures and dangers, deserves special consideration. We had better pay attention.

QUESTIONS FOR DISCUSSION AND REFLECTION

+ What sorts of living things are meaningful or significant? How likely is it that a chemical squeezed from an insect's body will somehow, someday, be useful to us? Should we work to preserve that insect—especially when preserving it entails some immediate economic sacrifice? Apart from any utilitarian purpose, is it worth our while to take the preservation of species seriously at all? In the end, are insects—even those unique in the entire history of the world—worth our concern and political effort?

+ What moral principle underlies our commitment to save endangered species? Is it purely utilitarian—that we might be able to use, for example, an esoteric secretion of an obscure species to solve a medical mystery someday? Is it aesthetic—that variety of life contributes to the beauty and wonder of the world and should be preserved? Is it metaphysical or religious—that each species is a unique creation, placed on Earth not by any labor of ours, and that we are therefore obligated to maintain it in being, to save it from extinction as Noah once did at God's command?

+ Human lives are certainly significant, but what about human lifestyles? Should the forest be preserved for indigenous peoples, simply because they (unlike you and me) will die if their forest is felled around them? Why should nonadaptive groups of humans be protected? What value is there in preserving remote and unfamiliar languages, cultures, occupations, and ways of living?

+ Edward Wilson, a nationally known biologist and champion of biodiversity, argues that one could reap tremendous economic benefits from developing sustainable uses of the rainforest, but he goes on to say, "I do not mean to suggest that every ecosystem now be viewed as a factory of useful products. Wilderness has virtue unto itself and needs no extraneous justification."[42] That "virtue unto itself" is the cutting edge of the inquiry for environmental ethics: How can we capture, in language and theory adequately respectful of human rights, our nagging sensation that the magnificent rainforest deserves our protection just because it is *there* and just for its role in the life of the planet?

+ How can we save the rainforest and still respect the national sovereignty of tropical nations? Policy problems surface at several levels. Can we, and should we, influence the use of Third-World resources? Why not just *buy* all the land we want and hold on to it? Would the land thus be safe from depredation? Would the United States inherit the opprobrium of the colonizing nations, who once held land in foreign countries to serve their own purposes?

✦ Finally, will we fail at compromise? Will we eventually be forced to abandon our attachment to individual rights and national sovereignty and declare the rainforest a global resource, with its protection enforced by the United Nations? Is such a course feasible? Is it desirable?

Notes

1. Unless otherwise noted, all biographical material on Chico Mendes is taken either from Andrew Revkin, *The Burning Season* (Boston: Houghton Mifflin, 1990); or Alex Shoumatoff, *The World Is Burning* (Boston: Little, Brown, 1990).

2. Revkin, *The Burning Season,* p. 8.

3. Shoumatoff, *The World Is Burning,* p. 48.

4. Ibid., p. 51.

5. Edward O. Wilson, *The Diversity of Life* (Cambridge, MA: Harvard University Press, 1992): p. 196.

6. Eugene Linden, "Playing with Fire," *TIME* (18 September 1989).

7. Phylum Arthropoda includes the crustaceans that we are familiar with, such as lobsters and shrimps, millipedes, centipedes, and spiders (arachnids), as well as insects, but insects comprise well over 90 percent of the species within this phylum.

8. Wilson, *The Diversity of Life,* pp. 190–206; Erik Eckholm, "Secrets of the Rain Forest," *New York Times* (17 November 1988): p. 20.

9. Wilson, *The Diversity of Life.*

10. Ibid.

11. Linden, "Playing with Fire."

12. James Brooke, "Plan to Develop Amazon a Failure," *New York Times* (12 November 1991).

13. Ibid.

14. Wilson, *The Diversity of Life,* pp. 272 ff.

15. Linden, "Playing with Fire," p. 82.

16. *EDF Letter,* "Brazil Creates Rainforest Reserve for Yanomamis," Environmental Defense Fund (April 1992).

17. Sandy Tolan and Nancy Postero, "Accidents of History," *The New York Times Magazine* (23 February 1992): p. 38.

18. Eugene Linden, "Lost Tribes, Lost Knowledge," *TIME* (23 September 1991): p. 46.

19. Stan Sesser, "A Reporter at Large: Logging the Rain Forest," *The New Yorker* (27 May 1991): p. 42.

20. Ibid.

21. Wilson, *The Diversity of Life.*
22. Shirley Christian, "There's a Bonanza in Nature for Costa Rica, but Its Forests Too Are Besieged," *New York Times* (29 May 1992): p. A6.
23. Jane Perlez, "Whose Forest Is It, The Peasants' or the Lemurs'?" *New York Times* (7 September 1991): p. 2.
24. Catherine Dold, "Tropical Forests Found More Valuable for Medicine than Other Uses," *New York Times* (28 April 1992).
25. Revkin, *The Burning Season,* p. 261.
26. Ibid., p. 8.
27. Ibid., p. 154.
28. Ibid., p. 10.
29. Ibid., p. 224.
30. Ibid., p. 219.
31. The *greening* of these banks has been a very slow process, but that's a topic for another volume.
32. Revkin, *The Burning Season,* p. 227.
33. Ibid., p. 266.
34. Ibid., p. 149.
35. James Brooke, "Brazilian Sequel: A Jailbreak, a Bitter Widow," *New York Times* (17 February 1993).
36. Presumably, this is the murder charge that Mendes had brought to light.
37. Brooke, "Brazilian Sequel."
38. Diane Ackerman, "A Reporter at Large: Golden Monkeys," *The New Yorker* (24 June 1991): p. 36.
39. Wilson, *The Diversity of Life,* p. 285.
40. Linden, "Playing with Fire."
41. Richard Preston, "A Reporter at Large: Crisis in the Hot Zone," *The New Yorker* (26 October 1992): p. 58.
42. Wilson, *The Diversity of Life,* pp. 282, 303.

Suggestions for Further Reading

Eckholm, Erik. "Secrets of the Rainforest." *The New York Times Magazine* (17 November 1988): p. 20.

Myers, Norman. *The Primary Source.* New York: Norton, 1984.

———. *The Sinking Ark.* Oxford: Pergamon Press, 1979.

Revkin, Andrew. *The Burning Season.* Boston: Houghton Mifflin, 1990.

Ryan, John C. *Life Support: Conserving Biological Diversity.* Worldwatch Paper 108. Washington, DC: Worldwatch Institute, 1992.

Sesser, Stan. "A Reporter at Large: Logging the Rain Forest." *The New Yorker* (27 May 1991).

Shoumatoff, Alex. *The World Is Burning.* Boston: Little, Brown, 1990.

Wilson, Edward O. *The Diversity of Life.* Cambridge, MA: Harvard University Press, 1992.

CHAPTER 5

To Reclaim a Legacy
The Tallest Trees in America

PREFACE: QUESTIONS TO KEEP IN MIND

What are we trying to save in the forests of the Pacific Northwest Coast?

Is it the endangered northern spotted owl—a diminutive raptor, uniquely adapted to life in the ancient forests of the region, and found nowhere else?

Is it the forest itself, with its millennial trees, likened by all who see it to the great cathedrals of Europe? People have been cutting down trees since there were people and trees—why do people find these evergreen forests, especially the old groves of northern California redwoods, so compelling?

Is it something more abstract, such as nature or biodiversity—or possibly a vision of a country worthy of being called America the Beautiful— a country that would protect these trees as part of our national gift and identity?

What are the lumber companies trying to gain in their operations on the Pacific Northwest Coast? Must they take into account stakeholders other than their shareholders?

Do the imperatives of maximizing shareholder wealth justify shutting down lumber mills and exporting raw logs (resulting in extensive unemployment)?

Can we use the tale of Pacific Lumber to illustrate the strengths and weaknesses of the present system?

The media have characterized the struggle between the loggers and the environmentalists as a class conflict: the working-class lumber workers against the elite professional class who typify the environmental movement. How can we sort out the stakeholders and their real interests in these conflicts? How can a balance be found among the interests, real and perceived, in such complex issues?

For the sake of clarity we will consider the issues in the following order:

1. *The owl and the trees.* The northern spotted owl (hereinafter, *the owl*) is found only in the ancient forests of the northwestern United States. Politically, it stands for the forests themselves. It is estimated that there are 2,000 breeding pairs left in the world.[1] The logging operations of the Northwest forest threatened it with extinction. To some extent, the owl is protected by the Endangered Species Act, but the issues go beyond the law. Why might we have a moral obligation to save endangered species? Why should we care about distant birds, anyway? What good is biodiversity, and what should we be willing to pay to maintain it?

   Meanwhile, the owl is not the central character. Ted Gup describes the owl as "a fine bird, yes, but...never really the root cause of this great conflict."[2] It is the trees themselves, great groves of sequoias and other cone-bearing trees, some of them more than 2,000 years old, that really fire the imagination. Do we have an obligation to preserve them, as a treasure for the whole world?

2. *The business.* Meanwhile, we live in a free enterprise system that generally serves us well. Do we have an obligation to protect businesses that operate in environmentally sensitive ways, or require that all businesses do so? The case of Pacific Lumber Company pits a company that preserved environmental values against hostile financial initiatives that were good for the shareholders' purses but bad for the trees. Does the fiduciary duty of the company extend to the environment? Should the trees have a vote at the annual meeting? Is there an obligation to protect the loggers in their specialized way of life?

3. *The government.* Consider the alphabet soup of government agencies that deal with environmental issues (see Appendix), and add the FBI for times when the confrontations get unpredictable. What is the government's role in protecting owls, trees, business, and us? What do we want it to be? What should the government be empowered to do, and at what cost?

All these questions turn on one indisputable fact: The Pacific Northwest Rainforests, ecosystems unlike any others in the world, have been logged for a century, to the point of the threatened extinction not only of the species housed there, but of the forests themselves. They are managed and regulated by an incredible mix of national bureaucracies, the actions of which affect the livelihoods of millions of people and the economies of three states. The loggers and lumber companies conflict with the environmentalists; both parties conflict with the regulators; the politicians land on differing sides of the controversy, depending on their constituencies; and everything ends up in court, though to this point, nothing has been finally decided.[3]

THE OWL AND THE TREES

For six months of the year, it rains every day in the Pacific rainforest. The currents of the Pacific Ocean have provided warmth and abundant moisture to this region for millions of years, ultimately engendering the ancient evergreen forests, or *old-growth forests*, at the heart of the controversy. The forests probably appeared in their present form about 6,000 years ago; at present, they have stands of trees up to one thousand years old, trees that are 300 feet tall with ten-foot diameters, at least twice as massive as those found in tropical rain forests. To put this in perspective, each tree contains enough lumber to build two houses. These forests extend from the Alaskan panhandle (Sitka spruce) south through Washington and Oregon (Douglas fir, western hemlock), to northern California (several varieties of redwood, ponderosa pine). Despite the poor, basaltic soil, these forests contain the largest examples of 25 species of conifers. The dead trees (*snags*) may stand for up to two hundred years, for it takes two to five hundred years for them to decay; nevertheless, the forest floor and streams are littered with decomposing trees that provide nutrients for the living ones, and a habitat for thousands of animal species (1,500 invertebrate species were counted on a single tree).

One of the vertebrate species has become, at least for legal and political purposes, the focus of this controversy. The northern spotted owl is a subspecies of the spotted owl; under the Endangered Species Act, the species as a whole is now officially listed as threatened. It weighs less than two pounds, has a wingspan of two feet, and must eat its weight each day to survive. Estimates of numbers surviving vary. A 1990 source states that a count of the northern spotted owl and the California spotted owl netted 2,900 pairs;[4] a later estimate suggests 2,000 pairs for the northern cousin alone.[5] For reasons not well understood, the owl breeds late (after three years old) and dies young, both factors working against survival. Without the loggers, though, it has held its own; the main cause of its threatened extinction is loss of habitat.

The owl is one of those species that requires unique stable conditions to survive: It seems totally dependent on old-growth forest and hunts there exclusively. To house the owl, the trees must be dense, and some proportion of them must be over 200 years old. Thus the future of the northern spotted owl and the old-growth forest are linked. As such, the owl is considered an *indicator* species; that is, a species the condition of which will indicate the condition of the entire ecosystem (like a canary in a coal mine). The owl requires not only old growth, but a lot of it. Studies show that each pair in Northern California ranged among 1,900 acres of old growth; that six pairs in Oregon averaged 2,264 acres as their range, and that six pairs studied in Washington averaged a range of 3,800 acres.[6]

Why the spotted owl requires old growth, and so much of it, is not fully understood, but it is well documented. (At great pain to the documenters: One researcher comments, "Critics who ceaselessly argue that more research is needed before any management decisions are made should spend a year or two tracking these nocturnal birds across the rugged terrain of the northwest.")[7] Evidently the owl requires such old-growth characteristics as broken branches that provide platforms, debris, and protective thermal cover, characteristics not found in new growth. Additionally, the owls' prey—squirrels, voles, rats—share the old-growth habitat and feed on the fungi that form on the decaying trees.

Further, the competition with other species may be forcing the spotted owl back into the old growth. The younger stands provide a habitat for the great horned owls, which feed on young spotted owls; the great horned owls also do well in clearings and edges of the old growth. So the spotted owl loses its protection from predators when it must leave the density of the old growth, even by flying across clear-cuts from one old-growth stand to another. Further, if the spotted owl survives predation in the clear-cuts and second growth, it has to contend with competition for food from the more aggressive barred owl. Finally, the owl's habitat is especially threatened by natural disasters— 5,000 acres of habitat were lost with the eruption of Mt. St. Helens— because it requires such a large area and so much of that area is already gone.

The northern spotted owl, then, is clearly threatened (still). To save it, we must save the oldest trees in large numbers. With 90 percent of that forest already cut, virtually all the remaining old growth, whether in private or public hands, must be preserved. For the sake of the owl, should we do that?

OUR OBLIGATIONS TO SPECIES

What is our obligation to preserve endangered species? For starters, what does *preservation* of a species mean? If we mean merely its genetic material, we can preserve the spotted owl by capturing a sufficient number of breeding pairs (say, 20), putting them in a climate-controlled zoo, and allowing them to produce little owls to their hearts' content—without gumming up the logging operations. Even if no zoos have room right now, we could freeze owl eggs indefinitely and regenerate the species later. Or does preservation of a species mean preservation *in the wild*, where it can live as it has evolved to live, naturally? If the latter, then what should we pay to preserve the habitat? Granted that the owl is worth something—we would not wish it extinguished, other things being equal—what is it worth when its preservation challenges jobs, regional economies, and the evolved lifestyles of the North Coast loggers?

Biodiversity

The preservation of a species contributes to the *biodiversity* of the area— literally, the number and variety of the species that live there. Is biodiversity good enough to sacrifice jobs for?

The first answer to that question is that while we may not be able to predict the future usefulness of any given species, we are aware that odd species may suddenly become dramatically useful; therefore, species ought to be preserved—not just cuddly ones like spotted owls, but fungus and insect species as well. Every unique grouping of chemicals found in a rare species may have contributed to that species' survival and may some day contribute to our own—as the obscure rosy periwinkle of Madagascar has yielded chemicals that fight childhood leukemia. We have no way of predicting just which of the vanishing species of the Pacific Northwest could provide a cure for cancer.

Where old-growth forests were concerned, that possibility remained hypothetical until the discovery of *taxol*, the drug that has shown better than expected results in treating ovarian and breast cancer and which originates in the bark (and maybe needles) of the Pacific yew, indigenous to the old growth. The Forest Service used to consider the yew a weed to be removed from a clear-cut and burned; now we know how valuable it is. Would we ever have found out about this if we had let the old groves die? Simple prudence argues for the protection of any species, no matter how humble, no matter what measures are required to preserve the conditions it needs to live. (Ironically, this very discovery poses a new threat to the yew's survival: pressure from many fronts to harvest as many trees as possible to manufacture more of the drug.)

A second reason to embrace biodiversity is that we know that in any ancient ecosystem the species have evolved in symbiosis; the destruction of one species, leaving its niche open and its role unfilled, tends to affect the system. Homeowners around the dwindling Eastern forests can testify to the effect of removing predators from an ecosystem: It allowed the white-tailed deer population to explode, and now they wander through yards, munching bushes in the summer and dying of starvation in the winter. What would be the effect of the extinction of the spotted owl? Perhaps not great, but who knows?

A third argument makes no such appeals to consequences. It holds, very simply, that a species is a unique grouping, whether specially created by God or uniquely evolved, and that we have no right to abolish it for all time from the possibilities of existence on this earth. Extinction is forever; it means that no member of the group could ever, even in theory, live on the earth again. Setting aside all considerations of consequences for our own future generations—who might, after all, want to see animals of this species—we have no right in principle to destroy forever that which we could never have created ourselves.

The Terms of the Act

Persuaded by such considerations, Congress passed the Endangered Species Act (ESA) in 1973. According to the act, the National Marine Fishery Service (Department of Commerce) and the Fish and Wildlife Service (FWS, Interior) are empowered to list marine and land species, respectively, as either threatened or endangered, after which they cannot be hunted, collected, injured, or killed. The bill also prohibits any federal agency from carrying out or funding any activity that could threaten or endanger these species *or their habitats*. This latter provision has caused the most controversy, in regard to not only logging in the old-growth forests, but also other projects such as dams and highways—any development receiving federal funding. Therefore, both the Bureau of Land Management (Interior) and the Forest Service (Agriculture) must consult the Fish and Wildlife Service (Interior) before undertaking any action that might threaten the owl.

The Act typifies environmental legislation in several ways. (1) Informed by the best science available, it is enlightened, far-reaching, and acknowledged as probably the world's most stringent species protection legislation. Noncompliance with the ESA is a criminal act; both civil and criminal penalties are provided, including imprisonment. (2) This act also receives pitiful funds. Funding for the act has averaged $39 million a year—a pittance, given the work that must be done to implement it.[8] (3) Three cabinet-level departments must work harmoniously for the act to work.

Implementation presents its own problems. According to the 1982 amendment of the act, economic implications of the protection of a species *may not* be considered in determining its status, whether or not it is endangered; that decision must be based "solely on the basis of the best scientific and commercial data."[9] Economic considerations *may* be considered after the listing, during the required preparation of a recovery plan for the listed species. In practice, because of the complexities involved, few plans have been prepared. The act also calls for a determination of the species "critical habitat," but up to a year after the listing, and acknowledging that because of complications, it may be indeterminable.[10] In determining the critical habitat, though, FWS *must* include economic considerations. On two occasions, court-ordered reconsiderations on the basis of economic impact have compelled the FWS to reduce the acreage required to preserve the owl. Additionally, there is the Endangered Species Committee (the "God Squad") to which appeal may be made by those who feel that their economic interests are damaged by species protection. The bureaucratic hurdles to actual protection of the owl daunt even the most hardened of Washington veterans; nevertheless, as a legal protection, it serves as the strongest statement that we, as a nation, can make about the value of the most threatened of our creatures.

The Oldest Trees

The cathedral groves of redwood trees, especially in northern California, are really the central characters of this drama, not owls. The redwood trees come in two species, *Sequoia gigantica* and *Sequoia sempivirens*. What's left of *gigantica*, largest of trees, grows almost completely within the boundaries of state and national parks. At issue for this chapter is *sempervirens*, the coastal redwood, to the best of our knowledge the tallest trees that have ever lived.[11] These giants, on the misty Pacific coast of northern California, have provoked the increasingly bitter disputes among environmentalists, the timber industry, loggers, and local communities.

Climactically unique conditions have produced these trees,[12] truly a breathtaking biomass. Coniferous evergreen trees (*gymnosperms*) dominated the planet before the evolution of flowering, deciduous trees (*angiosperms*). The latter are generally more successful than the former, because the reproductive strategy of a flower becoming a seed-bearing fruit is much more likely to result in a new tree than a cone bearing a naked seed. Extended areas of coniferous trees are now found only where conditions discourage deciduous plants. In the Pacific Northwest, peculiar climatic conditions—cold, wet winters and summer droughts—hinder photosynthesis in deciduous trees, allowing the more adaptable conifers to take over. Once established, this forest has proved almost immune from change by natural forces. Most ecosystems are characterized by succession—moving from pioneer species, through more stable species, to the most stable, climax species, only to change again when some violent event upsets its balance (the eruption of Mount St. Helens provides a good example). No such event has disrupted the redwood forests for millennia; the forest has remained, grown, and reproduced itself, resulting in some individuals as old or older than Christendom. To quote an admirer of old growth, Sallie Tisdale, "There is little on this earth so close to immortal."[13]

BUSINESS AND THE TEMPTATION TO OVERHARVEST

Unfortunately for those who hope for their survival, these trees are the most commercially valuable in the United States. The extent of the original forest and the acreage that remains is debatable, depending on one's definition of *old growth*, usually described as the largest old trees, living and dead, standing and fallen, within a multilayered canopy. Estimates of the extent of the original forest range from 20 to 70 million acres, depending on the threshold for calling a tree *large*, some 70 to 95 percent of which has been logged over the last century. The rate of logging has increased dramatically over the last three decades. Estimates are complicated by the fragmentation of the forest by clear-cutting, which leaves stands isolated in a barren landscape.

Clearly, this harvest is strictly limited. Once those old-growth trees are logged, there will be no more: The trees are gone forever. The second growth does not have the characteristics of the old growth in its resistance to insects, disease, fire, and decay; we may suppose that the twentieth century remainder of a 2,000-year-old forest is composed of the best survivors of all attacks, with the less resistant succumbing centuries ago. Nor, of course, is this new growth as massive. The old growth is thus an unreplaceable asset, more valuable every year, demanding care and conservative forestry practices. Wise management requires sparing the old growth and planting new trees to satisfy demands for ordinary lumber.

The failure to manage lumber harvesting wisely has effects beyond the loss of the wood. Besides the imprudent depletion of a valuable resource, rapid harvesting has serious environmental effects on the region and perhaps on the world. The fish and wildlife of the area may suffer severely from the same destruction of habitat that disrupts the owl. Once the trees go, the erosion of the denuded hillsides in the ceaseless rain carries topsoil into the streams. Once the topsoil is gone from the hills, where it formed only a thin layer, the land is useless for growing trees even if a lumber company conscientiously replants; once layered into the streams, the topsoil smothers salmon fry that must hatch in clean pebbles at bottoms of streams.

One serious environmental effect of overharvesting, presently unmeasurable, is its contribution to global warming. The old growth is a veritable storehouse of carbon, and carbon dioxide is the most important of the gases credited with causing global warming. While alive, the trees absorb huge amounts of that gas from the atmosphere in the photosynthetic process. Though nature's recycling laws require that the same amount of the gas be returned to the atmosphere, as through the trees' respiration and eventual decay, that can happen over hundreds of years. When the trees are felled, the photosynthetic carbon dioxide absorption stops. Further, when any of the *slash* (the branches and other valueless debris from the logging operation) is burned, the stored carbon is abruptly added to the atmosphere as more carbon dioxide. In response, the timber industry has claimed that by cutting old growth and planting young trees that have a faster photosynthetic rate, they actually ameliorate the global warming threat. This claim ignores the relative size of the area of photosynthetic activity. To be sure, a rapidly growing tree absorbs more carbon dioxide than a mature tree of the same size; but a small seedling does not approach the chemical activity of the enormous trees of the Northwest forest, trees many times as massive as those found anywhere else in the world.

Business and the Lumber

From the corporate viewpoint, rapid logging is just good business sense. "The woods," as one popular show has it, "are just trees, the trees are just wood." Timber appropriate for lumber—for houses, boats, fences, furniture—has been cut and processed by humans since their beginning. Particularly suitable for such harvest, redwoods provide lumber that is durable, light, and strong; holds nails well; resists insects and fire; and is beautiful. Each tree yields about 12 or 13 thousand board-feet, on the average—again, enough to build two houses.[14] It has always provided great profits.[15]

What constitutes *wise management* by a publicly owned company? The theory of business enterprise claims that investors put their money into a company solely to make money for themselves. It follows that, in the immortal words of Milton Friedman, "the social responsibility of business is to increase its profit."[16] Money now, as every first-year economics student knows, is more money than money later. Business managers fulfill their fiduciary obligation to the shareholders when, and only when, they put profit in the shareholders' pockets as quickly as possible. No other considerations may intrude on that objective. Since cut timber brings financial returns, while uncut timber just sits there as a tax burden, then the quickest and most cost-effective (least expensive) harvest of all the trees available for cutting would be the best business approach to old-growth forests. So, in contrast to the conservative forestry practices demanded by the long-run interests of trees and corporations, the interests of the current shareholders would be best served by clear-cutting old groves as quickly as possible.

Rarely do we see a direct face-off of the conservative business approach (oriented to the long-term maximization of value from assets, the long-term competitive positioning of the company itself, and the continuity of its arrangements with suppliers, customers, and employees) and the radical grab-the-profits-and-run approach made famous in the 1980s. Just such a confrontation arises in the Northwest forest, in the story of the Pacific Lumber Company.

PL: A Short History and Apologia

Before 1985 the Pacific Lumber Company (PL) was a model of family-style business enterprise. Run for three generations by the Murphy family, it was characterized by community service, environmental sensitivity, and the most scrupulous care of its workers. So successful was it as an old-fashioned paternalistic company that a pair of fascinated left-leaning sociologists (Hugh Wilkerson and John van der Zee) wrote a book about living in its employment and in the company-owned town, *Life in the Peace Zone.*[17] From this chronicle emerges a unique story. The company and its headquarters, Scotia, were founded about 1869. For the first part of their history, there was no limit on the harvest. Because through the 1920s it took four to five days for a team of men to cut down a single giant tree and about a week to complete its processing, the forest sustained little damage from such lack of regulation.[18]

In the 1930s, the company adopted a policy of *perpetual sustained yield*: Mature trees were marked for selective cutting, felled, snaked out by the "Cat" tractor, and milled. With more light in the forest, the younger trees matured faster; where bare spots were left, the company reseeded. In theory, such practices should "keep the company supplied with redwood logs from its own lands in perpetuity."[19] The sustained yield policy is economically sound and kind to shareholders. Pacific Lumber's financial statements for the years through 1984 show small cyclical adjustments to demand but steady earnings on its outstanding shares.[20]

It took just as good care of its workers.

> After he has put in ninety days on his mill job, [the worker] can get on the list to move into Scotia, where a comfortable one-bedroom company bungalow, with a garden and a lawn on a quiet residential street rents from under sixty dollars a month. Water and sewage and garbage removal are free. Every five to seven years, the company will

repaint his house, inside and out, free. As he moves up in the company, or as his family grows, he can move to a larger house in another part of town.... He has good accident and health coverage, and a choice of pension plan or an investment program.... And, in the remote future, as a Pacific Lumber employee, if his son or daughter qualifies for a four-year college, he or she will receive a thousand-dollar scholarship from the company."[21]

Further, Pacific Lumber hired any of the workers' sons who wanted a job, never laid people off, rarely fired, and promoted entirely from within. The pension plan, overfunded past all worry, was generous; a secure old age was certain. Workers could be forgiven a certain amount of complacency. Corky, one of the workers the sociologists interviewed in depth, was happy with his job and everything else in his life. "Golly, for the rent, you can't match this." He was twenty-four at the time of the interview. "I got forty-one years to go, and I can't see any reason I'd leave."[22]

Conscientious efforts to find something outrageously wrong in this secure life availed the authors nothing. One schoolteacher pointed out that the children's conviction of utter security, in some cases buttressed by two or three generations at Pacific Lumber, was based on faith alone: "What they don't know is that PL could fold tomorrow. And then what?" But that seemed so unlikely, even to the authors, that they dismissed it:

> "Most people,... recognizing that Pacific Lumber with its high-quality line of products and enormous timber holdings is not about to fail overnight, decide to...settle for the obvious rewards of a relatively comfortable and untroubled future..."

> "What Scotia is really offering those dismayed with the world outside, the tie that pulls men back who vowed to leave, is not the promise of fulfillment but an assurance of moderation, the possibility of living a humane life in a humane community. And for that, there will always be a waiting list."[23]

The hostile takeover. And then, in 1986, came the hostile takeover. Pacific Lumber failed its workers overnight. Charles Hurwitz, the CEO of MAXXAM, seized control of Pacific Lumber (with $900 million in Drexel Burnham junk bonds) and immediately terminated the pension plan, accelerated the traditionally measured timber harvest, and told the employees about his "Golden Rule: He who has the gold, rules."[24] He used $55 million of the pension funds to pay down part of his buyout debt.[25] An insurance company controlled by Hurwitz, Executive Life, bought more than one-third of the junk bonds, and issued the "annuities" required by Federal law to replace pension funds when their managers deplete them. Executive Life collapsed when the junk bond market did, leaving the workers without pensions beyond what the truncated company could temporarily supply.[26] Repayment of the same debt required that Hurwitz get money off the land as fast as possible, and Pacific Lumber's old-growth forest was certainly available for cutting. Immediately, forestry practices changed, attacking groves that the old Pacific Lumber had been saving for the end of the century, clear-cutting where selective cutting had been the rule, speeding up the pace of logging, and abandoning the costly projects of replanting that had insured the future harvest.

Besides providing for future harvests, the selective cutting and replanting had held the soil in place after logging, preventing erosion of the steep slopes in the relentless rainfall of the region. Under new management, the soil began to wash into the streams. As we know, erosion depletes the slopes (which cannot then grow more trees); destroys the banks of the stream, which overflow with regular spring floods; and kills off the salmon, which cannot breed when soil from erosion covers the gravel at the bottom of the streams.[27] These practices continued without limit until 1991, when U.S. District Judge William Dwyer declared a moratorium on the cutting of the old-growth habitat critical for the spotted owl.

Of course, it was takeover time all over the industry; Sir James Goldsmith had acquired two foresting companies, and Rupert Murdoch had made a run at Regis, driving it into the arms of Champion International. Champion itself was protected by a substantial purchase of its stock by Warren Buffett, an investor with an interest in stabilizing solid managements; otherwise it too might have gone the way of Regis.[28] A lumber company's attractiveness to a raider is easy to understand: If it owns huge tracts of timber, as PL and the others did, those trees represent cold cash as soon as they are "monetized"—cut and sold—and that cash can be distributed to the shareholders. Should there be different ways to evaluate such assets, to make companies that protect the forests less vulnerable to such hostile actions?

The rationale of destruction. The only way a company can be taken over like that is by offering the shareholders more money for their shares than they could get otherwise. Hurwitz certainly did that, obtaining the cash to do so from the sale of the junk bonds and other loans against the assets of the company. The shareholders of record at the time of the takeover made out very well indeed, though the shareholders later in this sort of game make out somewhat worse.[29] Hurwitz may have hurt the environment and the pensioners, but he enriched the shareholders.

If the CEO's fiduciary duty is to shareholders and shareholders alone, how can we condemn Hurwitz for making retired employees miserable? If it was legal to terminate the pensions under the conditions Hurwitz terminated them, and very much in the shareholders' interest to do so (because it was the condition for the high price they received for their stock), we could even argue that Hurwitz was obligated to do it. As John Boland points out, "The only direct, clear legal obligation of corporate fiduciaries (beyond obeying civil law and contractual constraints in general) is to the corporate owners who pay them."[30] After all, the government will take care of the retired workers. Corporations are not in the business of running charities for pensioners.

As for the environmental concerns, those too lie beyond the competence of business to decide. Everything Hurwitz did was legal. If the American people, through their elected officials, wish to keep more of certain kinds of products (such as trees) away from the market, let them pass a law to that effect, and law-abiding businesses will adhere to the law. But in a publicly held, profit-oriented corporation, it should not be management's obligation, or option, to look after the long-term fate of the trees. Pacific Lumber was in business to make money for the stockholders, not to act as unpaid trustee for the North Coast forest.

As for the laws to protect the trees, a good businessperson would regret, as a citizen, the loss to the economy that such a restriction would represent and would feel obliged to point out the potential cost in jobs, tax revenues, and so forth. In this effort, the company presidents, contemplating profits and prices per share, would be joined by the loggers, contemplating their jobs. As a matter of fact, the major initiatives to limit the effect of the Endangered Species Act, and to free more acreage of old-growth timber for cutting, have come from the workers and the small businesses of the affected regions, with the major timber companies, Pacific Lumber included, taking a back seat. The loggers have very few options. Most of them were raised in the region, either in the Pacific Lumber family or in areas with similar expectations. They do not see themselves as having the skills to move elsewhere; for them, only a job cutting down trees (or milling them, or serving those who do) stands between them and permanent unemployment. "Jobs or woodpeckers?" their signs demand; their bumper stickers insist that they "Love Spotted Owls: Fried, Boiled, Barbecued..." or that "Loggers, Too, Are an Endangered Species." Backed up by such strong political alliance, the companies have little motivation to retrain them for other employment.[31]

CAN WE RECLAIM THE REDWOODS FOR OUR OWN?

We have here a direct and serious confrontation of environmental value and short-term economic imperatives—the imperatives that rest on the rights of private property and the responsibilities to shareholders. Adam Smith, claiming that business enterprise of all kind is limited by supply and demand, would have held out hope for the trees in the very saturation of the market. There is a demand for only so much redwood lumber, he would argue; ultimately it will cost PL more to mill the logs it cuts than they will sell for, and then they will have to scale back logging until the demand returns. But if the market includes players operating by different rules—the Japanese, say, who pursue long-term instead of short-term economic interests—this reasoning fails to apply.

For most of the industry's history, market discipline has kept the cutting in check. There was a certain market for finished lumber in the United States, a much smaller market abroad, and the lumber companies, PL included, cut and milled as much lumber as they could sell. By the beginning of the 1980s, the industry was not sufficiently profitable (compared with real estate, for example) to compete successfully on the capital markets; investors chose other investments, and the industry began to starve for new capital. Stocks fell. But by the middle of the decade, a new market opened up: Japan was willing to buy raw logs at a price higher than domestic mills could pay, including the mills owned by the lumber companies themselves (once costs and income were factored out for the lumbering operations and the mills). Japanese merchants had figured out that those logs were unique, and if stored in fresh water (to prevent rot or insect damage) would fetch a fantastic price on the international market as soon as the United States ran out of them, which it was well on its way to doing. So the lumber companies closed their own mills, casting its workers into the sea of the unemployed, and started selling logs to Japan, which has placed no limit on the number they will buy. So the lumber companies now enjoy sales completely unlimited by domestic demand, and leave their workers to be taken care of by the government.[32] The closing of the mills, not the restrictions on the logging, seems to be the real cause of unemployment in the area.

Aristotle and Adam Smith both proved, in very different ways, that *property* (specifically, land and all resources for production) was better off, more likely to be taken care of, in private hands than public. The assumption that the private owner is the best caretaker underlies the importance we attach to the right of private property. In these cases, is this assumption false? The redwoods of Pacific Lumber are clearly not safe in Charles Hurwitz's hands. Do we have a legal right, or structure, to take the land away from him? We know that under the doctrine of "eminent domain" we can seize the redwoods for a new park; but can we seize all that land just to continue a more conservative logging operation?

Pacific Lumber's trees could be protected under the doctrine of eminent domain only if the Federal Government named the land as a park and compensated Pacific Lumber for its acquisition. This is a very expensive course of action. If we are going to spend that kind of money, we might simply offer to purchase the old groves. Charles McCoy, writing in the *Wall Street Journal* in August 1993, gives us an account of just that proposal—offered by Charles Hurwitz himself. In a suggestion "that brings new meaning to the term greenmail," Hurwitz "wants the U.S. government to pay him hundreds of millions of dollars for 4,500 acres of the ancient redwoods, in a remote California grove known as the Headwaters Forest. Otherwise, he says, he will press ahead with his plans to cut the trees down."[33]

Only a small part of the 45,000-acre tract on which the ancient forest sits, that acreage would probably not be adequate to preserve the habitat. Dan Hamburg, a Democratic representative to the U.S. Congress from California, has proposed a bill to purchase the entire tract; Hurwitz has expressed no interest in selling it all, demanding $600 million for the smaller piece alone. If he does not get his price, the trees die.

Payback

From two disparate sources comes another theory on which the American people might reclaim Pacific Lumber's remaining ancient forests—especially the Headwaters Forest. The environmentalist author G. Tyler Miller, in his ninth edition of *Living in the Environment*, and two Democratic Congressmen, George Brown and Pete Stark of California, in a joint Op-Ed in the *New York Times,* pointed out that Charles Hurwitz owes the taxpayers a very large amount of money and that the old grove might be a proper repayment.[34]

Primarily a financier, not a lumberman, Charles Hurwitz has a history of running financial enterprises, successful and otherwise. One of the least successful was the United Savings Association of Texas (USAT), a savings and loan institution that went bankrupt some years ago, leaving the taxpayers to pay back up to $1.6 billion, the amount on which USAT had defaulted. There seems to be no disagreement that the grove would be better off in public hands—why couldn't Headwaters be a partial payment of the debt owed by Hurwitz to the American people? As Brown and Stark point out, presidential action would be required to initiate such a "debt-for-nature" swap, because it involves coordinating several executive branch agencies, including the Federal Deposit Insurance Corporation, the Department of the Interior, and possibly the Justice Department.[35]

Action will have to be soon and decisive: The statute of limitations is running out on the debt; as long as the trees remain in Hurwitz's control they are in peril; and Pacific Lumber has shown no interest in adhering to agreements, or even court injunctions, that forbid the cutting of trees or destruction of habitat. In 1990 PL "reamed a broad, mile-and-a-half corridor into the middle of the Headwaters forest and called it, with a wink and a snicker, `our wildlife-biologist study trail.'"[36] Two years later, the damage was more extensive. Charles McCoy recounts the precedent of Owl Creek, a 465-acre stand of ancient redwoods, second only to Headwaters in its extent and home to the endangered marbled murrelet: "In June and November of 1992, over weekends and holidays when wildlife regulators weren't working, Pacific Lumber cut down hundreds of redwoods and firs in Owl Creek—despite warnings from regulators that doing so might violate wildlife protection laws, and despite previous agreements that regulators insist committed the company to hold off logging."[37] Particularly galling was the renegade logging of the November portion, the "Thanksgiving massacre": PL broke off ongoing talks with the state of California and the U.S. Fish and Wildlife Service to cut down as many trees as they could during the 1992 Thanksgiving weekend. The company claimed that Governor Pete Wilson had approved the cut, but a state appeals court brought it to a halt at the beginning of the next week. The environmentalists sued; Fish and Wildlife officers considered but did not pursue criminal charges; and in February 1995, a federal district court judge ruled that PL's logging of Owl Creek was illegal, was a threat to endangered species, and must be stopped. Immediately, PL announced that it would begin logging the Headwaters tract and filed a new timber harvest plan declaring its intention to do so. The only way to stop such plans is by further slow and expensive litigation, and the environmental organizations that bring such suits are running out of time and money.[38]

The Company's Position

When asked to give an account of its running of Pacific Lumber, MAXXAM stresses continuity with the old firm as run by the Murphys—environmentally responsible, committed to a policy of sustainability into perpetuity, public spirited, community oriented.[39] It insists that the spotted owl, the fish, and above all the trees, are flourishing under its administration, and that they will continue to do so into the future (it sees no natural limitation on redwood harvests). The company voluntarily runs a fish hatchery; it has performed at its own expense numerous studies of the marbled murrelet; it plants half a million seedlings on its land each year; it has nesting boxes for the northern spotted owl. Observing the spotted owl living comfortably in marginal new growth and nesting boxes, the company disputes the observations of the conservation ecologists that the owl can only live in old growth.

A separate "White Paper" is published on the Headwaters forest, with its position clearly stated: "Valued by an independent appraiser hired by the U.S. Forest Service in 1993 at about $500 million (including a 1,500 acre buffer), Headwaters is zoned by the state of California exclusively for the growing of commercial timber used to make wood products.

Accordingly, Pacific Lumber wants to manage Headwaters as a working forest."[40] It is not being permitted to do so, however, because crews of "environmental extremists and special interest groups" raise "judicial and administrative roadblocks." Conceding that Headwaters is the largest old-growth tract in private hands, the "White Paper" goes on to argue that Headwaters is inaccessible, surrounded by working tree farms, and therefore unsuitable for a park, even if the United States could raise the $600 million dollars the company requires for its purchase. Meanwhile, the company wants to harvest that old-growth wood, because, as it candidly admits, it can get a higher price for shipments of wood if some old-growth wood is enclosed with the newer, because the old wood is so rare and of such high quality.

Against the bulk of the popular attacks on the company, PL simply argues that it is the victim of a bum rap. The takeover itself was legitimate because of the previous officers' "undermanagement"; the junk bonds were later turned to investment-grade bonds. Besides, Drexel Burnham didn't hit the skids for years after its association with PL. The Executive Life annuities replaced an "overfunded" pension plan, and no one knew at the time that it would go bankrupt. In any case, PL picked up the pension obligations for most of its workers until other arrangements were found. The acceleration of the tree harvest schedule was "to make up for past underharvesting." Profits are up, employment is up, and "were it not for the emotional nature of the redwood debate, the acquisition would be held as a model of a sound business transaction in which all sides won."[41]

On the whole, the company sees itself as an environmentally sensitive and conscientious property owner, understandably committed to its right to use that property, but cooperating with all reasonable parties to achieve the best for the community and the natural environment. It sees its opponents either as committed radicals opposed to the institution of private property or as immature sentimentalists irrationally attached to the nurturing trees, not noticing that the very tracts they write and newspapers they circulate depend entirely on the industry they are trying to cripple.

Pacific Lumber typifies American companies. It neither insists, Friedman-like, on some absolute right and duty to make all the profit it can nor refuses to acknowledge the right of any nonshareholder to be taken into account. It takes the environment seriously and carries out many projects that protect it. PL wants to see itself, and have others see it, as a company with a strong sense of social responsibility. This fact suggests another tactic, in addition to the debt-for-nature swap just suggested: We ought to take that desire very seriously and see what can be done to construct a reality to match it.

The Role of Government

Even timber executives agree that competitive climates require government regulation to limit environmentally destructive practices. Then by what means, and to what end, shall the government regulate? At various stages in the effort, Congress has opted for (1) preservation of the woods for people to enjoy forever, (2) conservation of the woods to support the timber industry into the indefinite future, and (3) protection of the right of private owners to cut all the wood they want, subject only to minimal regulation.

Preservation is administered by the Department of the Interior, which supervises the national parks and wilderness areas. *Wilderness areas* are just what they sound like: places protected from all invasion. The *National Parks* are a different matter: The values of wilderness preservation and easy access for tourists will never sit easily together, and we will never be at peace over the way to love our parks. But in neither of those areas can the trees simply be cut for lumber. The national forests, on the other hand, were established under Teddy Roosevelt by his chief forester, Gifford Pinchot, to make sure that there would always be trees for the timber industry, although even at the beginning there were recreational and educational purposes thrown in. Here, the trees can be cut, and here the controversy begins for purposes of this section.

The Forest Service, a division of the Department of Agriculture, manages the national forests, federally owned lands that include some 36 million acres in the northwestern United States. From its founding in 1904 to World War II, the Forest Service had no problem reconciling its two charges: to promote logging while preserving wilderness for study, watershed protection, recreation, and other uses. At that time, the major timber companies, cutting on private land, discouraged Forest Service timber sales as unwanted competition. With the war, however, came an abrupt increase in timber demand, at a time when much of the more accessible privately owned land had already been cut; the transformation of the Service from "guardian, to arm of the timber industry" began.[42] In the postwar years, the Forest Service's reputation as a "federal timber company"[43] grew as logging on federal land began to exceed the Service's own guidelines, with the warm approval of loggers, paper and pulp companies, lumber interests in general, and the congressional delegation of the Pacific Northwest.

Along with more extensive logging came technological advance in the form of giant machinery capable of clear-cutting the woods. The economic advantages of clear-cutting, immediately apparent to lumber companies, caused them to adopt the practice. National ambivalence on the justifiability of such a practice, felt by the lumber companies as well as their regulators, is reflected in the Forest Service requirement that keeps the ordinary citizen from viewing it. *Visual protection corridors*, a suitably broad band of trees left in place alongside highways, are required by service regulations; insiders call them the "fool-'em strips."[44]

Occasionally the Forest Service's management of the national forests suggests that it has become an auxiliary to the lumber industry. It is supposed to sell the timber to the companies, at a profit for the taxpayer, but it does no such thing. It runs at a loss. The price charged to lumber companies for the right to cut and sell the lumber on these lands has been notoriously low. Some economists estimate that the Forest Service loses up to $200 million a year. Financial horror stories abound: spending $3 million to log $40,000 worth of timber, a loss of 90 to 99 cents on every dollar spent by the Forest Service, selling trees so cheaply "that loggers would be foolish to say no. [The Forest Service] builds roads, pays rangers, absorbs the risks of fires and insects, then sells at a loss."[45] Taxpayers may be expected to dislike this result. One way the Forest Service makes the situation look better is by amortizing the cost of roads over hundreds of years, to which one critic commented, "It's as if the current Italian government was still paying for the Appian Way."[46]

Congressional action to halt the situation is unlikely. As Jane Fritsch notes in the *New York Times*, Senator Frank Murkowski, chair of the Senate Natural Resources Committee, which oversees logging in the National Forests, turns out to have a personal financial interest in the Ketchikan Pulp Company, which will profit enormously from the bill that Murkowski introduced to increase logging in the Tongass National Forest.[47] The same senator has actively threatened appropriations bills when the executive branch does not interpret law favorably to the lumber industry.[48] While we tell our government to keep watch over private enterprise as it affects the environment, who will watch the watchers?

The strongest indication that the Forest Service and its allied agencies in Federal government may not be the true villains lies in the work they do when the law asks them to think creatively about these forests and their future. Pursuant to the Multiple Use Sustained Yield Act (MUSYA), the Forest Service, the Bureau of Land Management (BLM), and the FWS were asked to describe ways that the owl might be saved and the trees might serve national interests—besides being cut down. They did a fine job: The combined report of the Forest Service and the BLM recommends a drastic cutback in the old-growth harvest by forbidding the exportation of raw logs, then recommends and describes extensive educational and retraining programs for the loggers put out of work by the ban. Technical assistance will make logging and milling more efficient, avoiding the extensive waste entailed by present practices; recreational facilities will make the forests better known and used and will create political pressure to conserve the trees.[49] Even more impressive is the FWS's report. Going beyond the multiple-use scenario, the report specifically addresses "Non-Use Values": the value to the nation just to have the forests *there*.

> Estimates of recreation user demand, benefits of scenic beauty, and benefits of water quality represent only a partial estimate of society's total value for the spotted owl and its associated habitat. The public also is willing to pay for the option of recreation use in the future, the knowledge that the natural ecosystem exists and is protected, and the satisfaction from its bequest to future generations.... The average willingness to pay higher taxes and wood product prices reported in a referendum contingent valuation format was $190 per year. The lower limit of the 98 per cent confidence range was $117 per household."[50]

These reports put the Federal government's environmental services in a new and better light—a much better light. On the whole, they have been open to serious criticism as the merest tools of the timber industry: ineffective in their rare attempts at regulation. These reports suggest that the idealists who once joined government service to protect the nation's environmental heritage may still be there, waiting only for public opinion to catch up with them. A new agenda for the environment will require a trained corps of experts in science and policy to articulate a national environmental ethic and frame the plans for its implementation. In developing these reports, the Forest Service, the BLM, and the FWS have made an auspicious start.

TOWARD A FOREST FUTURE: SUMMARY REFLECTIONS

The heart of the problem, from an environmentalist's point of view, is the old-growth forest. From the loggers' point of view, it is jobs. The owl, the financier, and the alphabet soup are bit players in an agonizing twentieth century drama of loss and conflict. We need not search for villains. Once, we all thought that the forests were unlimited. The timber industry's managers, as they watched the old growth disappear before their eyes, did not know that it could not be restored—that once gone, it would be gone forever. They were no more ignorant than their regulators, their customers, their fellow citizens. The environmental movement is not the sole property of Eastern elitists, as loggers suspect, nor is the timber industry a series of tintypes of Charles Hurwitz, as environmentalists claim. Protecting the forests will require the abolition of a way of life that we have honored and valued. It will raise a series of questions that will not go away.

What, for instance, are the business imperatives of a company that logs redwoods? Is it sufficient to replace 2,000-year-old-groves with young stuff that one can harvest in 40 to 80 years?[51] Sufficient for what? What, exactly, will we do to compensate and redirect the people orphaned by preservation? On the other hand, will we spare ourselves that difficult decision by allowing the forests to be destroyed?

Are there environmentally friendly ways to carry on logging operations? Once the trees are gone, the industry will die and the workers will be unemployed, but then it will be their problem, not ours. How much are we willing to lose in order to avoid the pain of making a decision? Our history suggests, quite a bit.

Should the environmental movement be taking new directions? Should they abandon the "endangered species" approach and adopt ecosystem integrity?[52] Or will that move succeed only in disorientation, discouraging followers by forcing an admission that previous efforts were wrongly conceived, and plunging them into indefinable terms and inchoate goals? The Endangered Species Act has at least the virtue of clarity.

Meanwhile, quite aside from efforts to protect the owl, the current recession has lowered the demand for lumber and depressed the industry. About 50 percent of the cut forest has been exported to be processed in mills abroad, not in the United States.[53] Even if permission were granted to cut every last old-growth tree, they would all be gone, and the jobs with them, in five to ten years. What then?

The ironies abound, not the least of which is that agencies within agencies fight each other. But the most disturbing aspect of our political response to these problems is the hypocrisy of the United States urging Brazil and other Third-World countries to halt the cutting of their tropical rain forests in the interest of mitigating global warming, while we cut ours at a rate of about twice theirs. To quote an official with the Oregon Natural Resources Council, "It's interesting that we're telling Third World countries, 'don't cut your forests' [while]... we're wiping out our fish runs, we're wiping out our biotic diversity, we're sending species to extinction.... we're not a Third World country. We're not so poor that we have to destroy our ancient forests. And we're not so rich that we can afford to."[54]

QUESTIONS FOR DISCUSSION AND REFLECTION

+ What problems present themselves when we try to strike a "balance" in the taking and consuming of an irreplaceable resource?

+ Can you present a rationale for saving *all* the remaining old-growth forests, regardless of economic worth or other features? Can you present a rationale for saving *none* of them? Put together a debate along those lines. Then try to figure out a rule that will pick out a "happy medium" between those two positions. What ethical grounds would you base it on?

✦ Is it time for a full-scale debate on private property in land (refer also to Chapter 10)? We have no private property in the ocean; why not? Is land, like air and ocean, somehow "given" to humanity collectively, not to be parceled out for private destruction for personal purposes? Present rationales, pro and con.

Notes

1. Manuel Velasquez, "Ethics and the Spotted Owl Controversy," *Issues in Ethics*, vol. 4, no. 1 (Winter/Spring 1991): pp. 1, 6.

2. Ted Gup, "Owl vs. Man," *TIME* (25 June 1990): pp. 56–62.

3. M. Lynne Corn, "Spotted Owls and Old Growth Forests," *CRS Issue Brief*, updated 19 August 1991, Environment and Natural Resources Policy Division, Congressional Research Service, Library of Congress, p. 2.

4. David S. Wilcove, "Of Owls and Ancient Forests," in *Ancient Forests of the Pacific Northwest* (Washington D.C.: Island Press, 1990): p. 27.

5. Velasquez, "Ethics," pp. 1, 6.

6. Wilcove, "Owls and Ancient Forests."

7. Ibid., p. 78.

8. G. Tyler Miller, Jr., *Living in the Environment*, ninth ed. (Belmont, CA: Wadsworth, 1996): p. 653.

9. Corn, "Spotted Owls."

10. That habitat includes "specific areas outside the geographical area occupied by the species...on which are found...features essential to the conservation of the species" and "areas outside the geographical area" at the time of listing, later deemed by the Secretary of the Interior "as essential to the conservation of the species." Ibid.

11. Catherine Caufield, "The Ancient Forest," *The New Yorker* (14 May 1990): p. 46.

12. Ibid.

13. Sallie Tisdale, "The Pacific Northwest," *The New Yorker* (26 August 1991): p. 54.

14. Hugh Wilkerson and John van der Zee, *Life in the Peace Zone: An American Company Town.* (New York: Macmillan, 1971).

15. D. L. Thornbury, *California's Redwood Wonderland: Humboldt County.* (San Francisco: D. L. Thornbury at the Sunset Press, 1923).

16. Milton Friedman, "The Social Responsibility of Business Is to Increase Its Profit," *The New York Times Sunday Magazine.* (13 September 1970).

17. Wilkerson and van der Zee, *Life in the Peace Zone.*

18. D. L. Thornbury has an excellent account of the industry in the early 1920s on pp. 38–41 of *California's Redwood Wonderland.*

19. Wilkerson and van der Zee, *Life in the Peace Zone.* pp. 112-113.

20. In the third quarter of 1984, for instance, PL reported that its net earnings rose 50 percent over the previous year ($11,337,000, or 47 cents per share, compared to $7,547,000, or 31 cents per share, for the third quarter the previous year). See Pacific Lumber annual reports, years 1981 through 1984.

21. Wilkerson and van der Zee, *Life in the Peace Zone*, p. 45.

22. Ibid., p. 49.

23. Ibid., pp. 83, 106.

24. Constance E. Bagley, "Pacific Lumber Company: Case Presentation," Unpublished paper, June 1991.

25. Gisela Botte and Dan Cray, "Is Your Pension Safe?" *TIME* (3 June 1991): p. 43.

26. Ibid., also Janice Castro et al., "A Sizzler Finally Fizzles: In America's Largest Life Insurance Company Collapse, California Officials Seize Control of Shaky Giant Executive Life," *TIME* (22 April 1991). *Nightline* (ABC) did a program on the dire straits of workers who have lost their pensions in the collapse of insurance companies in general, with special attention to Pacific Lumber, on June 18, 1991. The program featured interviews with aging retired workers, bewildered and frightened, demonstrating in the streets, demanding the return of their pension fund.

27. Grant Sims, "Can We Save the Northwest's Salmon?" *National Wildlife* (Oct.-Nov. 1994): pp. 42–48.

28. Forest L. Reinhardt, "Champion International Corporation: Timber, Trade and the Northern Spotted Owl," Harvard Business School Case Study 9-792-017, March 15, 1993.

29. Because the assets are spent down so quickly. For another account of how Hurwitz's financial dealings and shareholders work in the market, see William Barrett, "Aluminum Cow," *Forbes* (6 January 1992) detailing Hurwitz's handling of Kaiser Aluminum.

30. *Wall Street Journal* (10 February 1988).

31. Timothy Egan, "Oregon Failing Forecasters: Thrives as It Protects Owls," *New York Times* (11 October 1994): p. A1. Incidentally, the loggers are all wrong. In 1994, after logging was drastically curtailed, Oregon had the lowest unemployment in years, gaining 10,000 nontimber jobs.

32. See Miller, *Living in the Environment*. pp. 296–298.

33. Charles McCoy, "Cutting Costs: For Takeover Baron, Redwood Forests Are Just One More Deal," *Wall Street Journal* (6 August 1993): pp. A1, A6.

34. Miller, *Living in the Environment*, p. 296; George Brown and Pete Stark, "The Last Stand: Only Clinton Can Save a Priceless Redwood Grove," *New York Times*, Op.-Ed. (1 December 1995).

35. McCoy, "Cutting Costs," p. A6; Brown and Stark, "Last Stand."

36. John Skow, "Redwoods: The Last Stand," *TIME* (6 June 1994): p. 59.

37. McCoy, "Cutting Costs," p. A6.

38. "Owl Creek Victory Triggers Pacific Lumber's Plans for Revenge Cut," *EPIC*, Environmental Protection Information Center, P.O. Box 397, Garberville, CA, 95542. (29 March 1995).

39. For the information in this section, I am indebted to Robert Irelan, MAXXAM's Vice President for Public Relations, and to Jim Noteware, President and CEO of MAXXAM Property Company.

40. Pacific Lumber Company publication, "The Pacific Lumber Company and the Headwaters Forest: A White Paper."

41. "White Paper", p. 7

42. Jack Shepard, *The Forest Killers* (New York: Weybright and Talley, 1975): pp. 18, 19.

43. Ibid., p. 31.

44. Caufield, "Ancient Forest," p. 60.

45. "News of the Week in Review," *New York Times* (3 November 1991): p. E1.

46. Ibid., p. 3.

47. Jane Fritsch, "Friend of Timber Industry Wields Power in Senate," *New York Times* (10 August 1995): p. B6.

48. John Cushman, Jr., "Court Fight over Timber Starts Immediately After Law Is Changed," *New York Times* (28 August 1995): p. A13. Editorial, *New York Times* (28 August 1995).

49. U.S. Forest Service and Bureau of Land Management, "Actions the Administration May Wish to Consider in Implementing a Conservation Strategy for the Northern Spotted Owl," Washington DC (1 May 1990).

50. United States Fish and Wildlife Service, "Economic Analysis of Designation of Critical Habitat for the Northern Spotted Owl," Washington, DC (August 1991).

51. Jack Shepard, *Forest Killers*, p. 33.

52. Kathie Durbin, "From Owls to Eternity," *E: The Environmental Magazine*, vol. 3, no. 2 (March/April 1992): pp. 30–37.

53. Tim Hamach, "The Great Tree Robbery," *New York Times* (19 September 1991).

54. Caufield, "Ancient Forest," p. 67.

Suggestions for Further Reading

Laurel Brubaker Calkins, "The Case Against Hurwitz," *Houston Press* (25 April–1 May 1996): pp. 17ff.

Daniel Glick, "Having Owls and Jobs Too: A Booming Economy Debunks the 'Owl-vs.-Jobs' Premise," *National Wildlife*, vol. 33, no. 5 (Aug./Sept. 1995).

Bill McKibben, "What Good Is a Forest?" *Audubon* (May-June 1996): pp. 54ff.

G. Tyler Miller, *Living in the Environment*, 9th ed. (Belmont, CA: Wadsworth, 1996).

David S. Wilcove, "Of Owls and Ancient Forests," *Ancient Forests of the Pacific Northwest* (Washington, DC: Island Press, 1990).

APPENDIX: AN ALPHABET SOUP FOR OUR TIME

We avoid, when we can, the technical jargon of government regulation, the esoteric debate that turns on the uncountable agencies and mystifying fragmentary legislation of federal and state governments. But this mass of information, as it dominates the corridors of Congress and governs the bureaucrats who actually make the day-to-day decisions, is occasionally crucial to an understanding of the real and major issues in contemporary affairs, the environment in particular. Here is a list of the most common (by no means all) of the agencies and laws that govern the fate of the redwoods, for your reference.

Selected Agencies Affecting Old-Growth Forests and the Owl

Fish and Wildlife Service (FWS)—an agency of the U.S. Department of the Interior. It administers the Endangered Species Act and the Migratory Bird Treaty Act; all other federal agencies must clear any action related to an endangered species with the FWS.

Forest Service—an agency of the U.S. Department of Agriculture. It manages national forests and, under the National Forest Management Act, has a mandate to ensure viable populations of wildlife in the forests it controls.

Bureau of Land Management (BLM)—an agency of the Department of the Interior. It manages timber lands, mostly in Oregon, under the Oregon and California Act and the Federal Land Policy and Management Act.

National Park Service (NPS)—an agency of the U.S. Department of the Interior that manages national parks.

Interagency Scientific Committee (ISC)—a committee formed by all of the above in 1988, specifically to find ways to save the owl.

Selected Legislation Affecting Old-Growth Forest and the Owl

Migratory Bird Treaty Act (MBTA: 1936)—protects the owl. A result of the 1936 Convention for the Protection of Migratory Birds and Game Mammals.

Oregon and California Act of 1937 (O&CA: 1937)—covering federal land management, in both states but mostly in Oregon, directs the BLM to manage those lands.

Federal Land Policy and Management Act (FLPMA: 1976)—extends the mandate of the O&CA.

National Forest Management Act (NFMA: 1976)—requires the Forest Service to protect indicator species on federal lands it manages, indeed all vertebrate species.

Multiple Use Sustained Yield Act (MUSYA: 1960)—The Forest Service is urged to encourage activities other than lumbering, e.g., tourism and camping, on federal lands.

National Environmental Policy Act (NEPA: 1970)—significantly, requires that all federal agencies include in any legislative recommendation or report, or any other federal action, an *Environmental Impact Statement* (EIS), an account of any aspects of the contemplated action that might affect the environment.

Endangered Species Act (ESA: 1973)—requires the FWS to determine what species are threatened or endangered and to guarantee protection for them and for their habitat.

CHAPTER 6

Oil and Waters

Exxon Valdez
and the Cleanup

PREFACE: QUESTIONS TO
KEEP IN MIND

On Washington's Birthday, 1996, the oil tanker *Sea Empress* was towed off the rocks on which it had foundered off Milford Haven in Wales; by that time it had "spewed more than 65,000 tons of crude oil into one of Britain's most sensitive areas."[1] Why haven't we solved this type of problem? What risk factors for oil spills, as the story of the *Exxon Valdez* demonstrates, make it so difficult to get spills under control?

How much should corporations do to ensure the safety of their operations? Were Exxon's safety rules sufficient? Was the problem in the rules or in their implementation?

What is *Alyeska*, the consortium that was supposed to clean up the spill? Why was it formed?

What went wrong with Exxon's reaction to the spill? What have we learned about the best way to deal with oil spills?

Why do we need so much oil? Do we have to drill for oil in the vulnerable ecosystems of Alaska? Is there some way we can fuel our lives with something else—something renewable, maybe, and less damaging to the environment?

REFLECTIONS ON RESPONSIBILITY

In the aftermath of the wreck of the *Exxon Valdez,* it became crucial, if only to save our own sanity in the face of such ugliness and environmental destruction, to place responsibility for the disaster somewhere, to hold someone to account for it. By the time the terms of the discussion had become clear, three levels of responsibility had surfaced. At the first level and most obviously, stood Exxon's corporate responsibility for the negligent seamanship that spilled the oil, as well as Exxon/Alyeska's corporate responsibility for the lack of preparation ashore—preparation that would have contained its spread within 2–3 hours. At the second level stood the citizen complicity in the whole "Alyeska syndrome"—their willingness to exploit oil resources at the peril of the pristine Alaskan environment, even against their better judgment. And third stands the accountability of us all, our cars and our heated houses, using all that oil despite our knowledge that the environment would be better off if we cut out, or cut down, on our use of this and all fossil fuels.

This chapter examines responsibility: individual, corporate, national, and environmental. At the end of the discussion we will raise the ultimate question arising from this incident: Must all our energy demands be filled? If we do need fossil fuels, are there safer ways to extract and transport them? What alternatives to fossil fuels exist? If we do not meet all our energy needs, how shall we live? What kind of society would have room for a decent human life and sea otters too?

THE EVENT: SHIP MEETS REEF[2]

From various accounts, including Art Davidson's book-length treatment of the incident, one can reconstruct the incidents that occurred March 23 and early on March 24, Good Friday, 1989. At 9:30 P.M. on March 23, the *Exxon Valdez,* a 987-foot oil tanker owned by the Exxon Shipping Company (subsidiary of Exxon U.S.A., part of Exxon Corporation), left the dock at the port of Valdez with a cargo of 1.26 million barrels of North Slope oil, brought in from Prudhoe Bay to the terminal at Valdez through the Alaskan Pipeline. Under the command of Captain Ed Murphy, an independent harbor pilot, it headed out through Valdez Harbor for Prince William Sound, the Gulf of Alaska, and onward to the open ocean. Captain Murphy took the ship safely through the Valdez Narrows, where the harbor ends, and out into Prince William Sound. At 11:24 P.M., he left ship, returning control to the master of the vessel, Captain

Joseph J. Hazelwood. One minute later Captain Hazelwood called the Coast Guard to tell them that he was leaving the outbound shipping lane and steering a course south (180 degrees) into the inbound lanes (empty at that time), to avoid ice floes broken from the Columbia Glacier to the north.

Hazelwood next gave a series of unusual orders: He told the lookout, Maureen Jones, to stand her watch from the bridge instead of 800 feet in front of it; he told the helmsman Harry Claar to accelerate to sea speed, although they were about to start maneuvering around icebergs of unknown dimension, and to put the ship on automatic pilot, which would complicate any course changes. Then, in direct contradiction to company policy, Hazelwood went below, leaving command in the hands of Third Mate Gregory T. Cousins, with orders to continue southerly to the lighted buoy off Busby Island, then return to the shipping lanes. When Cousins discovered that the ship was on autopilot, he put it back into manual mode. Then he turned to the radar to concentrate on missing the ice.

Why was Hazelton acting so strangely? He was probably under the influence of alcohol. By four days after the accident, both Coast Guard Lieutenant Thomas Falkenstein (the first to reach the *Exxon Valdez* after the grounding) and Captain Murphy told a federal investigating team (headed by William Woody of the National Traffic Safety Board) that they had smelled alcohol on Hazelwood's breath just before and just after the accident.[3] He was still legally drunk (0.061 percent) when the blood tests were finally made, nine hours after the accident.[4] This was not some recent deviance, and the record was not difficult to find. By March 29, an unsigned article appeared in the *New York Times,* datelined Hauppauge, Long Island (Joseph Hazelwood's home town), that tracks Hazelwood's drinking history. During the five years preceding the accident, he was twice convicted on charges involving drinking and driving; his license to drive a car had been suspended or revoked three times, and was suspended at the time of the accident.[5] Exxon had known of Hazelwood's alcohol problems and had sent him through rehabilitation and reinstated him. Still he drank openly.[6] How far does the company's responsibility— and right to monitor behavior—extend in such cases?

Meanwhile, the condition of those left on the bridge may not have been much better. The crew was exhausted. To save money, the company had cut back the crews on their ships, so that only 20 served aboard the *Exxon Valdez.* That left the members of the crew with an average of 140 hours of overtime a month per person.

Further, Third Mate Gregory Cousins was not licensed to navigate the ship in Prince William Sound. Did his inexperience cause the accident? On the one hand, the channel as marked and as normally traveled presents no difficulties for navigation. Paul Yost, Commandant of the Coast Guard, commented on the accident a week after it happened: "Remember, we've got 10 miles of open water there, and for that vessel to have come over and hit a reef is almost unbelievable," he told reporters. "This was not a treacherous area, as you people in the press have called it. It is not treacherous in the area they went aground. It's 10 miles wide. Your children could drive a tanker up through it."[7]

On the other hand, Hazelwood had planned a course that would skirt the southern edge of that 10-mile opening in order to avoid the ice. "A well-timed right turn would be necessary to avoid Bligh Reef, which lay six miles ahead in the darkness. There would be little room for error. The vessel needed at least six-tenths of a mile to make the turn, and the gap between the ice and Bligh Reef was only nine-tenths of a mile wide. The tanker itself was nearly two-tenths of a mile long. The tanker would have to start its turn well before the gap between the ice and the reef if it was to make it through."[8] Absorbed in his computations, Cousins missed the Busby Island light, where he was supposed to have started his turn, and had no idea how far off course he was until lookout Jones called his attention to the flashing red light off Bligh Island off his *starboard* side, where it had no business being if he was headed out.

After the *Exxon Valdez* hit the first rock, Cousins tried very hard to make the turn back into the shipping lanes, but the ship's momentum kept her going south to the reef where, 15 minutes later, she grounded. The reef punched eight holes in her hull, spilling a quarter of a million barrels of oil (about 11 million gallons) into the clear waters of the sound. Cousins called Captain Hazelwood to the bridge immediately, and Hazelwood spent 15 to 20 minutes trying to dislodge the ship from the reef, to no avail. At 12:27 A.M., Hazelwood radioed the Coast Guard and told them that he had fetched up north of Goose Island, at Bligh Reef. Coast Guard Commander Stephen McCall promptly warned off all ships, sent Lieutenant Falkenstein and Dan Lawn of Alaska's Department of Environmental Conservation (DEC) out to investigate, told incoming tankers to drop anchor, and closed the port of Valdez.

What had gone wrong? As with many such cases, including others in this volume, there are more than enough predisposing factors for the accident, and by foul chance they all converged on one hapless third mate and one beautiful ecosystem, causing death and destruction in the animal communities of the sound and anger and confusion in the human communities that were affected by the spill. To understand the impact of the spill, we need to know the environmental background of the sound and the kind of damage done by oil in those waters.

Prince William Sound: The End of Innocence

Every account of the monster spill includes a reference to the "pristine" beauty of the sound before the accident: the wealth of birds, fish, wildlife, kelp, living things of all sorts; the complex web of interdependence that makes a threat to any of those species a threat to them all. *Pristine* is not a word in common usage, primarily because it designates a rare condition: the original condition, according to Webster's—pure, untouched, unspoiled, uncorrupted. Prince William Sound had never been fouled, polluted, cut over, industrialized, or settled by environmentally intrusive human groups. It had been the home of Chugach Eskimos and Aleut Indians, recorded for the West by Captain James Cook in 1778 and named by him for the British Crown; Spanish explorers had christened Valdez and the nearby town of Cordova; Russian fur trappers had set up bases on Hinchinbrook Island; but none of these had affected the stunningly beautiful natural setting. Prior to the Alaskan Pipeline, the sound had been immune to the usual depredations of the twentieth century.

Prince William Sound is roughly 70 miles long and 30 miles wide, with many bays, inlets, and islands to break up its shoreline. There are approximately 2,500 square miles of open water, 1,800 miles of mainland shoreline, and 1,200 shoreline miles on islands and rocks. The depth ranges from 2,850 feet at its deepest, averaging 480 feet in the shipping channel—to virtually nothing over Bligh Reef at low tide. It is bounded by rocky peninsulas and towering mountains, most prominently the glacier-covered Chugach Mountains to the north.

The wildlife is diverse and abundant: "ten species of marine mammals, including sea lions, whales, seals, porpoises, and 10,000–12,000 sea otters; more than 30 species of land mammals,... more than 200 species of birds, including swans, cormorants, more than 15 million shorebirds, and 3000 bald eagles."[9] All of these were at risk.

> The sound is ... the crossroads for huge migrations of fish and birds ... The Copper River delta at the east end of the sound, 75 miles from the Exxon Valdez, is home to an estimated 20 million migratory birds in late April and early May, including one-fifth of the world's trumpeter swans.... One bay in the sound is home to the largest concentrations of orcas, or killer whales, in the world; its sea otters make up perhaps one-fourth of the total U. S. sea-otter population; marshes and estuaries near Cordova on the eastern side of the sound support the entire nesting U. S. population of the rare dusky Canada goose.[10]

Because the sound was enclosed, and therefore any oil slick continuous, the risk from spilled oil was great. The oil could not break up as it would in the open ocean, so the benzene and other volatile components of the spill, instead of evaporating, soon dissolved in the water to be consumed by zooplankton and other microorganisms at the beginning of the food chain, crucial for the life of the sound.[11] The enclosure of the oil made matters worse; it "delayed dissipation of the spill, exposing animals to oil for a long period of time and allowing oil to soak deeply into beaches and sediments."[12]

The Deadly Invasion of Oil

How does oil kill an animal? Diving birds and sea otters are most at risk. The birds catch their food by plunging into the water, diving to catch their fish, coming to the surface, and taking off to fly to their nests. Any weight on their feathers makes such flight impossible. If they do get to shore, they try to clean the oil off their feathers with their beaks *(preening)*, thereby ingesting the oil, which is fatal. Because oil makes their insulation (the inner layer of down feathers) matted and useless, most of them freeze to death before they have time to die of poisoning. Of particular concern were two rare birds, the yellow-billed loon and the merlet, which may have been particularly affected. We will probably never know just how badly: To get a bit ahead of the story, when Exxon applied for permission "to dispose of oil-soaked wastes some weeks after the spill, its list of throwaway items included twenty *tons* of dead birds [italics ours]."[13] A wildlife photographer counted 650 dead birds on a half mile of beach on Barren Island. But as David Cline, the National Audubon Society's regional vice president for Alaska, has pointed out, "You see only the birds that have managed to struggle to shore, where they shiver to death. And you find only a fraction of them. The majority of the dead you never see. Their oil-sodden plumage weighs them down and they drown." Up to 90 percent of oiled birds sink to the bottom.[14]

The sea otters suffered equally. Unlike seals and sea lions, otters have no blubber to keep them warm but insulate themselves with the air trapped in their thick soft undercoat. Because oil destroys their insulation, only a little on them will quickly freeze them to death in the frigid water. The oil also destroys their eyes, lungs, and intestines (when they ingest it from attempting to lick their coats clean).

The damage to fish caused the greatest monetary loss to humans, however. The fishing industry earns $100 million annually in Prince William Sound (out of $2 billion for all of Alaska). Herring and salmon are the mainstays, but those fish "are just the start of a rich web of major species, including crab, shrimp, Pacific cod, Alaska pollack, rockfishes, halibut, flounder and sharks."[15] In 1988, Prince William Sound salmon fishers earned $70 million from a harvest of 14.9 million salmon, 15 percent of the state harvest. King crabs (48,422 pounds in 1988) and shrimp (178,000 pounds) were the species most endangered by dissolved benzene.[16] The herring roe, which sells for up to $80 a pound in Japan, provides $13 million of business annually. The herring need clean kelp to lay their spawn; after the spill, the kelp was covered with oil. Most of the towns, and most of the independent businesses on the sound, make their living one way or another through the fishing industry, which employs 6,000 people all by itself. It is a growth industry—the average American consumption of seafood has nearly doubled in the last 20 years—and the fishers at the time were looking forward to a good year.

The fish do not merely provide a means to make a living. The fishers are united in a love both for their way of life, which is why they accept without protest the complex web of restrictions on fishing licenses, gear, and seasons, to preserve the fish runs for the future, and for their spectacularly beautiful home. If the spread of the oil could not be stopped soon, the fishing seasons would have to be canceled, and a year's income lost, or at least placed at the mercy of Exxon to make good; homes might also be lost, with all their value destroyed. The fishers had a tremendous amount at stake in stopping the oil. Would the Alyeska plan for stopping the oil work well enough, and quickly enough, to save the fishing season?

THE RESPONSE: STUDIES IN DYSFUNCTION

There is no way to characterize the Alyeska/Exxon response to the situation except as failure—dismal failure. Its causes are instructive: the unpreparedness; the dysfunctionality of large size; the incentives for ineffectiveness built into the system, especially the clouding of the boundary between appearance and reality (between public relations and environmental remediation); and the distractions of the law. These factors, which recur in all such situations either by themselves or generously mixed with human villainy, are worth noting in the discouraging tale of the response to the spill.

A Very Unprepared Consortium

The Alyeska Pipeline Service Company is a consortium of seven oil companies (including Exxon) that actually owns the oil pumped out of the North Slope. They had promised, when seeking approval for the pipeline, that the operations in Prince William Sound would be "the safest in the world."[17] Alyeska's plan, approved by the Alaska DEC, had specified that containment booms and skimming equipment (machinery for mechanically lifting the thick oil off the top of the water into transfer barges, which would take the oil to shore) would be on the scene of any spill in five hours, with backup equipment (lasers for burning off patches of oil, chemical dispersants) available if the booms and skimmers could not do the job. There was no doubt in anyone's mind that speed was essential to contain a big spill, as Alyeska's containment plan spelled out: "Speed in deploying booms is essential in order to contain the maximum amount spilled oil." The plan also promised that "the necessary equipment is available and operable to meet oil spill response needs."[18] That equipment was supposed to be available at the dock.

Unfortunately, Alyeska had estimated that such a large spill as that of the *Exxon Valdez* could happen only once every 241 years, which made it seem pointless to keep all that equipment around and all those experts on the payroll. "Alyeska fought steadily to cut back safety measures. The oil-spill contingency plan was trimmed and weakened. A twenty-man oil spill emergency squad was disbanded" in 1981. "Instead of the twelve miles of boom materials that the state wanted Alyeska to have on hand, Alyeska insisted that a fourth that much was sufficient."[19] The pattern of cost cutting and crew reduction that had perhaps contributed to the spill in the first place now crippled the response. Barges were supposed to be available for transporting oil and equipment: Alyeska's one barge, on the morning of the spill, was in dry dock. Workers had to dig out skimmers and boom from a local warehouse.

So even at the outset, when Alyeska's obligations were well understood and the weather was calm—ideal for containing and skimming the oil—the "Great Promise" (as Davidson calls it) was simply broken. A barge carrying 25 tons of cleanup equipment did not arrive at the accident site until 14 hours after the spill, after agonizing efforts to find, load, and operationalize the equipment that they could find. Even then, there was not enough containment equipment at that time to encircle the spill.

The Alaskans had been betrayed. Alyeska's cleanup plan had been crucial for the authorization of the pipeline to begin with. When the right-of-way permit was in doubt, back in 1971, "British Petroleum's top pollution specialist, L. R. Beynon, testified at Department of Interior hearings that Alyeska's contingency plan "will detail methods for dealing promptly and effectively with any oil spill which may occur, so that its effects on the environment will be minimal. We have adequate knowledge for dealing with oil spills.... The best equipment, materials and expertise—which will be made available as part of the oil spill contingency plan—will make operations in Port of Valdez and Prince William Sound the safest in the world."[20] Dennis Kelso, a DEC commissioner, at one point labeled that plan "the biggest piece of maritime fiction since *Moby Dick*." Even so, "it was Mr. Kelso's office that approved of the contingency documents. He said later he placed too much trust in industry to live up to its paper promises."[21] "Too much"? Should we not rely on citizens to live up to promises this specific and detailed, promises leaving no room for misunderstanding? In this sense of betrayal, what grated with particular harshness was the value at risk—the incredibly fertile beauty of Prince William Sound—and the clear fact, that without such promises, there would have been no pipeline.

As the spill spread across the Sound, where *was* Alyeska? As the DEC's Dan Lawn put it, "The people of the United States didn't want 4,700 different oil companies coming in here with 47,000 different cleanup contractors. They wanted one. That was Alyeska. And Alyeska was going to take care of everything. We've got a plan that says that. Where the hell were they?"[22] Why was Exxon suddenly the responsible party, and Frank Iarossi of Exxon Shipping Company in charge? In all the discussion afterward and to this day, there has not been a good explanation for the sudden disappearance of Valdez-based Alyeska and the ascendance of the Houston-based Exxon Shipping Company as responsible for the accident and charged with the cleanup.

Cleanup Efforts

Meanwhile, the balmy weather turned rough two days after the spill, making skimming very difficult. One could use *dispersants* (detergents that break up the oil spill), which wave action makes more effective. Dispersants have problems of their own, however. They do not really remove the oil from the water. They just sink it a few feet below the surface in an emulsion of oil and detergent, killing all marine life in that area just below the surface; the emulsion ultimately diffuses in the ocean. It kills young fish, and there is no doubt that it would hurt the otters and birds even more (since the detergent would dissolve the natural oils that insulate fur and feathers); the only real good that dispersants do is make the oil spill disappear.

On a practical level though, this problem was moot. Exxon had only 69 barrels of dispersant on hand in Alaska.[23] At great expense, Iarossi flew in dispersant from around the world. But it would have taken nearly 10,000 barrels of dispersant to treat that spill—there was not that much in the world.

The damage, at any rate, was done. A crucial 48 to 72 hours of calm weather had passed without the booms being deployed and the oil skimmed from the water to waiting barges. The transfer of the remaining million barrels from the stricken *Exxon Valdez* to the *Exxon Baton Rouge* had begun and continued through the winter storm that tore through the area on the fourth day after the spill and spread the oil from 100 square miles to 500. Forced to improvise, how did the agencies faced with this massive disaster respond?

The first major problem was one of authority. Davidson describes it as follows:

> Alyeska, which the state had relied on for spill response, had disappeared. Exxon was trying to respond but needed authorization. Most of Exxon's people, having flown up from other parts of the

country, had little knowledge of Alaska and virtually no connection to the land and to Prince William Sound. They didn't know Alaska's weather, Alaska's waters, Alaska's shorelines, or Alaska's people. But the state and the Coast Guard, which could have provided the needed direction, strained against the limits placed on their own authority.[24]

The fishers of the fishing towns on the sound then mounted their own initiative. After all, they had very little to do. On April 3, 1989, Alaska officials had canceled the herring fishing season. That was good news for the herring fishers, for it meant that they would surely get restitution for the season from Exxon (although the impact on the future of the herring is still not known.) It also left their boats free to work. As the oil continued to advance, it became clear that the precious salmon hatcheries were in danger. Because nothing was being done to protect them, the fishers decided to act.

The hatcheries had been built in the early 1970s, when overfishing had reduced the pink salmon run so low that the season had to be closed. The fishers borrowed $18 million from the state to build the Sawmill Bay and Esther Island hatcheries. "By 1989, the Koernig Hatchery, once an abandoned cannery on Sawmill Bay, was producing more than $20 million worth of salmon each year. The Esther had become the world's largest salmon hatchery, releasing 200 million pinks, 100 million chum, 4 million kings, and 2 million silvers."[25] The fishers were afraid that even a few gallons of that oil, sweeping through the rearing pens, could wipe out an entire generation of pink salmon.

So they took their own boats and went to work, dipping oil and laying booms to protect their hatcheries. Difficulties attended every step of getting better supplies from Exxon: "There were so many people in the chain of command that if one link goofed, nothing got done. Some of the Exxon people were trying their damnedest, but there simply wasn't enough equipment available."[26]

Heroic efforts staved off the oil until a more solid containment boom was available; the hatcheries were saved. But they were saved by people acting on their own, with no chain of command or formal plan, voluntarily cooperating with each other. The proper authorities—the huge state, the corporation, and the Coast Guard, acting together—found themselves in one vast unworkable gridlock.

Much the same observation could be made for other phases of the cleanup. The animal-rescue efforts, for instance, recruited some of the best people available to clean, cure, and release wild birds and sea otters, and volunteers worked tirelessly to save the lives of the oil-slicked wild creatures. Yet this effort continually ran afoul of the U.S. Fish and Wildlife Service, which ordinarily catches the oiled birds and animals and brings them to the veterinarians. In Alaska, the FWS instructed the experts brought up from the Berkeley-based International Bird Rescue Research Center (IBRRC) that they would have to find their own animals to rescue and talk Exxon into paying for these efforts. The role of the FWS was to "monitor" the operations. Eventually the IBRRC decided, just as the fishers had, that they would have to run the entire operation themselves without help from the corporate and government giants that had, at least on paper, authority over such decisions.

Systemic Disincentives

There may have been more at work than simple bureaucratic bungling in Exxon's handling of the extended cleanup effort. In the complex job of managing human interaction with nature (and each other), we must make sure that the incentives are in the right place: that agents perceive the task at hand as being in their best interest. With routine tasks, the incentive patterns are known, used, and generally reliable. One of the best analyses of such patterns, for instance, is the treatment of voluntary economic exchanges in Adam Smith's *The Wealth of Nations,* in which he proves that government management of the market is unnecessary to protect justice, and counterproductive in the accumulation of national wealth.

But in unfamiliar territory, we grope and sometimes fail. In the case of oil spills, for example, European nations immediately assume public responsibility for the spill, clean it up, and then send the offending oil company the bill for the damage. That approach has problems, for the government workers have no incentive to be frugal and to minimize the cost of the cleanup. With Alyeska, therefore, a different approach was adopted: Alyeska and the spiller would assume responsibility for the cleanup if they could and would. The federal government would not step in and start running the operation ("federalizing" the cleanup) unless the spiller denied responsibility or admitted the inability to continue dealing with it. Exxon did neither. At the beginning of operations, there was no doubt that the Exxon officers, especially Frank Iarossi, were doing their best to help the cleanup. Only as the oil spread across the sound—to ever more remote islands and to the Katmai National Park, 400 miles southwest of Bligh Reef—did the faltering of the cleanup begin to seem systematic.

By this time, support from Washington had begun to fade. Much of the fading seemed caused by Vern Wiggins, a Reagan appointee (deputy undersecretary of the Interior for Alaska) who honestly believed that oil development was essential to the state of Alaska; therefore it was essential to underplay the effect of this spill and the dangers of spills generally. His influence extended to the Coast Guard as well as the entirety of the park service.[27]

Meanwhile, strong signals came from Exxon that it was time to wind down the cleanup. There were never enough boats to transport the oily sludge that the volunteers had collected. When transport boats did show up, the Exxon employees did not want to transport the oil, because it contained oil-soaked sand, pebbles, and kelp—Exxon's position was that it was committed to transport *oil,* not all that the oil had penetrated. In some places, Exxon workers had to pick up oil with their hands because the trowels picked up pebbles. "Oil's hard to pick up just in gloves," commented one of the volunteers. "It goes through your fingers."[28] After a while of this, workers began very sincerely to doubt Exxon's commitment to getting oil off the beaches. The doubt was reinforced by days of sitting on beaches with no assignments and reinforced again by the observation that those who worked hardest, especially those who came up with better ways to remove oil from the beaches, tended to get fired.[29]

Appearance and Reality

What were the incentives? Clearly Exxon had a major incentive not to let the spill be federalized, for then they would lose control of the cleanup expenditures; therefore, they wanted to keep up the appearance of cleaning, at all costs. So trips were arranged, for Secretary of the Interior Manuel Lujan, boatloads of reporters, Exxon officers, and members of Congress, to beaches where 40 Exxon employees could be found skimming oil, mopping rocks, and scrubbing pebbles.[30]

But eventually an incentive to keep up an appearance of doing something is not the same as an incentive to do it. And the greatest incentive Exxon had, of course, was to make the spill appear to be gone and not as serious as people thought, so they could end the cleanup. To preserve that appearance, it is necessary not to appear to find very much oil damage. The best way to preserve *that* appearance is to make sure that one way or another, not very much oil is recovered and brought back to town for the news media to see and measure. And so the citizens and volunteers began to detect a pattern in the way Exxon conducted the cleanup in the later beaches—no vessels available to cart the spill back to Valdez; haggling reminiscent of Shylock and Portia over whether the oil may contain sand or other oiled debris; all initiatives and hard work punished by termination. Beaches were not to be "cleaned," they were to be "treated" and then left.

The chronicle of the *Exxon Valdez* leaves many questions unanswered. How shall we allot the tasks of cleanup after a major oil spill if our objective is to get it cleaned up as quickly and as frugally as possible? How can we allot the tasks of cleanup, authority, and responsibility so that the responsible parties will have an incentive actually to clean up and not to retreat to the appearance of a job?

A Slick of Lawyers over Alaska

Further disincentives to real remedy flowed from the operations of the law. By now we are familiar with the kind of legal wrangling that goes on when people are injured by the actions of a large corporation. Acutely aware of this wrangling, Exxon swiftly promised to recompense anyone injured by the spill (the fishers, for instance). This did not stop the lawsuits. Exxon and Alaska competed for the best law firms; at a preliminary hearing on some 150 lawsuits (58 of them class-action suits) held in Anchorage, 65 law firms were represented. Calculating damages, even where Exxon promised to pay, was extremely difficult. No problem arises in paying a fisher for a missed season, given solid figures on last season, but the damage to the species, especially genetic damage, to wildlife habitat, and to microscopic life was incalculable.

The legal actions that had followed the *Amoco Cadiz* spill off France in 1978 suggested that the ultimate liability of the parties to disputes of this nature depends on a judge's perceptions of the relative contributions of oil-company and government actions. Judge McGarr had found in that case that the French Government's refusal (on environmental grounds) to authorize the use of dispersants in water less than 50 meters deep was "without scientific justification," and "seriously interfered with the success of the dispersant method," thus relieving Amoco of much of the financial liability for the damage to the victims of that spill. Accordingly, Exxon immediately claimed that authorization for use of dispersants had been refused by Alaska—and Reagan's secretary of the interior, Manual Lujan, backed them up. There was no doubt that the wrangling drained energy from the cleanup

> as the state and Exxon fought each other for moral high ground in the press and for billions of dollars in court.
>
> The protagonists, entrenched with their lawyers and press agents, became increasingly isolated from each other. The result in many instances was that the battles took precedence over the problem. Too often the oil cleanup effort appeared to be driven more by legal and public relations strategies than by scientific considerations. And the common goal of restoring the coastal environment frequently seemed to get lost in the shuffle.[31]

THE BLAME

While the state and the company remained locked in a death grip of public relations and financial liability, the citizens of Alaska had an opportunity to reflect on their own complicity in the spill. "We're not victims of

Exxon," said Tom Copeland, the fisher whose bucket brigade had out-skimmed Exxon's best, "we're reluctant participants. Basically, Alaskans are addicted to that oil money. We've got that needle in our arms.... We don't deserve another dollar from that pipeline."[32] The oil companies had paid enough oil royalties in 1988 that each citizen of the state had received a royalty check in excess of $800. There is no record that any-one sent back their checks. And when Exxon offered to hire the fishing boats to fight the spill, at the rate of $5,000 per day, most fishers took them up on the offer. Somehow, it seemed in the historic opportunistic spirit of Alaska to do it.[33]

Ray Bane of the Katmai Park Service summed up the feeling of many of the residents. "Exxon caused this mess, but it had plenty of assistance. I think all of us who have benefited from that oil have a responsibility to bear. Alaskans take too much for granted. It's a big land—good fishing, lots of animals, wild rivers. We take it all so damn much for granted. The oil spill is only a symptom of all of us closing our minds to the fact that there is always a price to pay when you develop oil, or cut down some trees, or build a road."[34] But that kind of complacency went beyond the Alaskans. Shortly after the spill, Greenpeace put an ad in newspapers nationwide, showing Joseph Hazelwood's face, with a caption: "It wasn't his driving that caused the Alaskan oil spill. It was yours." Because the truth is, it continued, "the spill was caused by a nation drunk on oil. And a government asleep at the wheel."[35] "And ultimately," the Cordova fisher Ed Monkiewicz concluded, "we're all at fault, every single one of us. We've got to have our cars. We use the fossil fuels. Maybe if we put more value on our environment, this wouldn't have happened."[36]

Aftermath in Court

Exxon offered to settle the whole case two years later, submitting guilty pleas in an agreement that would have taken care of both criminal charges and civil claims of federal and state governments arising from the spill. Under that agreement, Exxon would have paid $100 million in criminal fines and as much as $1 billion for civil claims. This was not very much; an editorial in the *New York Times* pointed out that by mid-April, Exxon had already paid an estimated $2 billion for the cleanup.[37] But on April 24, 1991, Judge Russel Holland ruled that the $100 million in fines was not sufficient, and the legislature of Alaska subsequently voted that the civil settlement also was not enough.[38] Eventually, Exxon agreed to pay $900 million over 10 years for "restoring, replacing, enhancing, rehabilitating or acquiring the equivalent of natural resources" damaged by the spill. Like most large settlements, it was immediately visited by the lawyers: Of the first $240 million spent, only $11.4 went to the environment; the rest went to "reimburse the expenses" of the governments involved.[39] And now the trustees of the fund, bitterly criticized by environmentalists for mismanaging the money, have to decide which of two environmental causes, marine research or purchase of forest land, should get the remainder of the money, for there is no agreement among the environmental organizations.[40]

After years of efforts by Exxon's scientists to show there was no long-term damage to Prince William Sound,[41] in 1993 a geochemist working for the United States Geological Survey concluded that much of the oil on Alaska's beaches comes from an unnoticed 1964 spill of oil from Monterey, not from the *Exxon Valdez.* Exxon's lawyers immediately drew the legal implications and began work to extricate the company from further blame.[42] They were not entirely successful. In September of 1994, after a 20-week trial, a jury awarded $5 billion in punitive damages to 34,000 fishers and other Alaskans. That is a great deal of money even for Exxon, although the *New York Times* did not find it excessive,[43] and the matter continues on appeal. Ten days later another jury awarded $9.7 million in land damages to six Alaska native corporations and a village that had sued for damages.[44]

HAZELWOOD WAS NOT ALONE

Even as the *Exxon Valdez* headed for the reef, Alyeska officials were holding a victory dinner celebrating their cleanup of a spill days previously in Valdez harbor. As Frank Iarossi reached for the ringing telephone in the small hours of the morning of March 24, 1989, he was still winding down from the Hawaiian spill of March 2, when the *Exxon Houston* broke loose from her moorings in a storm off Barber's Point, about 15 miles from Waikiki Beach, and went aground on a coral reef about 2,000 feet off the west coast of Oahu.[45] Three months later, the nation watched three major spills take place in 12 hours. On June 23, 4:40 P.M., the *World Prodigy* struck a reef in Narragansett Bay, RI. Apparently, the ship had blundered into unfamiliar waters without waiting for a pilot and repeated the error of the *Exxon Valdez,* straying to the wrong side of the red channel buoys; 420,000 gallons of Number 2 fuel oil flowed into the bay. At 6:20 P.M. the same day, an oil barge collided with a tanker in the Houston ship channel, spilling 250,000 gallons of crude oil, about half of which had been cleaned up four days later. At 4:00 the next morning, the Uruguayan tanker *Presidente Rivera* managed to stray from its channel in the Delaware River and hit a rock, spilling 800,000 gallons of Number 6 fuel, little of which was recovered.

"The three spills reopened many of the questions that maritime lawyers, environmentalists and lawmakers had debated after the Exxon Valdez spill. Some environmentalists were asking whether the spills were a coincidence or an indication that something was so wrong that long-established maritime rules need to be changed." A bit of investigation showed that these incidents were not at all unusual. Captain Gerard Barton, chief of the Coast Guard's investigations division, told a House subcommittee that in 1988 "there were 5000 to 6000 spills involving oil and other toxic substances along the coasts and in other navigable waters," 12 of them major (more than 100,000 gallons or more), but that that was "down sharply from about 13,000 a year a decade ago." Unimpressed by the improvement, the House called for change in the oil transport system.[46]

This change did not occur in time to prevent the next rash of dreadful spills, in the winter of 1992–1993. On December 3, 1992, the tanker *Aegean Sea* grounded off the coast of Spain; 23 million gallons of crude oil were lost, most in the fire that followed the explosion, the rest in the sea.[47] In the first week of January, the Liberian-registered tanker *Braer* lost power and went aground, eventually spilling all its 22 million gallons of oil and severely damaging wildlife, including salmon hatcheries.[48] Then the Danish tanker *Maersk Navigator* collided with another tanker on January 21, 1993, whereby its 78 million gallons of cargo began to spill into the sea, much of which burned off. None of these, though—including the wreck of the *Exxon Valdez*—claim the title of largest: 88 million gallons of crude was lost off Trinidad and Tobago in 1979 when two oil tankers collided; 79 million gallons went into the ocean off Cape Town, South Africa, in 1983.[49] As if to remind us that the safety problem continues unaffected by all our efforts, the most recent spill off Wales, cited at the opening of this chapter, has already spilled almost twice as much oil as the *Exxon Valdez*.

Tanker and barge accidents account for only two-thirds of the oil that spills into the waterways each year (an estimated 91 million gallons, for instance, in the period 1980–1986). The rest comes from pipe ruptures, like the rupture of an Exxon pipe that filled the Arthur Kill, off Staten Island, with oil in January 1990. Because a detection system had malfunctioned for a year without repairs, operators had simply ignored its warnings when the real spill came.[50] That spill would cost Exxon $15 million, and there was no chance of restoring the environment.[51] Probably the worst spill of all came from the largest act of eco-sabotage known to history: the deliberate destruction of the oil wells of Kuwait by the retreating Iraqi army during the Gulf War in 1991, which released 250 million gallons into the desert and the Persian Gulf.[52]

Opinions on the ultimate significance of these spills will differ, of course. Some, for example, disagree on the facts, since the effect of oil on fragile environments is often completely unknown. Others simply show different perspectives. In Philip Revzin's reassuring article about the *Amoco Cadiz*, which sank off the coast of France, we are told that "for a year after the gooey oil washed up...business [fishing, oyster-growing, tourism] all but stopped. For five to eight years the aquatic food chain was disrupted, costing crab fishers three generations of their most prized catches." And oil remained, in pockets. "But generally, it's finished, all is back to normal,'" says Lucien Laubler, chief scientific advisor to a French oceanic research institute. Back to normal? The French were suing Amoco for $600 million—eleven years later.[53] The *New York Times* angrily editorialized that it was time to stop the self-deceptions and make rational plans for safety and cleanup for the next spill.[54]

SO IT WILL NEVER HAPPEN AGAIN

Ultimately, the big story is the story of oil and energy—not Hazelwood's driving, but ours. From the renewed public discussion that followed the spill, three sets of imperatives emerged to avoid another *Exxon Valdez* (*Amoco Cadiz, Aegean Captain, Sea Empress...*).

Safe Operation

First, there arose imperatives to enforce the law, monitor compliance to existing policies, and implement known technology for the safe transport of oil. There are sufficient laws on the books, and clauses in the contracts, to make the oil industry operate safely. Complacency, carelessness, and criminal negligence produce these spills. Tankers can be required to have double hulls, more effective containment booms can be developed (the ones in use in Prince William Sound kept breaking), and we may develop new technology for the containment of spills. For instance, one interesting suggestion involves using fly ash—a pollutant removed from the chimneys of many industrial plants—fused with titanium dioxide into tiny glass beads, which will absorb a spill, permit burning it off, and incidentally get rid of the fly ash.[55] More important, if the penalties are sure enough and severe enough, the industry will find it to its advantage to monitor the state of preparedness of its cleanup crews, not to mention the state of inebriation of its employees.

There has been little improvement. A spokeswoman for the Skomer Island Dyfed Wildlife Trust, after the 1996 *Sea Empress* spill, "blamed the Government, charging that it had 'failed to provide an adequate and rapid response' to what she called 'an ecological disaster.'"[56] But at least in theory, that set of imperatives is not controversial; if we pass a law, or set a policy, we presumably have no objection to carrying it out. The other imperatives present greater problems.

Preservation of the Land

The second set of imperatives aims to protect forever the last remaining tracts of unspoiled land in the world, to the extent that it is in our power to do so. Whatever we thought we would gain by building the Alaskan Pipeline from Prudhoe Bay to Valdez—and we certainly had our doubts about it at the time (1973), when the vote of Spiro Agnew was required to break the tie in the Senate—the sight of the beaches mired with oil changed at least some of our minds. Everything else in this world—energy, money, production, recreation—is ultimately fungible; we can find some sort of substitute that will do just as well. The land alone is unique; once polluted, it can never be fully restored.

Protection of the land means setting it aside from human use and exploitation. It may mean leaving oil under the ground forever in the Arctic National Wildlife Refuge, the Bristol Bay fishery, the Florida Keys, and New England's Georges Bank fishery. It will surely mean protecting it from all mining, timbering, and other exploitation of resources. What other sources of oil are there? Prospecting for new oil all over the world, the major oil companies are drilling dry hole after dry hole.[57] In an increasingly crowded world, to what extent can we prefer the interests of land—that only a handful of people may ever see—to the material interests of people presently alive?

Energy

The third set of imperatives has to do with our use of energy, specifically the energy supplied by fossil fuels. Conservation of fuel can, realistically, relieve the pressure on some of the lands proposed for exploration. "Merely improving the efficiency of existing oil and gas furnaces and water heaters to the fullest cost-efficient extent would save the equivalent of 4.5 billion barrels of oil. This is roughly the same amount of oil that is believed to underlie the most sensitive areas. Moreover, aggressive weatherization programs for America's 53 million oil- and gas-heated homes would save twice the oil believed to be in these areas."[58] There are limits to what can be accomplished by conservation measures, like those above, that entail no change in lifestyle. Beyond these, we know that we must scale back tremendously on the use of automobiles, on long-distance travel, on the scattering of residences and shopping malls across the land. How can we persuade the people of the world—and that means the people of the United States to begin with—that lifestyle expectations and practices require drastic change?

One excellent suggestion is the imposition of a significant federal tax on sales of gasoline (a dollar per gallon, maybe two), and a modest tax on heating oil. The advantage of a tax—simply raising the cost of the gallon of oil or gasoline—is that it conscripts the infinite ingenuity of the consumer to the work of conservation. If the law tells me to conserve, I will try to get around the law; if my immediate material welfare relies on conservation, I will discover ways of conserving that I would have thought impossibly burdensome, such as carpooling, keeping the speed of the car to 50 mph, or keeping my home at 65 degrees in the winter. The suggestion for a tax has been around for a long time. It received renewed currency after the *Exxon Valdez* and again when the Persian Gulf embroilment reminded us of the real costs of imported oil.[59] The idea was mentioned briefly during the 1992 presidential election campaign, but in the rapid change of political climate that followed, all such ideas were put in mothballs. (Now, incredibly, opportunists on the political scene are suggesting a *cut* in the very modest gasoline tax now in place. Stay tuned.)

There are limits to expectable lifestyle changes, too. Suggestions that we go "back" to some pre-fossil fuel civilization are not only unrealistic but antienvironmental; the use of wood for fuel and animals for transport had all but turned Connecticut into a desert before the discovery of fossil fuels, and the rest of the country could not have been far behind. "Renewable resources" work only as long as the population is low enough to let the resources renew, and ours has long outstripped that point. Fossil fuels actually saved the environment once. We need a new fuel breakthrough to save it a second time.

QUESTIONS FOR DISCUSSION AND REFLECTION

+ Until we find a way to do without oil, we are going to have to transport it over long distances, sometimes through dangerous passages. How can we make that transport as safe as possible?

+ Above all we are going to have to learn to conserve energy. What form would conservation take? Are we prepared to change lifestyles—to band together in apartment houses to save oil, to abandon our malls and do all shopping at stores within walking distance?

+ What kind of political balance should we seek between the pursuit of energy sources and the preservation of wild land and other valuable real estate? What sorts of places should be off limits?

+ We will take up energy questions once more in the epilogue. Meanwhile, what technologies should we explore immediately to raise the amount of energy available without further harm to the planet?

Notes

1. Sarah Lyall, "Oil Tanker Refloated off Wales: Spilled Cargo Makes 25-Mile-Long Slick," *New York Times* (22 February 1996): p. A8.

2. This account is taken from Art Davidson, *In the Wake of the Exxon Valdez* (San Francisco: Sierra Club Books, 1990), and from contemporary newspaper accounts, as noted.

3. Philip Shabecoff, "Captain of Tanker Had Been Drinking, Blood Tests Show; Illegal Alcohol Level; Coast Guard Opens Effort to Bring Charge of Operating Ship While Intoxicated," *New York Times* (31 March 1989): pp. A1, A12.

4. Ibid.

5. "Captain Has History of Drinking and Driving," Special to the *New York Times* (28 March 1989): p. B7; Timothy Egan, "Elements of Tanker Disaster: Drinking, Fatigue, Complacency," *New York Times* (22 May 1989): p. B7.

6. Egan, "Elements of Tanker Disaster," p. B7.

7. Shabecoff, "Captain of Tanker," p. 12.

8. Davidson, *Wake of Valdez*, p. 16.

9. Catherine A. Dold and Gary Soucie, "Just the Facts: Prince William Sound," insert in George Laycock, "The Baptism of Prince William Sound," *Audubon* (September 1989): pp. 74–111.

10. Ken Wells and Marilyn Chase, "Paradise Lost: Heartbreaking Scenes of Beauty Disfigured Follow Alaska Oil Spill," *Wall Street Journal* (31 March 1989): pp. A1, A4.

11. Malcolm W. Browne, "Spill Could Pose a Threat for Years," *New York Times* (31 March 1989): p. A12.

12. Malcolm W. Browne, "In Once-Pristine Sound, Wildlife Reels Under Oil's Impact: Biologists Say Spill Could Set Records for Loss of Birds, Fish and Mammals," *New York Times*, Science Times (4 April 1989): pp. C1, C5.

13. Laycock, "Baptism," p. 81.

14. Ibid.

15. Wells and Chase, "Paradise Lost," pp. A1, A4. Other sources for this section include Laycock, "Baptism," and Michael D. Lemonick, "The Two Alaskas," *TIME* (17 April 1989): pp. 56–66.

16. Browne, "Spill Could Pose Threat."

17. Laycock, "Baptism," p. 84

18. Davidson, *Wake of Valdez*, p. 24–25.

19. Laycock, "Baptism," p. 84.

20. Statement by L. R. Beynon for Alyeska Pipeline Service Company, Trans-Alaska Pipeline hearing, Department of Interior, Anchorage, February 25, 1971, exhibit 48, vol. 3. Cited in Davidson, *Wake of Valdez*, p. 81.

21. Egan, "Elements of Tanker Disaster," p. B7.

22. Cited in Davidson, *Wake of Valdez*, p. 81.

23. Egan, "Elements of Tanker Disaster." Iarossi claimed that Exxon had 365 barrels ready to use. Davidson, *Wake of Valdez*, p. 53.

24. Davidson, *Wake of Valdez*, p. 58.

25. Ibid.

26. Ibid., p. 110.

27. Ibid., pp. 242–243.

28. Ibid., p. 261.

29. Ibid., p. 262.

30. Matthew L. Wald, "Cleanup of Oily Beaches Moves Slowly," *New York Times* (23 April 1989): p. A30.

31. Davidson, *Wake of Valdez*, p. 199

32. Ibid., p. 109

33. Ibid., p. 147

34. Davidson, *Wake of Valdez*, p. 273.

35. Greenpeace USA, 1436 U Street NW, Washington, DC 20009.

36. Davidson, *Wake of Valdez*, p. 277

37. "Dolphins and Double Hulls," Editorial, *New York Times* (14 April 1990): editorial page.

38. Charles McCoy and Allanna Sullivan, "Exxon's Withdrawal of Valdez Pleas Will Maintain Pressure to Settle Case," *Wall Street Journal* (28 May 1991): pp. A3, A6.

39. Keith Schneider, "Dispute Erupts on Settlement in Valdez Spill," *New York Times* (16 October 1994): p. A22.

40. Ibid.

41. Caleb Solomon, "Exxon Attacks Scientific Views of Valdez Spill," *Wall Street Journal* (15 April 1993): p. B1.

42. Agis Salpukas, "Spilled Oil May Not Be from Exxon Valdez," *New York Times* (1 December 1993): pp. A2, D7.

43. "Long Shadow of the Exxon Valdez," Editorial, *New York Times* (21 September 1994).

44. "$9.7 Million Land Damages Won in Valdez Case," *New York Times* (26 September 1994): p. A12.

45. "Tanker Spills Oil Off Hawaiian Coast," *New York Times* (4 March 1989): p.6

46. Philip Shabecoff, "The Rash of Tanker Spills Is Part of a Pattern of Thousands a Year," *New York Times* (29 June 1989): p. A20.

47. Ken Wells, "Ship Spews Oil After Collision off Indonesia," *Wall Street Journal* (22 January 1993): p. A7.

48. William E. Schmidt, "The Afflicted Shetlands Pray, For Man and Beast," *New York Times* (11 January 1993). Also, William E. Schmidt, "Storm Batters Wrecked Tanker, Worsening Oil Spill in Shetlands," *New York Times* (12 January 1993): pp. A1, A9; Ken Wells, "Oil Spill Drifts; Salmon Farms Are Threatened: Shetland Fishing Operations Face Millions of Dollars in Immediate Damages," *Wall Street Journal* (11 January 1993): p. A11; Ken Wells, "Volunteers Battle Storm, Pollution, but Oil Spill's Wildlife Toll Mounts," *Wall Street Journal* (11 January 1993): p. A11.

49. Wells, "Ship Spews Oil," p. A7.

50. Craig Wolff, "Exxon Admits a Year of Breakdowns in S.I. Oil Spill," *New York Times* (10 January 1990): pp. A1, B3; Craig Wolff, "Leaking Exxon Pipe Ran Through Regulatory Limbo," *New York Times* (11 January 1990): pp. B1, B7; Tim Golden, "Oil in Arthur Kill: Publicity and Peril for Urban Marsh," *New York Times* (18 January 1990): pp. B1, B4.

51. Allan R. Gold, "Exxon to Pay Up to $15 Million for Spill," *New York*

Times (15 March 1991): p. B1.

52. Wells, "Ship Spews Oil."

53. Philip Revzin, "Years Temper Damage of Worst Oil Spill: Starkest Fears of 1978 Amoco Disaster Weren't Realized," *Wall Street Journal* (4 April 1989): p. A10.

54. "On Oil Spills: Trust Turns Into Anger," Editorial, *New York Times* (28 June 1989): p. A22.

55. Malcolm W. Browne, "Experts See Glass Beads as Low-Cost Tool for Oil-Spill Cleanup," *New York Times* (11 April 1992): p. 12.

56. Sarah Lyall, "Oil Tanker Refloated," p. A8.

57. Caleb Solomon, "The Hunt for Oil: Petroleum Industry Pins Future on Finding Large Overseas Fields," *Wall Street Journal* (25 August 1993): pp. A1, A4.

58. Sarah Chasis and Lisa Speer, "How to Avoid Another Valdez," *New York Times* (20 May 1989): p. 27.

59. See, for instance, the lead editorial in the *New York Times* September 4, 1990, in response to the war in the Persian Gulf; also L. H. Newton, cited in Andi Rierdon, "Connecticut Q & A," *New York Times* (11 December 1988).

Suggestions for Further Reading

Audubon Magazine, entire issue (September 1989).

Davidson, Art. *In the Wake of the Exxon Valdez.* San Francisco: Sierra Club Books, 1990.

CHAPTER 7

Wounded Air

Global Climate Change

PREFACE: QUESTIONS TO KEEP IN MIND

In January of 1996, a climatologist speculated that El Niño, an oddball current in the Pacific Ocean, may have prolonged its stay in 1994 because of global warming.[1] How would we ever know? How could the observation ever be repeated?

What do we mean by "Science has proved...?" Why is this always a persuasive line in advertisements for new products? Why is science more certain than other disciplines (say, philosophy)?

Why does there seem to be so much uncertainty about global warming, or "the ozone hole"?

How do policymakers usually proceed when they are not sure of the facts? How do you think they should proceed? Does inaction have as many consequences as action? How would you balance the relative advantages and disadvantages of decisions to do nothing and decisions to do something?

ON NOT REALLY KNOWING

Summing up the worst dilemmas of our discipline, one of my colleagues posted a cartoon on his office door: Two worried men pace the executive suite, as one concedes to the other, "It's really still too early to know if it's too late to do anything about it." Global warming is like that—as is pollution of the oceans, coral reef bleaching, and, until recently, the deterioration of the ozone layer. We are still not really sure what we are seeing, and by the time we can be sure that the effect is there, that there really *is* damage from pollution and unsound use of resources, it will be much too late to reverse that effect.

On the other hand, we must be very wary of acting without being sure of the effect. With only suspicions, untested logic, and computer projections to go on, we can justify advancing hypotheses and schedule symposia in the annual conventions of learned societies—but can we justify suspending economically beneficial activities, throwing people out of work, and damaging the economic infrastructure of whole regions, solely from computer-projected horror scenarios? After all, the jobs lost are real, and the poverty endured for lack of them is very real, but the computer's fantasies are not, certainly not yet. Where putatively preventive measures cause no disruption, of course they may be recommended. But may we sacrifice the present welfare of real people for the future possible welfare of future possible people? What ethical obligations exist between metaphysically disparate generations?

Jim Hansen Blows the Whistle

On June 23, 1988, Dr. James Hansen, Director of the National Aeronautics and Space Administration's (NASA) Goddard Institute for Space Studies, testified before the U.S. Senate Committee on Energy and Natural Resources, "It's time to stop waffling so much and say that this evidence is pretty strong that the greenhouse effect is here."[2] This testimony was given in Washington, D.C., always steamy in summer. This summer, however, would be the hottest on record (with warmer ones yet to come) and produce one of the worst droughts in U.S. history. There were banner headlines the next day, and many scientists were shocked at such an unequivocal statement coming from a scientist with impeccable credentials. This was the first time that a member of the club, as it were, had exhibited such candor before a public and highly visible forum. Many of his colleagues felt he had been too absolute; others agreed with him but wished that he had hedged his bets a bit or had given more attention to the imperfections of computer climate models. Nevertheless, six years later, his testimony is still credited as the single most effective witness—the first voice that cried out in the wilderness near enough to be heard. Jim Hansen's testimony may well be the event that raised, in the public eye, the distinct possibility that humankind is changing the planet's climate.[3]

THE GREENHOUSE EFFECT

The "greenhouse effect" is the (imperfect) analogy used to explain the atmospheric phenomena that keep our planet warm enough to sustain life. Our atmosphere allows about half the incoming solar radiation to reach the earth's surface. The balance is either directly reflected back into space or absorbed and held (for a while). The energy that reaches the ground is either bounced back as heat or is used to do work (e.g., photosynthesis, evaporation, fuel the climate), degraded to heat energy, and then returned to the atmosphere. Here is where the greenhouse effect kicks in: Some gases in the atmosphere, notably water vapor and carbon dioxide, can hold on to that heat for a while, just as the glass panes in a greenhouse do. Without this heat-holding action, the earth's surface would cool to about −18°C. (−4°F.) instead of maintaining an average temperature of 14°C. (57°F.), and there would be no life as we know it.

The current concern is not that the greenhouse effect exists—we wouldn't be here if it didn't—but that it may be being exacerbated by anthropogenic increases in the effective gases, threatening a disruption to the equilibrium between incoming and outgoing energy, and a resulting average global warming. Since the start of the industrial reveolution, humankind has been adding to the natural amounts of carbon dioxide entering the atmosphere, primarily by burning fossil fuels. Additionally we have caused increases in other "greenhouse gases," among them methane from rice paddies and cattle flatulence and nitrogen oxides from fertilizers, combustion, and other activities.

A Brief History of Temperature

If we go back just 100 million years to the age of the dinosaurs, the temperature was about 10°F to 14°F. warmer than today. About 65 million years ago, the dinosaurs became extinct. We once assumed that the extinction was caused by a gradual cooling leading to an ice age, but the theory of choice among scientists now is that the climate change was more sudden, brought about by the dust from a huge meteor impact. Whether the change was sudden or gradual, the dinosaurs didn't make it;

the climate grew colder, the mammals survived, and the primates, including *Homo sapiens*, evolved.

Agriculture and civilization began in the warming interglacial period begun some 15,000 years ago, and paleontologists tell us we should be on the verge of another ice age. Shouldn't the earth be getting colder? It's not.

The Past as Cracked Mirror

What does all this tell us about global warming today? Certainly that there is a lot of uncertainty. We know that carbon dioxide and other gases have increased in the atmosphere, that they have the capacity to hold heat, and that the contributions of these gases from human activity is increasing. We know that temperature fluctuation over geological time is the rule rather than the exception, but we also know that seemingly small temperature changes have had significant effects on the history of life on the planet. Scott L. Wing, a Smithsonian paleontologist, points out that "none of us feel the past is a crystal ball. It's a cracked and warped mirror, but it's the only mirror we've got."[4] Wallace Broecker of the Lamont-Doherty Laboratory comments, "We're living in a system that can do strange things. Small forcings have produced large things and to say a priori that this gas [carbon dioxide] can't produce large changes is just bloody insanity."[5] From 1880 to today, by many measurements, the global average temperature has increased by 0.5°C. The most recent predictions for the twenty-first century, without a change in the current emissions, range from an increase of 1°C to 3.5°C.[6] To put this into perspective, at the height of the last ice age, 18,000 years ago, when the ice had reached as far south as Long Island, New York, and had covered the Great Lakes, the average temperature was only 3°C to 5°C. cooler than it is now.[7]

There has been significant division in the scientific community, to say nothing of the political community, as to the cause of an increase in global temperature, specifically whether or not the increase is merely the result of natural temperature fluctuations. The uncertainty increases when predictions based on computer models are published. Hansen's interpretation of the data accumulated from the computer runs of climate change models led him to 99 percent certainty that the earth is warming; it convinced him that the warming is due to the accumulation of greenhouse gases; and that signal events, like droughts, will increase. Hansen's critics, the "greenhouse agnostics," claimed that the temperature record is not reliable; there are too many climate variables to lay cause to greenhouse gases; and that, in short, we don't understand the climate.

Programming computer models to predict the climate of the future is clearly an imperfect science at best. As Michael Oppenheimer said in *Dead Heat*, "In short, we face uncertainty, indefinitely."[8]

Cassandra's Trail

As long ago as 1827, Jean-Baptiste-Joseph Fourier compared the atmosphere to a greenhouse, and in 1896 Svante Arrhenius predicted a rise in temperature by some 4°C to 6°C. with a doubling of carbon dioxide in the atmosphere.

In 1957, C. David Keeling started making CO_2 measurements from the observatory in Mauna Loa, Hawaii, 11,000 feet high. To this day, these observations are probably the most quoted or graphed as indicators of the CO_2 rise. The 1957 measurement was 315 parts per million (ppm); the 1988 was 350 ppm, a 25 percent increase since the estimated 280 ppm of 1800. At this rate it is estimated that atmospheric CO_2 will double from its 1800 level by 2075.

Keeling's work sparked an academic interest, if not a public outcry; computer simulations of the future climate followed rapidly in the wake of his announcement. By 1975, a number of respected scientists, including Hansen, had sounded the first alarms about CO_2, adding that other gases, especially methane, nitrous oxide, and possibly CFCs, together equaled the effect of CO_2. In 1983 both the National Academy of Sciences and the Environmental Protection Agency released studies. The former proclaimed that there was cause "for concern, but not panic"[9]; the latter predicted a doubling of CO_2 would occur by 2030, accompanied by major agricultural, economic, political, and climatic disruptions. Now the public was aroused; by 1985, global warming had global attention.[10]

In 1988, Jim Hansen's models, using the average temperature from 1950 to 1980 as the baseline from which to make comparisons, found an increase of 0.5°F. from 1880 to the baseline and the same increase from 1980 to 1988. By then it was clear that 1981, 1983 and 1987 were the warmest years since record keeping started, and 1988 was on its way to break another record. Even though many models had predicted a 2° increase rather than 1° by then, even that increase seemed significant, given the cooling effect of volcanos—and the presumption that we should be entering a new ice age.[11]

FIRST ATTEMPTS TO ACT

In November of 1990, at the second World Climate Conference, 700 scientists called for cuts in emissions of CO_2 and other greenhouse gases, saying it could be done without economic disruption. The United States was the only industrialized nation other than the oil producers (Middle East, USSR, Venezuela) that did not concur. The chair of the International Council of Scientific Unions, the biologist Maurice la Riviere, said that "given what we know, there is absolutely no excuse for governments not to save on energy."[12] Two studies released by the United States and the United Kingdom simultaneously ranked 1990 the warmest year yet, and documented that the seven warmest years since 1880 have all occurred since 1980.

The findings prompted a number of comments. Hansen said that "the case for a cause-and-effect relationship is becoming harder to deny" and that "seasonal temperature is still a crap shoot, but the global warming is loading the dice." However, Tim Barnett, a climatologist at Scripps Institute of Oceanography, said the warmest year can't be attributed "to any single cause. Is it green house gases or is it natural variability?" James K. Angell of the National Oceanic and Atmospheric Administration's Air Resources Laboratory admitted, "I've been a skeptic, but as these warmish years come one upon the other, you begin to waver a little bit." And many think of science as the domain of "hard facts," of the irrefutable evidence of carefully calibrated instruments!

Complicating the Climate

Shortly after it became evident that 1990 was the hottest year on record, in mid-1991, the Philippines' Mount Pinatubo erupted, throwing tons of dust and ash into the atmosphere and disrupting predictions by exerting a cooling effect. The same year, the Pacific El Niño current reappeared with its warming effect and climatic disruptions. It is just such events as the Mt. Pinatubo eruption and the El Niño current that confound the computor modelers and provide considerable grist for the mills of the "global warming agnostics," to use Jim Hansen's phrase. The number of variables involved in producing our climate are huge and probably not all known.

Clouds are the most difficult factor in the overall climate picture. They reflect shortwave radiation from the sun but absorb the long-wave (heat) radiation from the earth's surface. The first action cools, the second warms. Different kinds of clouds have different effects on temperature, with cirrus the most reflective. The variables go on—the paths that carbon takes as it cycles through the biosphere, the capacity of the oceans to absorb CO_2, the role played by coral reefs—but effects of the Mt. Pinatubo eruption and the El Niño current are beginning to be apparent.

It was predicted that the fallout from the eruption would be complete by 1994, and sure enough 1994 became the third warmest year.[13] But El Niño was still around into 1995, outlasting its usual stay of 12 to 18 months. And the frequency of the current's appearance has increased, occurring more often since 1976 than it ever has over a period of 113 years. According to a report to the National Center for Atmospheric Research, "this opens up the possibility that the [El Niño] changes may be partly caused by the observed increases in greenhouse gases."[14] So El Niño was given some of the credit for the warmth of 1994. However, another factor entered the picture when a study demonstrated a correlation between temperature and pollution particles (primarily sulfur dioxide). This analysis provided evidence for the proposition that sulfur dioxide pollution may be preventing predicted warming levels.[15]

The picture clears a bit: 1994 was warmer than the two previous years, presumably because the effect of Pinatubo diminished, but also because of the continuing effect of El Niño; however, it might have been even warmer if we didn't have the present level of sulfur dioxide pollution (which shades the sun) in the atmosphere. (That level is high, despite the Clean Air Act's aim to cut emissions in half; the act has not had much effect yet.)

Well, what of 1995, after Pinatubo *and* El Niño? *It was the hotttest year ever.* Despite the volcano, the 1991–1995 period was the hottest five years on record, and the earth has warmed about 0.2°C. per decade since 1975.[16]

Unfortunately, the delegates from 120 countries to the climate talks held in Berlin in April 1995 didn't know how hot they were. The meeting was dictated by the agreement reached in Rio in 1992 that industrialized nations would cap greenhouse gas emissions at 1990 levels by 2000. Generally, their efforts are behind schedule; however, despite considerable disagreement among oil producers, island nations, and some heavy energy users, including the United States, the meeting produced a pledge to complete negotiations regarding emissions after 2000 in two years.[17]

They may be back at the table sooner than they think. They went home to find that 1995 was the hottest year ever. They also read headlines such as "Global Experts Call Human Role Likely," "It's Official: First Glimmer of Greenhouse Warming Seen," and "Warm up to the Idea: Global Warming *is* Here." For the first time ever, the prestigious Intergovernmental Panel on Climate Change (IPCC)—2,500 scientists from around the world, mandated by the U.N to study climate—came flat out and said that human activity was the likely cause of global warming. The official wording agreed upon was "the balance of evidence suggests that there is a discernable human influence on global climate."[18] This event is probably second only to Hansen's 1988 testimony in influencing the climate change debate. Whether it will silence the doubters remains to be seen.

PREDICTED EFFECTS OF GLOBAL WARMING

Why is global warming so dangerous? To begin with, melting icebergs and expanding oceans may cause floods. The Alliance of Small Island

States has been publicizing its potential plight wherever possible. Some predict that a one-foot rise in sea level could cover whole islands. Beyond the concerns of the islanders, Stephen P. Leatherman, director of the Laboratory for Coastal Research of the University of Maryland, predicts that a three-foot rise would displace 72 million people in China, 11 million in Bangladesh, and 8 million in Egypt. (Twenty-five percent of the world's population lives less than 1.1 meter above sea level).[19] The IPCC report predicts a 1.5-foot rise in sea level by 2100, flooding river deltas and cities. In the United States, 53 percent of the population lives within 50 miles of a coast. If predictions are borne out, the East Coast beaches will be gone in 25 years and 45,000 people in the Marshall Islands will have to be evacuated.[20]

A harbinger of future flooding occurred with the breaking loose of an iceberg the size of Rhode Island from the Larsen Ice Shelf in Antarctica in 1995, causing quite a stir among global warming watchers. Ice shelves have been shrinking there; the temperatures in the area and in the continent of Antarctica have increased considerably more than over the planet as a whole.[21]

The IPCC report also predicts droughts, heat waves, expanding deserts, ecosystem disruption—and increasingly severe weather. Anecdotal evidence from practically all U.S. citizens can testify to the last, and now there's data to back up these perceptions. A study has found increases in drought, temperature, winter precipitation, and heavy rainstorms in much of the United States from 1980 to 1984.[22]

A less-well-known concern, contrary to popular movies and books, is the spread of tropical diseases in conjunction with the increase in insect vectors (see also Chapter 2 for the increase caused by rising populations). The IPCC predicts an increase of some 50 to 80 million cases of dengue, yellow fever, and viral encephalitis, as well as malaria.[23] In Thailand, right now, drug resistant malaria is on the rise. "While AIDS and terrifying illnesses like...Ebola...have captured public attention, malaria may be the most deadly disease in the world."[24]

On the other hand, amid the myriad disaster predictions, some have suggested potential advantages to the warmer climate of the future. There's a general reluctance to point out possible advantages accompanying warming because of the fear that it could defuse the effort to cut the emissions of the causative gases. But northern Europe, the northern United States, Canada, and the former USSR might all benefit from warmer and wetter conditions to grow crops.

In the same vein, some have hoped that an increase in CO_2 would act as a fertilizer to plants (especially crops) in general. Experiments, however, indicate that CO_2 alone does not provide such an increase in crop productivity, and that other nutrients (water, trace minerals), the availability of light, and competition from other species are just as important.[25] Other studies indicate that U.S. agriculture should not suffer more than the northward shift just mentioned, depending on the intensity of the warming.[26]

Surely the projected miseries outweigh these putative benefits, but there are also cautions against jumping in with expensive solutions to unproven problems. Jedde H. Ausubel points out that "a stitch in time saves nine if you know the right stitch."[27]

THE SEARCH FOR SOLUTIONS

What might that stitch be? There appears to be general agreement that energy efficiency is the wave of the future. One argument states that efficiency could reduce carbon dioxide emissions by 60 percent over the next 20 years and save money; but another claims that a reduction of 20 percent below 1990 levels would cause a drop in the U.S. Gross Domestic Product (GDP) by 1 to 2 percent.[28] This latter argument adheres to the position that any decrease in energy use, by definition, equals a decrease in GDP, so staunchly defended by much of corporate America. Nevertheless, a number of corporations are reducing emissions via energy savings through changed lighting and other measures; however, these measures become offset by the recent love affair Americans are having with gas-guzzling vans and four-wheel-drive vehicles.[29]

As great as the challenge of reducing carbon dioxide emissions in the industrialized world is, the challenge of reductions in the rapidly industrializing developing countries is huge. China, with its vast coal reserves, one-fifth of the world's population, and a firm policy of providing its citizens with modern conveniences such as autos, appliances, and air conditioners, offers perhaps the most daunting foreign policy problem facing Western nations. China is expected to be the largest emitter of carbon dioxide by 2020 or 2030. Between 1970 and 1990, their energy consumption increased by 208 percent—and that's just the beginning. In 1994 they burned 1.2 million tons of coal, more than any other nation, and they're expected to burn 3.1 billion tons by 2020.[30] The issue is inevitably entwined in the North versus South confrontation (see Chapter 2). The South points out that because the industrialized North caused the problem, they should clean it up as well as pay for any changes that are required of the South. These challenges are exacerbated by the current political climate in the United States, as illustrated by the comment of one Republican congressman who dismisses the threat of global warming as "liberal claptrap."[31]

So where are we? We've been assured by 2,500 scientists of the Inter-governmental Panel on Climate Change that global warming is a real threat, there's hard evidence that some of its effects are already being felt, island nations are scared stiff, and many industrialized nations, including our own, are still loath to commit to major changes in energy policy, while the industrializing countries continue to want their share of the planet's bounty. Yet, study after study demonstrates that reductions in energy use can be accomplished with minimal social disruption. Also, perhaps most important, international dialogue continues. As Steven Schneider, a noted climatologist, states, "I'm not 99 percent sure, but I am 90 percent sure [that the climate is changing]. Why do we need 99 percent certainty when nothing else is certain? If there were only a 5 per-cent chance the chef slipped some poison in your dessert, would you eat it?"[32]

In conclusion, repeated consideration of this subject at international conferences demonstrates that climate change and other environmental issues have moved to the global front burners. With the end of the cold war, increasing attention is being paid to the "new" international conflict, that between the rich, industrialized North and the poorer, arguably exploited, South. Thanks primarily to the threat of global warming, they are at least talking to each other. If international cooperation on address-ing global concerns, or at least an accepted set of procedures for address-ing those concerns as they arise, evolves as a by-product of the threat of drastic climatic change, it will be worth all the fuss it has caused.

QUESTIONS FOR DISCUSSION AND REFLECTION

✦ What does the future hold? As has been abundantly demonstrated, no one really knows. The data that supports an increase in the planet's average temperature over the next 50 years or so is becoming increas-ingly accepted, not only by scientists but by policymakers. How much will the temperature rise? When? What will be its effects? These ques-tions are still honestly arguable.

✦ How shall we best serve our long-term interests in the face of global warming? The interest of the European community and Japan in coop-erating with the Third World on this issue will likely influence United States policy eventually, especially since their interest springs from what they see as economic advantages in energy conservation and pollution-control technologies. Does our economic advantage also lie in the direc-tion of climate-sensitive technology and cooperation with the South?

Notes

1. J. Travis, "The Loitering El Niño: Greenhouse Guest?" *Science News*, Vol. 149, (27 January 1996): p. 54.

2. Michael Oppenheimer and Robert Boyle, *Dead Heat* (New York: Basic Books, 1990). p. 51; George J. Mitchell, *World on Fire* (New York: Scribner, 1991): p. 26.

3. Oppenheimer and Boyle, *Dead Heat*; Richard A. Kerr, "Hansen vs. the World on the Greenhouse Threat," *Science* (2 June 1989): p. 1041.

4. Richard Monastersky, "Swamped by Climate Change?" *Science,* vol. 138: p. 184.

5. William K. Stevens, "In the Ebb and Flow of Ancient Glaciers, Clues to a New Ice Age," *New York Times* (16 January 1990): p. C1. For more information on the history of our climate, see the books just noted and articles from the bibliography by William F. Allman and Betsy Wagner, Richard Monastersky, James Kasting et al., J. Raloff, and William K. Stevens.

6. Richard A. Kerr, "Greenhouse Report Foresees Growing Global Stress," *Science* (3 November 1995): p. 731.

7. For more detailed descriptions of greenhouse warming and the history of the earth's climate, see Steven H. Schneider, *Global Warming* (San Francisco: Sierra Club Books, 1989); Oppenheimer and Boyle, *Dead Heat*; and Mitchell, *World on Fire.*

8. Oppenheimer and Boyle, *Dead Heat*, p. 57.

9. Ibid., p.39.

10. Virtually all of the foregoing is taken from Oppenheimer and Boyle, *Dead Heat*, pp. 18–39.

11. Philip Shabecoff, "Temperature for the World Rises Sharply in the 1980s," *New York Times* (29 March 1988).

12. Marlise Simons, "Scientists Urging Gas Emission Cuts," *New York Times* (5 November 1990).

13. William K. Stevens, "A Global Warming Resumed in 1994, Climate Data Show," *New York Times* (27 January 1995): p. A1.

14. Travis, "The Loitering El Niño," p. 54

15. Richard A. Kerr, "Study Unveils Climate Cooling Caused by Pollutant Haze," *Science* (12 May 1995): p. 802.

16. William K. Stevens, "'95 the Hottest Year on Record As the Global Trend Keeps Up," *New York Times* (4 January 1996): p. A1.

17. William K. Stevens, "Climate Talks Enter Harder Phase of Cutting Back Emissions," *New York Times* (11 April 1995): p. C4.

18. William K. Stevens, "Global Warming Experts Call Human Role Likely," *New York Times* (10 September 1995): p.1; Richard A. Kerr, "It's Official: First Glimmer of Greenhouse Warming Seen," *Science* (8 December 1995): p. 1565; Colum F. Lynch, "Warm up to the Idea: Global Warming Is Here," *The Amicus Journal* (Spring 1996): p. 20.

19. Paul Lewis, "Island Nations Fear a Rise in the Sea," *New York Times* (17 February 1992); Paul Lewis, "Danger of Floods Worries Islanders," *New York Times* (13 May 1992).

20. William K. Stevens, "Scientists Say Earth's Warming Could Set off Wide Disruptions," *New York Times* (18 September 1995): p. A1.

21. "Giant Iceberg Breaks off Antarctica," *Science News* (29 April 1995): p. 271; William K. Stevens, "Ice Shelves Melting as Forecast, but Disaster Script Is in Doubt," *New York Times* (30 January 1996): p. C4.

22. William K. Stevens, "In Rain and Temperature Data, New Signs of Global Warming," *New York Times* (26 September 1995); p. C4.

23. Kerr, "Greenhouse Report," p. 731.

24. Seth Mydans, "Along Thai Border, Malaria Outpaces New Drugs," *New York Times* (3 March 1996).

25. Fakhri A. Bazzaz and Eric D. Fajer, "Plant Life in a CO_2-Rich World," *Scientific American* (January 1992): p. 68.

26. R. Monastersky, "Warming Shouldn't Wither U.S. Farming," *Science News,* vol. 137: p. 308.

27. Jesse H. Ausubel, "A Second Look at the Impacts of Climate Change," *American Scientist* (May/June 1991): p. 21.

28. William K. Stevens, "Price of Global Warming? Debate Weighs Dollars and Cents," *New York Times* (10 October 1995): p. C4.

29. William K. Stevens, "With Energy Tug of War, U.S. Is Missing Its Goal," *New York Times* (28 November 1995): p.A1.

30. Patrick E. Tyler, "China's Inevitable Dilemma: Coal Equals Growth," *New York Times* (29 November 1995): p. A1; Elizabeth Economy, "China's Power to Harm the Planet," *New York Times,* Op. Ed. (10 September 1995).

31. Stevens, "Energy Tug of War."

32. J. T. Houghton et al., *Climate Change 1992: The Supplementary Report to the IPCC Scientific Assessment* (New York: Cambridge University Press, 1992): p. 14 (as quoted by the Union of Concerned Scientists, *Sound Science Initiative* [Summer 1995]).

Suggestions for Further Reading

Flavin, Christopher. *Slowing Global Warming: A Worldwide Strategy.* Worldwatch Paper No. 91, Washington, DC: Worldwatch Institute, 1989.

Mitchell, George J. *World on Fire.* New York: Scribner, 1991.

Oppenheimer, Michael, and Boyle, Robert. *Dead Heat.* New York: Basic Books, 1990.

CHAPTER 8

The Silence of the Birds

Rachel Carson and the Pesticides

PREFACE: QUESTIONS TO KEEP IN MIND

What evidence convinced Rachel Carson, and others, that pesticides, especially DDT, were harmful to birds?

What role do insecticides play in American agriculture? Could we do without them? What are the alternatives? What effect would their prohibition have on the way we grow our food?

What role do pesticides in general play in the American economy? If they were generally prohibited, what effect would it have on the economy?

What new ethical concerns are raised by the practice of exporting pesticides banned here but not abroad?

THE WAKE-UP BOOK

It was 1962. For over 15 years, the United States had been the main—indeed, the only—industrial power in the world, developing new products and new technology with magical skill, doubling and tripling its citizens' real standard of living, effortlessly dictating to the world a new measure of achievement in productivity and convenience. We created a new class—the working-become-middle class, employed in the rapidly growing corporations with the first generation of college degrees, thanks to the GI Bill. We also created a new area of living ("suburbs"), settled into the new mode of transportation that it required (the automobile, with attendant highways); we reformed religion, politics, economics, and the household (with the deep freeze, washing machines, and vacuum cleaners). In short, we showed the world how to live.

Leading the way in the technological parade of miracles was the chemical industry. It had developed the pharmaceuticals (antibiotics, especially penicillin) that saved the GIs during the war and sent the infant mortality rate plummeting immediately after it. And it developed insecticides. The focus (villain?) of this chapter, DDT was first synthesized by a German chemistry student in 1874, but it was only in 1939 that a Swiss chemist, Paul Muller, recognized its use as an insect killer. Its worth in World War II cannot be measured: Sprayed liberally by the Allies in all theaters, it killed the mosquitos that carried malaria, filiariasis, and yellow fever; the lice that carried typhus; and the fleas that carried, for yet another century, the bubonic plague.[1] This is no small accomplishment. Wars have always been races between the generals and the insects, with the generals rarely winning: "Typhus, with its brothers and sisters—plague, cholera, typhoid, dysentery—has decided more campaigns than Caesar, Hannibal, Napoleon, and all the inspector generals in history."[2]

This huge outpouring of technological progress—in construction, in automobiles and the roads to drive them on, in plastics, fuels, pharmaceuticals and all products of chemistry—came about because of the war that we had fought to protect our nation. As such, a widespread impression arose that opposition to progress—or, further development of goods and services for the health, enjoyment, and convenience of the American consuming public—was downright unpatriotic. The American victory was a gift from God; the attendant prosperity, the greatest *relative* prosperity the world has ever known, came as part of that gift; one does not look gift horses in the mouth, especially divine ones.

Until, that is, 1962, when a noted author and naturalist, Rachel Carson, published *Silent Spring*. She largely demonstrated that the pesticides kill not only insects but birds and will eventually kill us. This was the first book (Ralph Nader's *Unsafe at Any Speed* did not come out until 1965) that raised doubts about the quality of our victory, that dared to wonder if concerns for human and environmental safety had possibly been ignored in the march from war to bigger and better consumption.

That insecticides kill birds was not news to much of the scientific community. The first warning had been sounded in 1945. Gove Hambidge, author of the article praising DDT just cited, worried at the end of that article that DDT "may be a little *too* effective for comfort. For it is capable of blotting out insect life so completely throughout large areas that it may upset the whole balance of nature."[3] He notes that it killed the pollinators of the crops and might well be poisonous to livestock and human beings. Other observations from the mid-1950s suggested that pesticides were killing the birds. In 1957, grebes were dying in California's Clear Lake, and biologists blamed DDD, a DDT relative that had been sprayed on local farms.[4] In 1958, Roy Barker of the Illinois Natural History Survey at Urbana documented the decline of local robins, and showed how the spraying of DDT to control Dutch Elm Disease had fed them a diet of poisoned earthworms.[5] By 1960, scientists generally recognized that there was something wrong, but it was certainly news to the rest of us. Where did these revelations come from? Why was the reaction against them so ferocious? How did we respond to them? For starters, who was Rachel Carson?

Rachel Carson, Naturalist and Prophet

Rachel Louise Carson was born on May 27, 1907, in Springdale, Pennsylvania, to a strong-willed mother and a father who farmed his 65-acre parcel and dabbled in real estate, both with indifferent success. Though the area was generally industrialized, Carson grew up in a rural setting.

Her interest in writing surfaced early (she published her first story at age ten[6]) as did her interest in nature, encouraged by her mother. Upon her mother's death, she wrote of her, "more than anyone else I know, she embodied Albert Schweitzer's 'reverence for life.'"[7] She particularly loved the sea, despite her inland upbringing. Though a quiet, good student and a bit of a loner, she was known for friendliness and kindness to other students and elders.

During her years at the Pennsylvania College for Women, conflict between the biology and English departments drove her to change her major from English to biology, to the intense consternation of the English department, which had supported her with scholarship funds for writing. She completed her education through a combination of work, financial aid, and loans, earning first her A.B. (summa cum laude) at Pennsylvania College and then an M.A. in marine zoology at Johns Hopkins, made possible in part by a summer fellowship at Woods Hole, Massachusetts. Her interest in writing never waned, however: "Eventually it dawned on me that by becoming a biologist I had given myself something to write about."[8]

After her father and sister died, Rachel took on the responsibility for her mother and her sister's two daughters; she abandoned academe to take a position at the Bureau of Fisheries (later the Fish and Wildlife Service), where she remained from 1935 to 1952.[9] By then she was gaining recognition as a science writer by both scientists and the literati; during this time her literary career took off. She believed that there was "no separate literature of science. The aim of science is to discover and illuminate truth. And that, I take it, is the aim of literature."[10] Her first book, *Under the Sea-Wind,* was published in 1941, followed by the immensely popular *The Sea Around Us* in 1951, and *The Edge of the Sea* in 1955.[11] These works and others brought her numerous awards, and literary as well as scientific praise.[12] While her published works showed scientific clarity combined with poetic expression, she was also blessed with a sense of humor, noted by friends and in her letters. She wanted to be taken seriously as a writer of science, and for a woman, that meant serious writing. When some readers could not believe that a woman had written *The Sea Around Us,* she commented (prophetically, given the forthcoming reaction to *Silent Spring),* "Among male readers, there was a reluctance to acknowledge that a woman could have dealt with a scientific subject."[13]

By 1952 she could buy a cottage on the Maine coast near her beloved ocean and devote full time to her writing. Here, her friendship with Dorothy and Stanley Freeman began, enriching her remaining years.[14] And here, parts of *Silent Spring* were written. By the time her mother died in 1958,[15] Carson had decided on pesticide poisoning as her next focus.

Aware of DDT and its potential for ecological disruption since 1944, she had joined other scientists in unpopular warnings that it might not be the panacea, sought since biblical times, that would finally win the war against the insects. These warnings fell on deaf ears. After all, DDT had saved American GIs from a typhus epidemic in Italy during World War II. After liberation in 1944, the sick, undernourished and flea-infested Dutch had roundly praised it. DDT stopped the spread of infection, permitting the Allied armies to operate, and saved the first crops after the war, establishing adequate nutrition in Europe.[16] But numerous communications detailing the pesticide's effect on birds and other species, as well as continuing rising concerns among scientists, led Carson to decide to take on this issue.[17]

"The time had come," she reflected later, "when it must be written. We have already gone very far in the abuse of this planet.... The ideas had to be crystallized, the facts had to be brought together in one place.... Knowing the facts as I did, I could not rest until I had brought them to public attention."[18]

This book would depart from her earlier paeans to the sea, "no longer the delights of ... Maine rocks at low tide.... the exploration of coral reefs."[19] This book would be a declaration of war. Rachel Carson was fully aware that the book would be controversial and that the response from the chemical industry and many policymakers would be intense. To make the response more manageable, she tried to keep the work under wraps until publication. She had been warned that upon its publication she would be subjected to ridicule. Typically, therefore, she proceeded with meticulous, time-consuming research that included correspondence with experts worldwide. Her interest in exploring the links between pesticides and cancer was perhaps more than academic. Diagnosed with breast cancer in 1957, she suffered from poor health for much of the writing of *Silent Spring*.[20]

Reaction to the Book

Robert Downs, reflecting on Rachel Carson's work in the year of the first Earth Day, comments that "*Silent Spring* was comparable in its impact on public consciousness, and demand for instant action, to Tom Paine's *Common Sense*, Harriet Beecher Stowe's *Uncle Tom's Cabin*, and Upton Sinclair's *The Jungle*."[21] Before the publication of the hardcover edition, the public had had a chance to learn its major themes. In June 1962, when *The New Yorker* started a three-issue condensation of *Silent Spring*, responses poured in. Excerpts were read into the *Congressional Record*, and President Kennedy was questioned about pesticides at a news conference. The official publication took place on September 27, 1962, to excellent reviews: Loren Eiseley, a well-known naturalist from the University of Pennsylvania, called it "a devastating, heavily documented, relentless attack upon human carelessness, greed, and irresponsibility"; Supreme Court Justice William O. Douglas called it "the most important chronicle of this century for the human race."

But even before the official publication of the book, in July the *New York Times* headlined a controversy: "Silent Spring Is Now Noisy Summer; Pesticides Industry up in Arms over a New Book. Rachel Carson Stirs Conflict—Producers Are Crying Foul." The article went on to describe the distress in the industry: "Some agricultural and chemical concerns have set their scientists to analyzing Miss Carson's work line by line. Other companies are preparing briefs defending their products. Meetings are being held in Washington and New York. Statements are being drafted and counterattacks planned."[23]

Reactions came from far and wide. The Toledo, Ohio, Library ordered gallons of ladybugs as a biological control for aphids. Friends wrote that *Silent Spring* was the prime topic of conversation in their communities. By way of typical contrast, the Bethlehem, Pennsylvania, *Globe-Times* surveyed local county farm offices and found that "no one in either...office who was talked to today had read the book, but all disapproved of it heartily."[24]

Even some in the scientific community reacted cautiously. Typical of Carson's thorough research was her consultation with experts in each field she wrote about, asking them to review appropriate chapters. Not all of them were prepared for war. A. W. A. Brown, a zoologist from the University of Western Ontario, had been consulted and had in fact made some helpful prepublication comments. Once the book became controversial, though, he complained publicly that his suggestions had not been taken and that, by using his name, Carson "had put him in a bad light with his colleagues." Searching her notes, Carson discovered that all of his material that she had used was already published. She pointed out icily that he had surely been free to complain when he reviewed her manuscript before it was in print, and she requested that he represent the facts accurately in the future. Though she expressed regret that he was unhappy with the result, she did not back down one inch.[25]

Typically, critics patronized Carson as a sentimental woman lacking scientific objectivity. *TIME* magazine reported that "Many scientists sympathize with Miss Carson's love of wildlife, and even with her mystical attachment to the balance of nature. But they fear that her emotional and inaccurate outburst in *Silent Spring* may do harm by alarming the nontechnical public, while doing no good for the things that she loves."[26]

But it was the chemical companies and other agricultural interests that launched the most vigorous attacks. The Velsicol Chemical Corporation, sole manufacturers of the pesticides chlordane and heptachlor, which Carson had criticized, responded rapidly and fiercely. Alerted by the *New Yorker* articles, they wrote Carson's publishers, urging them not to publish a book so full of "inaccurate and disparaging" statements designed to sabotage Western capitalism. A portion of what has become a notorious letter reads, "Members of the chemical industry in this country and in western Europe must deal with sinister influences, whose attacks on the chemical industry have a dual purpose: (1) to create the false impression that all business is grasping and immoral and (2) to reduce the use of agricultural chemicals in this country and in the countries of western Europe, so that our supply of food will be reduced to east-curtain parity. Many innocent groups are financed and led into attacks on the chemical industry by these sinister parties."[27]

Other comments from those threatened by the book were less formal but equally revealing. Some dismissed Carson as an unimportant member of some fringe group. The director of the New Jersey Department of Agriculture spoke for many: "In any large scale pest control program we are immediately confronted with the objection of a vociferous, misinformed, group of nature-balancing, organic-gardening, bird-loving, unreasonable citizenry that has not been convinced of the important place of agricultural chemicals in our economy."[28] Others leveled personal attacks such as that from a member of the Federal Pest Control Review Board, who said, "I thought she was a spinster. What's she so worried about genetics for?"[29]

Many of the chemical and agricultural interests treated the publication of *Silent Spring* as a public-relations problem. The Nutrition Foundation put together a "fact kit" that contained defenses of pesticides, negative reviews of the book, and a letter written by the Foundation president claiming that Carson's supporters and advocates included "food faddists, health quacks, special interest groups, [that are] promoting her book as if it were scientifically irreproachable and written by a scientist." These "kits" were distributed among universities; agricultural organizations; public health officials; women's organizations; state, county, and local officials; and libraries.[30] Another approach used the National Audubon Society's annual Christmas Bird Census to point out that, contrary to Carson's warning, birds are abundant. (The Audubon Society tends to discount the accuracy of this annual event.)[31] As Paul Brooks, her editor, said in his book about her work, "Perhaps not since the classic controversy over Charles Darwin's *The Origin of the Species* just over a century earlier had a single book been more bitterly attacked by those who felt their interests threatened."[32]

Nevertheless, by the end of 1962, *Silent Spring* had made a tremendous impact on the ordinary public. Forty bills had been introduced to various state legislatures to regulate pesticides, and on the public side, *CBS Reports* scheduled "The Silent Spring of Rachel Carson" for April 3, 1963. Some of the sponsors of that program predictably opted out, including Standard Brands and Ralston Purina. On May 15, 1963, President Kennedy's Science Advisory Committee echoed the criticism Carson had initiated against chemical pesticides. Their report strongly agreed with her evaluation of the danger inherent in the insect eradication program—the danger posed by pesticides that persist, and the apparent lack of concern in dealing with the application of synthetic chemical pesticides. This report was headlined in the *Christian Science Monitor* as "Rachel Carson Stands Vindicated."[33]

By the summer of 1963, she knew she was dying; nevertheless, before her last trip to Maine, she detoured to testify before a Congressional committee at which she urged regulation, research, education, and registration for pesticides. The chemical offense was not yet stilled. A consultant to Shell Chemical Company testified that "Miss Carson is talking about health effects that will take years to answer. In the meantime we'd have to cut off food for people around the world. These peddlers of fear are going to feast on the famine of the world—literally." During a recess, one of the agricultural "experts" commented, "You're never going to satisfy organic farmers or emotional women in garden clubs."[34]

Rachel Carson died on April 14, 1964. Her funeral in the National Cathedral in Washington, D.C., was attended by many dignitaries. Among them was Senator Ribicoff (CT), before whose committee she had testified. He eulogized her as "this gentle lady who aroused people everywhere to be concerned with one of the most significant problems of mid-twentieth century life—man's contamination of his environment."[35]

THE TROUBLE WITH DDT

Now dead for more than thirty years, Rachel Carson is a national insti-tution—almost a national icon. But let's backtrack. *Why* is she so justly celebrated on this issue? How do pesticides work—what makes them at once so valuable to some people and so deadly to the birds?

The trouble with DDT is that it kills things and that it persists in the environment. That's also what's good about it. Insecticides are designed to kill the insects that eat the same types of food that we do. If such chem-icals were not toxic, they could not do their job. And they stay around—they do not disappear in the next rainstorm; otherwise their effectiveness would be very limited. But this persistence is also the root of their harm-fulness.

DDT is an organochlorine, a synthetic insecticide of the chlorinate hydrocarbon group. In ways that are not completely known, these organochlorines destroy living cells, affecting the nervous system in par-ticular, and thus end the life of the organism that ingests them.[36]

They are distinguishable by the range of their toxicity, their solubility, their persistence, and the breadth of their killing spectrum. If one wanted to kill every insect in sight (and many other creatures along the way), one would use a broad spectrum, highly toxic, fat-soluble, and very persistent insecticide, such as DDT. Historically, many have taken this approach. Its drawbacks soon became apparent. The *broad-spectrum* insecticides kill nontarget insects, including those that prey on the target insects and the pollinators essential to flowering crops. *Fat-solubility* means soluble in fat rather than water; thus it cannot be cleared from animal bodies by the kidneys and washed out in the urine. *Persistence* means that the poison does not begin to break down into other chemicals for years, but accu-mulates and concentrates in food chains. That is, each organism higher in the food chain will have a higher concentration of a poison than their prey. To survive, consumers must eat more than their own weight in the plants or animals they eat. So, to use the rule of thumb, 0.1 part per mil-lion (ppm) concentration of an insecticide in algae becomes 1.0 ppm in zooplankton that eat algae, 10 ppm in minnows that eat zooplankton, 100 ppm in small fish that eat minnows, and 1,000 ppm in large preda-tor fish.

Rachel Carson recognized this problem: "One of the most sinister fea-tures of DDT and related chemicals is the way they are passed...through all the links of the food chains. Hay containing residues of 7 to 8 parts per million may be fed to cows. The DDT will turn up in the milk in the amount of about 3 parts per million, but in the butter made from this milk the concentration may run to 65 parts per million."[37]

Meanwhile, the undiscriminating toxicity of DDT has threatened with extinction numerous unintended species, especially the birds of prey (the raptors) that ate the owls that had eaten the snakes that had eaten the mice that had eaten the acres of insecticide-treated plants. *Silent Spring* contains myriad descriptions of senseless unintended poisonings. The next thought of course is, what is the effect on humans, who are high on the food chain? The effect is terrible. That is why eating fish caught in contaminated waterways is banned, and why some poisons exist in human milk in higher concentrations than allowed in cow's milk.

All this devastation—but the effectiveness of the insecticides is quite limited. There are more than 1 million insect species. That's *species*—not individuals—including only those known to us. If we talk *individuals,* there are about 4 billion insects per square mile. Carson put it this way: "70 to 80 per cent of the earth's creatures are insects. The vast majority of these insects are held in check by natural forces....If this were not so, it is doubtful that any conceivable volume of chemicals...could possibly keep down their population."[38] Given these numbers, it is reasonable to expect that among an insecticide target species, some would be genetically immune to the poison (just as some humans are immune to poison ivy). Now, an effective insecticide will kill all those that are not immune. Left behind are those unaffected by the poison, who reproduce like crazy, passing the trait along to a population presented with a feast, such as a corn field, with *no competition* from either their own species or predator species, also dead from the insecticide. We now have an insecticide-resistant strain of an insect species. The next step for the farmer is usually to try a different, usually more expensive insecticide, and the process starts all over again. This is often referred to as "the pesticide treadmill."

Documenting many observations of worldwide insecticide resistance, Carson mused that "Darwin himself could scarcely have found a better example of the operation of natural selection than is provided by the way the mechanism of resistance operates." She explained that "it is the 'tough' insects that survive chemical attack. Spraying kills off the weaklings. The survivors are...the parents of the new generation, which, by simple inheritance, possesses all the qualities of 'toughness' inherent in its forebears. Inevitably, it follows that intensive spraying with powerful chemicals only [makes] worse the problem it is designed to solve. After a few generations...there results a population consisting entirely of tough, resistant strains."[39]

In 1938 there were seven insect species that exhibited pesticide resistance. In 1984 there were 447. Today about the same percentage of our crops—15 percent—are lost to insects and weeds as were before the development of synthetic pesticides.

Rachel Carson's comment made in 1962 is as relevant today as it was then: "To have risked so much in our efforts to mold nature to our satisfaction and yet to have failed in achieving our goal would indeed be the final irony. Yet this, it seems, is our situation."[40]

NATIONAL RESPONSE: REGULATION

As we have seen, when the book came out, cries arose for regulation of pesticides in general and DDT in particular. DDT was generally banned for all use and sale in the United States in the Federal Insecticide, Fungicide, and Rodenticide Act (FIFRA), the first comprehensive approach to the problem. The act has been amended a number of times, most recently in 1988. It provides that all pesticides used in the United States must be approved by the Environmental Protection Agency (EPA). The pesticide manufacturer submits data to the EPA regarding their product, then the EPA, using that data, determines an acceptable daily intake of the poison as a residue on food. EPA approval does not constitute an endorsement of the chemical, but merely a judgment that if used as directed, its benefits exceed its risks. No pesticide can be advertised as safe.

Enforcement of the act has always posed a problem. The EPA does not have the resources to evaluate the 450 active ingredients and 1,820 "inert" ingredients used in pesticides today. Although the EPA can ban a chemical at any time, it must compensate the manufacturer for stored supplies and the like, which would bankrupt the EPA if no other way can be found to sell the pesticides legally. The upshot is that many chemicals on the market have not been fully and reliably tested by an objective organization.[41]

UPDATE ON PESTICIDES

Unbelievably, pesticide problems and controversies continue. DDT is showing up in albatrosses at Midway Island in the middle of the Pacific Ocean. A World Resources Institute report indicates that many pesticides seem to affect the immune system. The institute reviewed a large number of studies on pesticides and immunity, including laboratory animal tests, as well as tests on animals in the wild such as Baltic seals and Soviet studies on changes in human immunity. In this last, the scientists report high levels of infections in areas containing pesticide residues beyond "accepted standards." In addition, a Canadian study of Inuit children whose mothers' milk contained high levels of organochlorides found that their immune response was so low that they couldn't be vaccinated, given their lack of antibodies.[42]

Where are these Canadian, Arctic, and Pacific residues coming from? Pesticides in use in the United States, and presumably other industrialized countries, are pretty well accounted for, but the United States and other countries export tons of pesticides to less-developed countries, especially in Africa and South America. Protecting the safety of workers and populations where these substances are used presents difficulties familiar to the nongovernmental organizations that monitor international health: Often those who use the imported substances cannot read the labels, are unused to sterilization and safe spraying practices, and cannot take remote dangers into account. The government agencies that monitor imported chemicals are understaffed, inefficient, and often corrupt. Because the pesticides in use are often banned or restricted for use at home, antidotes and special precautions are never developed. Between 1992 and 1994, the United States exported 4,950 tons of unapproved pesticides, 11,000 tons of "severely restricted" pesticides, and 100,000 tons of pesticides with some U. S. restrictions. In 1992 alone, the U.S. exported 1,950 tons of pesticides banned, suspended, or discontinued at home. The farmer tends to believe that if the product comes from the United States, it's safe — the label, if there is one and it's understandable, doesn't tell him it's banned there.

It is estimated that the United States exports 250,000 tons of *recorded* pesticides per year, but the export data is scarce and unreliable. That from the EPA is also spotty, given that the EPA doesn't track unregistered pesticides and the staff is overwhelmed because of budget restrictions. Many pesticides are volatile and sprayed indiscriminately, causing numerous local poisonings and resulting in airborne chemicals deposited all over the world. Atmospheric scientists are just now beginning to think of monitoring pesticide "emissions" as they do other air pollutants. Dr. John Giesy, a toxicologist from Michigan State University who was a member of the team studying Midway Island, suggests, "Our research demonstrates that global controls on the distribution of persistent, bioaccumulative, toxic compounds need to be considered. The problem can't be approached on a country-by-country basis."[43]

Consider that insecticides are only the most visible of the pesticides, a billion-dollar industry. This in turn is dwarfed by the other petrochemical operations—plastics, synthetic fibers, and thousands of other chemicals. There are 100,000 synthetic chemicals used worldwide, with about 1,000 new ones put on the market each year, "most of them without adequate testing."[44] A movement is afoot to eliminate all synthetic chlorinated hydrocarbons (including the pesticides like DDT) in some U.S. quarters. Recently, all chlorinated hydrocarbons, such as PCBs, and dioxins as well as pesticides have come under attack on account of these effects. A study done by the World Wildlife Fund found that of 42 chemicals that affect the reproductive system, 55 percent contained chlorine. A senior economist with Environment Canada posits that "no other class of industria—or natural—chemicals is known that exhibits so many detrimental properties at the same time."[45] Greenpeace, the environmental activist association that started the attack, has adopted the position that "no further organochlorine pollution should be permitted,"[46]entailing the complete cessation of the use of chlorine in manufacturing. Though the chemical industry is pursuing substitutes for chlorine, it tends to view the proposed chlorine ban as "an extremist position" and generally ridiculous. "We're not well served by blanket solutions to complicated problems."[47]

ALTERNATIVES TO PESTICIDES

What can we do? Alternatives to chemical warfare against the insects are under study, some of them on the horizon. For starters, not all pesticides have to be chlorinated hydrocarbons; a number are organophosphates, which do not persist in the ground as long as the organochlorines, and some have less dangerous chemical formulas, such as carbamates. Interesting research concerns Integrated Pest Management (IPM), or using carefully measured minimal doses of pesticide along with biological and mechanical controls on insect pests. The cultivation of insect predators is already under way; perhaps we should also look into the capacity of plants to defend themselves. "Besieged by armies of voracious creatures but unable to run away, plants over the eons have evolved cunning defenses that include deadly poisons, oozings of toxic glue and hidden drugs that give leaf-eaters serious indigestion.... Many plants...wait until a predator actually starts munching before they unleash their most noxious washes of chemicals."[48] The obvious suggestion is to learn how they do that and figure out how to have our agricultural staples do the same. Then we would not have to use chemical pesticides at all. That would be good for the farmers, good for the land, and a fitting tribute to the foresight of Rachel Carson.

CONCLUSION

It seems fitting to let Rachel Carson have the last word. She finished *Silent Spring* with the following castigation:

> The "control of nature" is a phrase conceived in arrogance, born of the Neanderthal age of biology and philosophy, when it was supposed that nature exists for the convenience of man. The concepts and practices of applied entomology...date from that Stone Age of science. It is our alarming misfortune that so primitive a science has armed itself with the most modern and terrible weapons, and that in turning them against the insects it has also turned them against the earth."[49]

QUESTIONS FOR DISCUSSION AND REFLECTION

✦ Where should we place responsibility, or accountability, for the deleterious effects of pesticides? On the chemical companies? On the farmers? Or on the consumers and their demands for perfect appearance in their fruits and vegetables?

✦ What is the difference between the way we ascribe blameworthiness to individuals and to corporations? Can you blame a whole country for taking a wrong turn? Can U.S. consumerism and reliance on technological fixes be regarded as morally blameworthy?

✦ What course should the chemical companies follow to ensure that their products are safe? What would follow from the Responsible Care initiative described in Chapter 3?

✦ Can pesticides be made completely safe for use around humans and on products consumed by humans? If not, why not? If so, how?

Notes

1. Gove Hambidge, "The New Insect-Killers," *Harper's Magazine* (February 1945): p 264.

2. Ibid., citing Hans Zinsser, p. 264.

3. Ibid., p. 265.

4. Frank Graham, Jr., *Since Silent Spring* (Boston: Houghton Mifflin, 1970): p. 16.

5. Ibid., p. 16.

6. Philip Sterling, *Sea and Earth: The Life of Rachel Carson* (New York: Thomas Y. Crowell, 1970): p. 2.

7. Carol B. Gartner, *Rachel Carson* (New York: Frederick Ungar, 1983): p.7.

8. Graham, *Since Silent Spring*, p. 5.

9. Mary A. McKay, *Rachel Carson* (New York: Twayne, 1993): p. 13. See Chronology as well.

10. Ibid., p. 2.

11. Gartner, *Rachel Carson*, Chronology.

12. Ibid.

13. Ibid., p. 17.

14. McKay, *Rachel Carson*, p. 19; Martha Freeman, ed., *Always, Rachel: The Letters of Rachel Carson and Dorothy Freeman* (Boston: Beacon Press, 1995).

15. Gartner, *Rachel Carson*, p. 21.

16. McKay, *Rachel Carson*, p. 63.

17. Ibid., p. 63ff.

18. Paul Brooks, *The House of Life: Rachel Carson at Work* (Boston: Houghton Mifflin, 1972): p. 228.

19. Ibid.

20. McKay, *Rachel Carson*, pp. 69 and 80; Gartner, *Rachel Carson*, pp. 21ff.

21. Robert B. Downs, *Upsetting the Balance of Nature* (London: Macmillan, 1970); quoted in McKay, *Rachel Carson*.

22. McKay, *Rachel Carson*.

23. Sterling, *Sea and Earth*, p. 172.

24. Graham, *Since Silent Spring*, p. 48.

25. Ibid., p. 60.

26. Brooks, *House of Life*, p. 293.

27. Graham, *Since Silent Spring*, p. 49; Marty Jezer, *Rachel Carson* (New York: Chelsea House, 1988): p. 95.

28. Graham, *Since Silent Spring*, p. 56.

29. Ibid., p. 50.

30. Ibid., p. 59.

31. Ibid., p. 60.

32. Brooks, *House of Life*, p. 293.

33. Ibid., pp. 72–79.

34. Ibid., pp. 86–88.

35. Graham, *Since Silent Spring*, p. 89.

36. Ibid., p. 15, note.

37. Rachel Carson, *Silent Spring* (Greeenwich, CT: Fawcett, 1962).

38. Ibid., p. 220

39. Ibid., p. 240

40. Ibid., p. 217.

41. G. Tyler Miller, Jr., *Living in the Environment*, 9th ed. (Belmont, CA: Wadsworth, 1996): p. 598.

42. J. Raloff, "Pesticides May Challenge Human Immunity," *Science News*, vol. 149 (9 March 1996): p. 149.

43. Janet Raloff, "The Pesticide Shuffle," *Science News*, vol. 149 (16 March 1996): p. 174; Leslie Line, "Old Nemesis, DDT, Reaches Remote Midway Albatrosses," *New York Times* (12 March 1996): p. B1.

44. "Hormonal Sabotage," *Natural History* (March 1996): p. 46.

45. Ibid.

46. Joe Thornton, "Chlorine, Human Health, and the Environment," *Greenpeace* (October 1993), quoted in J. A. Raloff, "The Role of Chlorine—and Its Future," *Science News* (22 January 1994): p. 59.

47. Ibid.

48. Carol Kaesuk Yoon, "Nibbled Plants Don't Just Sit There: They Launch Active Attacks," *New York Times* (23 June 1992): p. C1.

49. Carson, *Silent Spring*, p. 261.

Suggestions for Further Reading

Brooks, Paul. *The House of Life: Rachel Carson at Work*. Boston: Houghton Mifflin, 1972.

Freeman, Martha, ed. *Always, Rachel: The Letters of Rachel Carson and Dorothy Freeman*. Boston: Beacon Press, 1995.

Graham, Frank, Jr. *Since Silent Spring*. Boston: Houghton Mifflin, 1970.

McKay, Mary A. *Rachel Carson*. New York: Twayne, 1993.

Sterling, Philip. *Sea and Earth: The Life of Rachel Carson*. New York: Thomas Y. Crowell, 1970.

Weir, David. *The Bhopal Syndrome: Pesticides, Environment and Health*. San Francisco: Sierra Club Books, 1987.

CHAPTER 9

Skunked

The Death of the
Great Fisheries

PREFACE: QUESTIONS TO
KEEP IN MIND

How do we catch fish these days? How did we used to? What difference does this change make in employment, technology, and the social structure of fishing towns?

What has happened to the total catch of fish since World War II? Why?

What measures seem likely to ensure plentiful fish into the future? Or are there any?

TOO MANY BOATS
CHASING TOO FEW FISH

In 1973, the Northwest Atlantic fisheries yielded 4.4 million tons of fish, but in 1992, only 2.6 million tons, a decline of 42 percent.[1] The take of Atlantic cod, crucial to the New England economy, had peaked in 1968 at 3.9 million tons; by 1992, it was down to 1.2 million tons—a decline of a horrifying 69 percent.[2] The next year saw further declines.[3] Worldwide, the marine catch had been stagnant since 1989, despite an increase in the number and capacity of all boats. From the New England fisher's point of view, the monetary loss has been staggering, especially in recent years: The Northeastern U.S. catch of the most popular commercial species was worth over $150 million in 1991, not quite $130 million in 1992, and less than $116 million in 1993. The value of the annual catch of Atlantic cod fell from almost $75 million in 1991 to $45 million in 1993, down 40 percent.[4] Given this unprecedented situation, the United Nations Food and Agriculture Organization (FAO) suggested that the only way to increase the supply of fish was "by reducing or temporarily eliminating fishing in many fisheries."[5]

What went wrong? In *Net Loss,* a 1994 Worldwatch paper, Peter Weber puts the problem very simply: There are too many fishers chasing too few fish. "Today, world fisheries have on the order of twice the capacity necessary to fish the oceans. Between 1970 and 1990, FAO recorded a doubling in the world fishing fleet, from 585,000 to 1.2 million large boats, and from 13.5 million to 25.5 million gross registered tons."[6]

Size alone creates difficulties: Each of those boats represents a hefty investment for its owner, who can only pay off the loans by bringing in ever more fish. Until very recently, the sorts of boundaries that can limit human predation on land did not apply on the sea;[7] management options are therefore limited to constricting the permissible time for catching fish: "Open access allows fishers to enter a fishery at will. If regulators limit the total catch, they must calculate the potential take of the fishers and adjust the length of the open season accordingly. Fishers then race each other to get the most fish possible. As the number of fishers or their capacity increases, the season gets shorter,"[8] tending to zero as a limit. Under these conditions, of course, the owner who fields the most or the largest boats brings in the greatest share of the prize; the incentive is to increase the capacity to catch and store fish, as well as the speed to get to the fishing grounds. In this way, building to overcapacity is structured into the system.[9] The only limit on entry comes when the latest entrant, no matter how efficient, cannot meet his or her marginal costs. Then the catch may stabilize—but at too low a level to sustain the fishery.[10] The situation is made bad by the free market system, which abhors limits on individual exploitation of the natural world, and then made worse by the tendency of developed nations to vote government subsidies for the financially distressed but politically popular fisher, thus keeping boats active in the water that pure market forces would scuttle.

Clearly something has to be done. But it is not in the nature of the fishing industry, carried on by thousands of entrepreneurs who own their own boats, to cooperate in making and enforcing rules to limit the catch, even though such rules are necessary to keep the fishery going in the long run. Like farming, fishing is not so much a business as a way of life—

inherited, valued, and tied up with regional institutions. The fishers keep on doing what they have been doing all their lives, even though it destroys the resource from which they draw. "Indeed what is fascinating," one observer comments, "and also tragic—about the fishing industry is that it so actively participates in its own annihilation."[11] Any remedial action, then, must begin outside the industry. Once begun and accepted as reasonable, it has a chance of obtaining the support of the fishers; it cannot succeed without their cooperation.

Before trying to crack the political nuts at the heart of this natural disaster, let us review some of the history of this craft, profession, and way of life. The analysis and conclusions of this chapter should hold good for any fishery in the world. Even so, each fishery has its own history, customs, and economic and social support systems, without which we cannot comprehend the environmental problem and possible solutions. Because we cannot cover them all, we will start with the nearest, the one made famous by Rudyard Kipling's novel, *Captains Courageous*—the Gloucestermen of Georges Bank. The rest of the Northwest Atlantic fisheries follow the same pattern.

THE CAPTAINS COURAGEOUS: FISHING IN NEW ENGLAND

The Natural History of Georges

The curious features of the water on the massive shoal known as Georges Bank ("St. Georges' Shoal," on the earliest maps) account for the tremendous concentration of fish. The currents on Georges Bank are strong and complex. In his *Oil and Water,* an account of the Georges as background for the 1980s dispute over the placement of oil rigs on it, William MacLeish includes a short account of these currents. Citing Brad Butman, a physical oceanographer associated with the U.S. Geological Survey, MacLeish reports that the current

> has three components. The tidal one is by far the strongest, about a knot and a half up by the shoals. Superimposed on that is the mean flow around the Bank, the clockwise gyre Bigelow [a pioneer in oceanography] found and others at Woods Hole have studied for years. That moves usually at about a tenth of a knot. The third component, only recently the subject of systematic measurement, is storm driven. Those currents have been clocked at near one knot at the bottom along the southern flank of Georges and are probably much stronger near the surface.[12]

There are also internal currents and eddies. The tidal currents are complex, because the water moves much faster over the shallow areas than the deep.

> Out of this swirl come hints, some of them quite strong, of what makes Georges Bank so productive. First, its waters are rich in nutrients like phosphorus and silicates, supplied in part by the cold oceanic water welling up from the depths onto the Bank and in part by planktonic organisms, whose excretions contain some of the nutrients they have ingested. Second, over much of the Bank, waters are sufficiently shallow so that sunlight—essential to the growth of phytoplankton, the tiny plants at the base of the food chain—penetrates all the way to the bottom. Third, tides and winds mix the shallows so that the surface waters, which otherwise would tend to lose their richness to grazing organisms, are constantly being replaced by richer waters from below. Fourth, the clockwise gyre, which appears at times to be a closed circuit, may act to keep nutrients and plankton—including fish eggs and larvae—captive in a productive environment far longer than is normally the case.[13]

The fish that thrive in this rich soup were first cataloged and described by Henry Bryant Bigelow, a turn-of-the-century enthusiast of the Western Atlantic. As the founder and first director of the Woods Hole Oceanographic Institute, he did research for the U.S. Fish Commission (predecessor of the National Marine Fisheries Service) on their schooner, the *Grampus*. He studied the Gulf of Maine, out into Georges Bank, from 1912 to 1929. The work that came from that study, *Fishes of the Gulf of Maine*, written with William Schroeder, is still the best starting place for understanding Georges Bank.[14]

Bigelow started with the haddock, then described all the other fish he found—yellowtail flounder, hake, whiting, pollock, and above all, cod. The cod, as MacLeish describes it, "is the eponym of the gadoids, the family that includes the haddock, the dark handsome pollock, the whiting, and other hakes. It is the largest gadoid. One that must have gone 180 pounds live came in on fishing schooner back in 1838, and another six feet long and 200 pounds was taken on a line off Massachusetts in 1895." The days of the giants are gone, he points out, "and that's an indication of a stock under pressure. Thirty pounds is a fine fish these days."[15] Sadly, there really is no good reason for a well-managed stock of cod to suffer the pressure; cod will eat anything, survive almost anything, and are enormously prolific. The mindless greed of the fishers is overwhelming a potentially infinite natural resource.

The importance of the industry for the northeastern section of the continent cannot be overestimated. In *The Cod Fisheries,* Harold Innis argues that despite possibilities for the coastal population to branch out into other industry, the United States and even more so Canada remained dependent on it. It is one of the stablest and most enduring industries in the Western Hemisphere.[16] As far as anyone knew at the beginning, fish would provide an unlimited resource. John Smith, soldier and adventurer, urged England early in the seventeenth century to embrace the industry as a source of unending prosperity. Indeed, the ready availability of inexpensive fish contributed enormously to Europe's prosperity before the American Revolution. Pickled in brine, cod could be shipped directly to Europe, but it was usually salted and dried on frames on the beaches. "Men killed and governments threatened war over which stretch of beach would be used by what ships."[17] Similarly, the newly constituted United States could not afford to lose the fish. Parceling out the fishing rights on Georges Bank between the United States and (British) Canada was an essential, and hotly contested, point in the Treaty of Paris in 1783. The same dispute surfaced again in the 1980s, leading to the "Hague Line," separating U.S. from Canadian fishing rights.

The Gloucester Fishing Industry

In *Down to the Sea*,[18] Joseph Garland presents an exciting history of the Gloucester enterprise, illustrated with a wealth of contemporary photographs. His account is essentially a celebration, with qualifications, of the fishing way of life.

> Three pinkies first tried fishing for cod on the tricky shoals of Georges Bank, 125 miles to the southeast of Gloucester, in 1821. They anchored and were so whipped around by the rip tides that nine years passed before Captain John Fletcher Wonson of East Gloucester and his crew screwed up the courage to tackle the Georges again. They found the great bank teeming with gigantic halibut, discovered they could anchor and fish without being dragged under by the current after all, and thus opened up the richest fishery in the North Atlantic. (p. 9)

> By 1859 [Gloucester's] fleet stood at 301 schooners crewed by 3568 men and boys, augmented by another fleet of smaller craft. Together they brought in, that year alone, 60,000 barrels of mackerel, 11,400,000 pounds of codfish and 4,590,000 pounds of halibut, and a few million more of haddock, hake, pollock, herring, sole and other species, lobsters and clams, tongues, sounds and oil. (p. 15)

The first codfishing on Georges, as Garland describes it, was *handlining*, over the rails along the side of an anchored boat. Fishers released the *Georges gear,* a sinkered tarred line with several hooks, which hung just off the bottom. They kept the lines apart with *sojers,* wooden pins every four feet or so on the fishing rails. When cod got on the lines, the fisher

> hauled back, maybe taking half an hour to wrestle a pair of big ones to the surface and gaff them aboard.
>
> The codfish were worked off the hooks, their tongues cut out for keeping tally, and the gangings replaced with a pair baited in the meanwhile, and back over with the lead. This way, a high-line fisherman [the best, or luckiest fisherman—the one with the highest catch] on his best day might boat nearly two hundred fish, and a lucky crew as much as thirty thousand pounds in the round, eviscerated. If he chanced upon a halibut, each man cut his own distinctive mark in it for counting in his favor. (p. 15)

By 1879, new fish products were bringing prosperity to Gloucester and the surrounding region. In that year, Gloucester packed off 14 million pounds of its widely advertised "boneless fish"—salt cod packed in boxes. By that time also the fish cake had become enormously popular. Potatoes would be brought down from Aroostook County, Maine, by the carload, with a stove (and stovetender) in the boxcar to keep them from freezing. They'd be shredded and mixed with chopped salt cod. Then, the mixture was tinned, ready to be scooped out, fried, and served up with ketchup (p. 143). As one might expect, the factory owners received most of that prosperity, with the fishers still scrambling for a living. "The average Gloucester fisherman in 1879 made $175, although the Goode study estimated that if he worked like the devil for twelve months, including winter, he stood to earn as much as $300 to $500, the skipper usually double that" (p. 143). By 1900 the town and the entire region depended on that catch for their livelihood.

Garland's celebration of fishing and its role in New England is sobered by his grim reminders of the cost. "The fish were there all right, but what a deadly game! The best fishing was in the worst place, naturally, the east and southeast rim of the shoals in two to twelve fathoms, where the waves broke in rough weather. This was one hell of a lee in an easterly storm." (p. 101). Brave souls but damn fools, observers at the time agreed. Fishers would not raise—or more realistically, cut loose—the anchor, in a storm, for fear of losing fish, for fear of losing face with their rivals, and for (a very Yankee) fear of expense: Their anchor cables, first to go in any rough weather, were not insurable.

Many fishers died in these efforts. Garland documents the loss and danger associated with that way of life, and the callousness of the capitalist system that underlay this example of American industry.

In the twenty-five years between 1866 and 1890 Gloucester lost 382 schooners and 2454 fishermen. All of those men didn't go down with their ships, nor did every ship let down its men. Dories capsized or went adrift. Men were washed overboard, fell out of the rigging, or were struck by booms. Schooners were lost through negligence or in storms and under conditions that no vessel could be expected to survive. All the same, as Chapelle has been quoted on an earlier generation of schooners, "...the men lost cost the shipowner nothing, and insurance could take care of the loss of vessel property."...

No one knows how many men and boys—fishing vessels usually carried one or two youngsters as apprentices—were lost from the town. One estimate, which seems high, puts the figure at 30,000 since the beginning 350 years ago. Ten thousand seems more like it, and still appalling. A good many went down tumbling in the wildness of Georges Bank. (pp. 17, 25)

There was, for instance, the storm of February 23, 1862, when a hundred or so boats, most of them from Gloucester, were fishing the Bank. Thirteen went down in collisions, all hands lost, while two more were abandoned. About 138 people drowned in 24 hours (p. 26). And on the night of February 20, 1879, a gale wiped out 13 Gloucester fishing boats, at a cost of 143 men. "Before the year 1879 was out, the count would be twenty-nine Gloucester schooners and 249 men, by far the most of them gone down with their vessels" (p. 104).

How long could such an industry have continued? There is no sign that the Gloucestermen were willing to give up their fishing because of the danger. And had they continued in their old wooden schooners, as Garland points out, their simple ways of fishing could have gone on indefinitely: There was a nice balance between human need and technology and the natural supply of fish (p. 18). We need only compare the proud yield of 5.7 *thousand* tons of cod brought in by the huge fleet in 1859 with the 3.9 *million* tons in 1968. When the technology changed, starting with the diesel engines and ending with huge factory trawlers, the balance was destroyed.

The Russians Are Coming!
And the Germans, Poles, Spanish...

The destruction began in the mid-1950s, when a new kind of fishing vessel began to sail the Atlantic waters. Huge—the earliest were over 300 feet—it fished from the stern instead of over the side, and it swiftly processed and froze everything it caught. This "factory-equipped freezer stern trawler," or factory trawler, spelled doom to any fishery it visited.[19] For the most part, the factory trawlers were foreign.[20] "The Soviets showed up with their giants at the beginning of the sixties, and then the Germans and the Poles and the Spaniards.... The new technology moved in floating cities, and it broke the back of the fisheries from Labrador to Georges and on southwest."[21]

At first the fleets fished for squid and red hake and the like, species not customarily marketed in New England ports. However, in the middle sixties, "there occurred one of those periodic blooms of haddock, or, more precisely, haddock surviving to a catchable size." The trawlers took most of them and came back for more.

> There were more Russians on Georges by then than there were Americans. The foreigners swept the bottoms and the midwaters. To them, Georges was just one of many shoalings in the high seas, places with names like Whale Deep and Flemish Cap off Atlantic Canada, No Name Bank off Greenland, Bill Bailey's Bank off Iceland, Viking Bank and Tiddly off Scandinavia, Skolpen and Parson's Nose off the Soviet Union. Processers and trawlers moved along the chain pulse-fishing, setting their nets for one species until the catch became too small to bother with, and then moving on or setting their nets for another. The system worked so well that shortly it failed.[22]

It is not clear whether it was concern for the preservation of the fishery or concern for national sovereignty that prompted the U.S. Congress to move, but move it did.

> [The] intolerable had happened: the Russians were now the highliners. In 1960, just before the foreigners arrived on Georges, American boats were taking 90 percent of the harvest there, and most of the remainder went to the Canadians. Twelve years later the Yankees were taking 10 percent and the foreigners the rest. It wasn't just the long-distance fleets. New England's total catch had been dropping, with some surges here and there, ever since 1950. But you couldn't tell that to the captains. From Rhode Island to Maine, they sat in their small, wood-hulled, fifteen-year-old boats and roared.

> The response from Washington was the Fisheries Conservation and Management Act of 1976, known as the Magnuson Act.... [which] extended United States fishery jurisdiction out to two hundred miles.[23]

Other countries claimed 200-mile limits too, of course; these Exclusive Economic Zones (EEZs) of 122 coastal states totaled 10 percent of the ocean's surface in 1992. This area included all the good fishing.[24] Ten percent of the total EEZs belonged to the United States. Even after the World

Court required the U.S. to shave off the eastern corner of the Georges Banks for Canada, the fishers thought that now there'd be plenty of fish for all of them, and no limits. "In 1980, fishermen caught about 294 million pounds of fish and shellfish from Georges Bank, worth a little under $200 million dockside and considerably more when processing and marketing are thrown in. The Americans, fishing all over the Bank, took three quarters of that poundage and two-thirds of the value. The Canadians, restricted by joint agreement to the eastern third, took almost all the rest, mostly scallops."[25]

The Bank continued to decline. The fishers were wrong: By this time U.S. fishing alone sufficiently overwhelmed the capacity of the Georges. The act gave the government power to set quotas to conserve threatened species; shortly, these became necessary.[26] For the fishing grounds did not recover; New England had "replaced overfishing by foreign fleets with overfishing by their own," and the catch continued to decline.[27] By 1993, cod and yellowtail flounder were at record lows off New England; after the haddock catch plunged 63 percent in one year, the federal government shut down part of the Georges Bank completely.[28]

The days of mass-production fishing are essentially over. According to William Warner, the factory trawlers were on their way out by the late 1970s. There were no more "floating cities—the massive concentrations of one hundred or more distant water vessels once so common on prime grounds."[29] Now they seemed not the wave of the future but dinosaurs; with a daily operating cost of about $13,000 each, and operations scaled to a very high catch of single species at one time, they could not possibly make a living on the quotas they had been assigned by coastal states. The 200-mile limit had made the difference.

By 1980, when the last German ships were recalled from New Zealand, the industry had just about folded in Germany. England had perhaps a dozen distant water ships in 1982; the Hull Fishing Vessel Owners Association (the port authority that ran the fishing docks in that city) went bankrupt in 1980, and Hull itself took on the aspect of a maritime ghost town. The Spanish boats continued to fish; less controlled by government or central agencies than the others, they simply went on doing what they knew how to do, catching fewer fish each trip.[30] Spanish and Portugese fishing boats, flying flags of convenience to evade international treaties which their nations had signed, have been seized by Canada as recently as 1994 for predatory overfishing with equipment that has been banned and in grounds where, according to the Canadians, they have no right to be.[31] We are looking at the tail end of an industry. The Grand Banks, like the Georges, are overfished, and large-scale fishing can no longer survive there. The question now is whether *any* fishing can survive.

Short History of a Short Controversy:
Oil versus Fish

In the late 1970s and early 1980s, when oil prices were high, several American oil companies tried to extend their offshore drilling operations from the friendly shores of the Gulf of Mexico to the decidedly less congenial shores of rocky New England. In a sense, the controversy provides only historical interest, since not enough oil was discovered in the drillings to make the enterprise commercially worthwhile. At the time, however, the strong interest in drilling and controversy over sale of drilling leases gave the nation an opportunity to weigh the value of the fishery against the value of a new source of petroleum. For the first time, the nation came to grips, in Congress and courtroom, with the importance of the Georges Bank fishery.

One of the first legal actions, for example, came about over Lease Sale Forty-Two—roughly translated, the government's sale to an oil company of the right to lease a particular patch of ocean for the purpose of drilling for oil. In January of 1978, the Commonwealth of Massachusetts brought suit to delay that sale, and Judge W. Arthur Garrity—the same judge who ordered the busing to integrate Boston's schools—granted a preliminary injunction against it. Here are some excerpts from his decision:

> This is no ordinary fishing ground. It is as important a resource as the people of this state will ever have to rely upon.... The plaintiffs are looking for a delay of a relatively few months to preserve a resource that has taken millions of years to accrue, and which will be with us, for better or for worse, for untold centuries to come.... The opposing considerations here are use for a period of about twenty years as a source for gas and oil, as against the preservation of the natural resource... for the indefinite future.... If there ever was a public interest case, this is it.[32]

The U.S. government and the oil companies promptly sued to stay the injunction. In the United States Court of Appeals for the First Circuit (Boston), Judge Levin H. Campbell said absolutely not; the decision of the "judge below" was quite correct: "There may be issues more serious than ones involving the future of the oceans of our planet and the life within them, but surely they are few."[33]

Similarly, in March 1983, a part of this controversy came to a head in a suit brought by the Conservation Law Foundation and several other environmental organizations (including Greenpeace and the Massachusetts branch of the Audubon Society) to obtain an injunction against another of the lease sales. In granting the injunction, Federal Judge A. David Mazzone emphasized the importance of preserving the fishery. "In short," he wrote, Georges Bank "represents a renewable, self-sustaining resource for the entire nation.... In light of the significance of the Georges Bank fishery resource that may be jeopardized by that sale, I find that the plaintiffs have adequately demonstrated that they will suffer irreparable harm if this injunction does not issue."[34] We will never know what would have happened if abundant oil had been found beneath the Georges. At least the dialogue on its value had begun—after two centuries—and a foundation had been laid for a discussion of what we lose when we destroy a major national resource.

PRESENT AND FUTURE

Taking Stock

Where are the North Atlantic fisheries at this point? Peter Weber, in *Net Loss,* points out that overfishing has long-term environmental consequences. The chief cause

> of the decline of the Atlantic cod and haddock fisheries off North America.... appears to be long-term overfishing, which has reduced the average size of the cod and haddock, as well as their overall numbers. By removing such a large number of these predators, fishers may have also caused a long-term transformation of the North Atlantic ecosystem. Populations of dogfish and skate—types of shark—have boomed and are now filling the niche left by the cod and haddock. Because dogfish and skate prey on young cod and haddock as well, they are reinforcing this ecological shift. Although the ecosystem is still producing fish, the fishers lose out because there is little demand in North America for dogfish and skate, which do not store well.[35]

If fish have become scarce, how can we reduce pressure on the fisheries? Weber points out that the first reaction of fishing nations tends to be to adopt programs (consolidation, licensing, quotas, etc.) that put fewer fishing boats on the water. These surviving boats tend to be the most efficient in terms of operating cost per unit of fish processed, but these, of course, turn out to be the biggest, the newest, and employing the least crew. In his concern for worldwide employment, Weber finds this solution perverse. He believes that what we need is a proliferation of small local fishers, who tend to employ many more people in the process of taking many fewer fish, and whose simple fishing methods can never damage a large fishery.

The employment issue on the Georges is addressed directly in documents prepared for the East Coast Fisheries Federation by its executive director, James O'Malley. He cites an estimate by the New England Fishery Management Council that the industry will have to cut back their fishing by one half to replenish the stock of fish on the Georges. The fishing fleet in the Northeast will shrink, but how? In many ways: "The contraction of the fleet may take place through bankruptcy, attrition by age, consolidation of fishing power into fewer hands, or through a buyout of existing vessels. Each of these alternatives has a cost. Widespread bankruptcy is socially unacceptable. Furthermore, the economic failure of any vessel does not mean that its fishing power is removed from the fleet; only that it will be resurrected at a lower price by the next purchaser, leaving the same level of fishing pressure on the resource."[36] Shades of the arrival of the Spanish and the Portugese. There is no sign that attrition will cause any significant effects soon; consolidation may mean fewer boats working at higher efficiency to bring in more fish per boat. As long as the marginal costs of the low-end producer are met, the fishing will continue; the market, unaided by government, does not hold a solution for the Georges.

The major obstacle to any rational plan is the entrenched opposition of fishers to *any* restrictions; this industry has never had them. For the families invested in the industry, all such measures are anathema, as Michael Parfit has observed:

> [This] I learned one evening in New England at a hearing on bluefin fisheries. All it took was a speaker to gingerly suggest limiting numbers of fishermen. A gray-haired man leaped to his feet, furious.
>
> "Don't go to limited access!" he shouted across the room. "I don't want to be limited! That's not American!"[37]

Is It Possible to Strike a Balance?

From a variety of sources, a pattern of suggested solutions emerges in order of priority.

1. Immediately: reduce the fishing, allow the fishery to recover. This means taking boats off the water—temporarily, for periods, or permanently. The Grand Banks has already been temporarily closed to fishing, to allow time for the fish to breed and grow. But we will need programs to help the transition. Weber identifies "a $30 million package for New England fishers and their communities. Twelve million dollars of this is earmarked to help individual fishers move into other fisheries and other industries."[38]

   This solution, a typical "bail out" designed to keep present fishers in business somehow, is admittedly less than ideal; there are no more unexploited fisheries in this world, and it makes little sense to take pressure off one fishing ground only to destroy another. And what "other industries" did we have in mind? New England would like to know.

2. We surely need international agreements to prevent the kind of flag-of-convenience raiding the outraged Canadians found the Spanish boats doing. In August of 1995, the *New York Times* applauded the first international agreement that might do some good: "The United Nations Food and Agriculture Organization, once an ardent booster of highly mechanized fleets that sweep up fish by the ton, now says that virtually every commercial fish species is either declining or at serious risk.... Last Friday, after two years of protracted and bitter negotiations, delegates from 100 countries meeting under the auspices of the United Nations approved the first international treaty to regulate fishing on the high seas."[39]

   The agreement only regulates "straddling" fish, which migrate from coastal waters to high seas. Still, the *Times* believes, it will reduce appalling waste of *bycatch*, undesirable fish caught in indiscriminate nets, rejected and dumped dead back into the sea. The agreement at least regulates the nets, prohibiting the kind that catch everything, and provides for some international inspection. It is also time, the editorial concludes, that we stop "bailing out" the fishing fleets through subsidies that allow inefficient fishers to continue in business.

3. Individually transferable quotas (ITQs) assign quotas of certain numbers of certain fish to present fishers; no one can fish at all without owning such a quota. Because the fishers may use, give, bequeath, assign, sell, or otherwise treat that quota as personal property, it is "individually transferable." For those presently in business, the ITQ is a pure bonus, a windfall. For the purchaser, it is a barrier to entry into the industry, which is the point.[40] Because the ITQs can be regulated—their number increased or decreased as the fishing ground waxes or wanes—we may theoretically control the amount of fishing effort. However, we must also enforce the quotas—someone has to inspect every boat coming in off those foggy and storm-tossed waters. Such quotas have not been tried.

4. A frank buyout might be a more adequate solution. A buyout would require that fishers turn in their licenses once and for all and scrap their boats, in return for some federally funded retirement or retraining package. Such plans have worked in the United Kingdom, and are currently proposed for New England.[41]

5. A buyout might work best in combination with severe limits on the hunting seasons. Because the least efficient boats would have the hardest time making a living in a short season, they would have an incentive to retire.

6. What about limiting the technology? Theoretically, limits on boats and methods should work—the Gloucesters could have fished indefinitely. But such measures are very difficult to implement. Recall the cry of Parfit's fisherman: Limits are not American! As such, American ingenuity might sabotage the effect.

7. For a long-term supply of fish for the world, we must encourage fish farming. It could be argued that the modern fish industry is about where the beef industry was at the time of Buffalo Bill—we find the wild species in their largest concentrations, then use our best technology to slaughter them. No wonder the fisheries are crashing. What could be accomplished if we put our technology to work breeding fish, experimenting with new breeds of fish, studying their diseases, and finding what combinations of food would produce the best flesh for the table?

Current fish farming, or *aquaculture,* involves many disadvantages. Only the most expensive species are raised, because they bring in the highest profit from those who can pay. More important, we currently depend on coastline locations for the farms, since we dare not try to raise marine fish without their native waters. But the coastline is our most valuable property, in demand for industrial, recreational, and residential purposes. Worse, the remaining coastal salt marshes provide the essential nurseries for the life of the sea; if we convert them to fish farms, we condemn all ocean wildlife to death.

The objections can be answered. As they do in animal husbandry, let the state farms sponsor experimentation in aquacultural food, diseases, and environments. Let new nutrient broths be discovered and tried. There is no reason, given such research, that aquaculture could not take place where real estate is cheaper than on the coasts.

The Sadness of It All

In the course of this chapter, we have spoken of the attitudes of fishers and their families in this crisis. They are concerned; they are intelligent; they understand precisely the nature of the problem, the catastrophe that attends inaction, and the probable direction of any effective action. Yet, they resist it to the core: They are against limits; against collectivization and consolidation, against being regulated, reformed, and brought in line with the common good for the long run. They view themselves as the last strivers for a heroic life, the last independents in a corporate country, the last real entrepreneurs who muster intelligence, tradition, and courage to wrest a living from the merciless sea.

All of this will be lost, whether we do nothing and allow the fish, fisheries, fishers, and fishing towns to perish together, or whether we do what has to be done to save the resource by telling fishers where and when and for what they may fish. The collapse of the New England fisheries has been compared well to the Dust Bowl in the Midwest; as went the family farm, so goes Gloucester. In the course of a community celebration of the fishing way of life in St. John's, Newfoundland, after the closing of the Grand Banks, Michael Parfit found himself meditating on this comparison:

> The Grand Banks disaster has been called the Dust Bowl of fishing. The Dust Bowl did not kill American agriculture, just changed it. It became big industry: highly regulated, tidy. Thus it may be with fishing. Fish farming, the only piece of world fisheries to show a real gain in recent years, will continue to grow. So will regulation of the sea itself. We will still have fish but not the fishermen we knew. In that auditorium in St. John's, the old life was turning from reality to myth before my eyes.[42]

Finally, the frontier is closed, and the government will have to come in and regulate. The old fisherman's protest against being "limited" hits home—in its genuinely American character and in its futility. As Parfit comments, "His words struck me as a cry of loss, and I imagined them rolling out across this world of inevitable limits, to the very edge of the sea."[43]

Notes

1. Peter Weber, *Net Loss: Fish, Jobs, and the Marine Environment*, Worldwatch Paper No. 120 (Washington, DC: Worldwatch Institute, July 1994): Table 1, p. 14.

2. Ibid., Table 2, p. 15.

3. Northeast Fisheries Science Center, *Status of the Fishery Resources off the Northeastern United States for 1994* (Woods Hole, MA: NOAA Technical Memorandum NMFS-NE-108, 1995).

4. James D. O'Malley, "Preliminary Findings" in "Draft Statement on Buyout Design" (Narragansett, RI: East Coast Fisheries Federation, Inc., 1994): p. 8.

5. Ibid., p. 16, citing Food and Agriculture Organization of the United Nations (FAO), *Marine Fisheries and the Law of the Sea: A Decade of Change*, FAO Fisheries Circular No. 853 (Rome, Italy, 1993).

6. Weber, *Net Loss*, p. 28.

7. In theory, the use of Global Positioning Systems should make it possible to put up electronic "fences" all along the 200-mile limits of the fishing nations and patrol them by remote control. No one has yet suggested this.

8. Weber, *Net Loss*, p. 28.

9. Ibid.

10. Ibid., p. 29.

11. James R. McGoodwin, *Crisis in the World's Fisheries* (Stanford, CA: Stanford University Press, 1990), Note 14.

12. William H. MacLeish, *Oil and Water: The Struggle for Georges Bank* (Boston: Atlantic Monthly Press, 1985): pp. 163–164.

13. Ibid., p. 164.

14. Ibid., p. 14.

15. Ibid., p. 17.

16. Harold A. Innis, *The Cod Fisheries: The History of an International Economy* (Toronto: University of Toronto Press, 1978). Cited in MacLeish, *Oil and Water*, p. 19.

17. MacLeish, *Oil and Water*, p. 21.

18. Joseph E. Garland, *Down to the Sea: The Fishing Schooners of Gloucester* (Boston; David R. Godine, 1983).

19. William W. Warner, *Distant Water: The Fate of the North Atlantic Fisherman* (Boston: Little, Brown, 1977): p. vii.

20. The United States has some of them, of course, but not for the New England fishery. An excellent diagram of such a ship, with all its activities, is found on p. 14 of Michael Parfit's "Diminishing Returns," an article on the state of fisheries worldwide, *National Geographic* (vol. 188, no. 5, November 1995).

21. MacLeish, *Oil and Water*, p. 201.

22. Ibid., pp. 201–202.

23. Ibid., p. 203.

24. Weber, *Net Loss*, p. 47.

25. MacLeish, *Oil and Water*, pp. 28–29.

26. Ibid., p. 203.

27. Weber, *Net Loss*, p. 53.

28. Frank Graham, Jr., "Defender of the Fishes," *Audubon Magazine* (Sept.–Oct. 1994): pp. 96–99.

29. Warner, *Distant Water*, p. 309.

30. Ibid., pp. 311–315.

31. Weber, *Net Loss*, p. 5. See also Clyde H. Farnsworth, "Canada Acts to Cut Fishing by Foreigners: Will Seize Boats Outside Its Waters," *New York Times* (22 May 1994); Colin Nickerson, "Pirates Plunder Fisheries," *Boston Sunday Globe* (17 April 1994).

32. MacLeish, pp. 72–73.

33. Ibid., p. 74.

34. Ibid., p. 245.

35. Weber, *Net Loss*, p. 19. He cites as his authority on this change, Massachusetts Offshore Groundfish Task Force, *New England Groundfish in Crisis—Again* (Boston: Executive Office of Environmental Affairs, 1990).

36. James D. O'Malley, "Draft Statement: Buyout Design" (September 1994); available from East Coast Fisheries Federation, Inc., P.O. Box 649, Narragansett, RI 02882. (401) 782-3440.

37. Parfit, "Diminishing Returns," p. 29.

38. Weber, *Net Loss*, p. 53.

39. Editorial, "A Modest Step to Save the Fish," *New York Times* (8 August 1995).

40. Weber, *Net Loss*, p. 35.
41. O'Malley, "Draft Statement."
42. Parfit, "Diminishing Returns."
43. Ibid., p. 29.

Suggestions for Further Reading

Garland, Joseph E. *Down to the Sea: The Fishing Schooners of Gloucester.* Boston: David R. Godine, 1983.

MacLeish, William H. *Oil And Water: The Struggle for Georges Bank.* Boston: Atlantic Monthly Press, 1985.

McGoodwin, James R. *Crisis in the World's Fisheries.* Stanford, CA: Stanford University Press, 1990.

Parfit, Michael. "Diminishing Returns: Exploiting the Ocean's Bounty." *National Geographic*, vol. 188, no. 5 (November 1995): pp. 2–37.

Warner, William W. *Distant Water: The Fate of the North Atlantic Fisherman.* Boston: Little, Brown, 1977.

———*Net Loss: Fish, Jobs, and the Marine Environment.* Worldwatch Paper no. 120. Washington, DC: Worldwatch Institute, July 1994.

CHAPTER *10*

Private Property and Takings

The Law and the Political Tradition

PREFACE: QUESTIONS TO KEEP IN MIND

The "Takings Clause,"the centerpiece of this chapter, is the last clause in the Fifth Amendment to the Constitution of the United States: "nor shall private property be taken for public use without just compensation." What does it mean to take something from someone? What did the writers of the Constitution mean to prohibit by this provision?

Why is *private property*, especially private property in *land*, so important in the Anglo-American political and legal tradition? What political developments led to the centrality of this right?

If environmental regulation can constitute a "taking" of private property, what other sorts of regulation might do so also? Zoning laws? Traffic laws?

INTRODUCTION: THE SLOW WAY

As the population grows, as technology changes, and as economic interests evolve, the environmental ground shifts under our feet. Sometimes it does this with great speed: A factory explodes, and whole nations are instantly aware of the dangers posed by chemical plants. Soon, measures are adopted to make those plants safer. Sometimes the process is much slower but at least visible and subject to public debate, as when a tanker spills oil over a pristine wildlife refuge or a scientist claims that the world is getting warmer and national and international councils take up the dispute over means to prevent oil or warming from harming the natural world. And sometimes the process is glacial, abstract, and almost invisible. Such is the issue of *takings*. An abstract debate has accompanied the issue since the drafting of the Constitution. As the Supreme Court's membership changed from conservative to liberal earlier in the century, it dropped out of sight; when the Court recently became conservative again, it reappeared. Eventually a case reached the Court, and the new Court handed down a decision, and as a result, all environmental law is radically changed. We begin with the decision itself; the facts and the consequences will be explained as we go along.

DAVID LUCAS' BEACH HOUSE

JUSTICE SCALIA delivered the opinion of the Court:

> In 1986, petitioner David H. Lucas paid $975,000 for two residential lots on the Isle of Palms in Charleston County, South Carolina, on which he intended to build single-family homes. In 1988, however, the South Carolina Legislature enacted the Beachfront Management Act, S.C. Code sections 48-39-250 *et.seq.* (Supp. 1990) (Act), which had the direct effect of barring petitioner from erecting any permanent habitable structures on his two parcels....Lucas promptly filed suit in the South Carolina Court of Common Pleas, contending that the Beachfront Management Act's construction bar effected a taking of his property without just compensation. Lucas did not take issue with the validity of the Act as a lawful exercise of South Carolina's police power, but contended that the Act's complete extinguishment of his property's value entitled him to compensation regardless of whether the legislature had acted in furtherance of legitimate police power objectives. Following a bench trial, the court agreed.[1]

It ruled that the prohibition "deprive[d] Lucas of any reasonable economic use of the lots,...eliminated the unrestricted right of use, and render[ed] them valueless." It concluded that Lucas' property had been "taken" by operation of the act, and ordered the State of South Carolina to pay "just compensation" in the amount of $1,232,387.50.

> The Supreme Court of South Carolina reversed. It found dispositive what it described as Lucas's concession "that the Beachfront Management Act [was] properly and validly designed to preserve...

South Carolina's beaches."...Failing an attack on the validity of the statute as such, the court believed itself bound to accept the "uncontested...findings" of the South Carolina legislature that new construction in the coastal zone—such as petitioner intended—threatened this public resource. The Court ruled that when a regulation respecting the use of property is designed "to prevent serious public harm,"...no compensation is owing under the Takings Clause regardless of the regulation's effect on the property's value.

Two judges of the South Carolina Supreme Court disagreed, arguing that the precedents established only that when law prevented the "noxious" or harmful uses of property could such law escape responsibility for lowering the value of the property. A single-family dwelling is not obviously a "nuisance."

To the dissenters, the chief purposes of the legislation, among them the promotion of tourism and the creation of a "habitat for indigenous flora and fauna," could not fairly be compared to nuisance abatement.

Scalia's Thoughts

After disposing of some technical difficulties, Justice Antonin Scalia, a Reagan appointee to the United States Supreme Court, gives us a short history of the case law on the subject as he sees it.

Prior to Justice Holmes' exposition in *Pennsylvania Coal Co.* v. *Mahon*, 260 U.S. 393 (1922), it was generally thought that the Takings Clause reached only a "direct appropriation" of property,...or the functional equivalent of a "practical ouster of [the owner's] possession."...Justice Holmes recognized in *Mahon*, however, that if the protection against physical appropriations of private property was to be meaningfully enforced, the government's power to redefine the range of interests included in the ownership of property was necessarily constrained by constitutional limits. 260 U.S., at 414–415. If, instead, the uses of private property were subject to unbridled, uncompensated qualification under the police power, "the natural tendency of human nature [would be] to extend the qualification more and more until at last private property disappear[ed]." *Id* at 415. These considerations gave birth in that case to the oft-cited maxim that, "while property may be regulated to a certain extent, if regulation goes too far it will be recognized as a taking." *Ibid.*

If regulation goes too far. That is the kind of pronouncement that creates perpetual headaches for Supreme Court justices, green fields for legal scholars, and lucrative careers for lawyers.

Justice Scalia concedes that the Court has never defined *too far*, but has generally dealt with contested regulations on a case-by-case basis. Yet there are two general situations where, he insists, the Court has always found an element of "taking": first, where there is a physical intrusion upon the property, no matter how small (an ordinance, for instance, requiring landlords to let cable TV companies put boxes—about 1.5 cubic feet—in their buildings) and second,

> where regulation denies all economically beneficial or productive use of land.... As we have said on numerous occasions, the Fifth Amendment is violated when land-use regulation "does not substantially advance legitimate state interests or denies an owner economically viable use of his land."[2]

The second sentence is much more sweeping than the first. If denying an owner *any* economically viable use of his land is unconstitutional (or constitutes a "taking"), then every zoning law in the United States falls. That can't be what it means.

Justice Scalia continues:

> We have never set forth the justification for this rule. Perhaps it is simply, as Justice Brennan suggested, that total deprivation of beneficial use is, from the landowner's point of view, the equivalent of a physical appropriation.... Surely, at least, in the extraordinary circumstance when no productive or economically beneficial use of land is permitted, it is less realistic to indulge our usual assumption that the legislature is simply "adjusting the benefits and burdens of economic life"... in a manner that secures an "average reciprocity of advantage" to everyone concerned....
>
> On the other side of the balance, affirmatively supporting a compensation requirement, is the fact that regulations that leave the owner of land without economically beneficial or productive options for its use—typically, as here, by requiring land to be left substantially in its natural state—carry with them a heightened risk that private property is being pressed into some form of public service under the guise of mitigating serious public harm.... As Justice Brennan explained: "From the government's point of view, the benefits flowing to the public from preservation of open space through regulation may be equally great as from creating a wildlife refuge through formal condemnation or increasing electricity production through a dam project that floods private property."[3] The many statutes on the books, both state and federal, that provide for the use of eminent domain to impose servitudes on private scenic lands preventing developmental uses, or to acquire such lands altogether, suggest the practical equivalence in this setting of negative regulation and appropriation....

We think, in short, that there are good reasons for our frequently expressed belief that when the owner of real property has been called upon to sacrifice *all* economically beneficial uses in the name of the common good, that is, to leave his property economically idle, he has suffered a taking.

Scalia points out that the trial court reached that conclusion and ordered compensation. When the case got to the South Carolina Supreme Court, however, the court asked a very different set of questions. Did petitioner concede that the beach and dune area of the shore was a beautiful and valuable public resource? He did—that's why he wanted to build the houses there. Did he concede that building houses on the dunes damaged that resource? He did. But he thus conceded, said the Court, that building his houses would cause public harm and was therefore "noxious," very much akin to "creating a nuisance." There are a long line of cases (starting with *Mugler* v. *Kansas*, an 1887 case refusing a moonshiner compensation for rendering his still economically valueless[4]) sustaining the state's use of police powers against due process and takings challenges. Lucas' case was simply part of that line, which includes, for instance, a variety of homeowner challenges to historic or landmark preservation ordinances.

Examining more closely the "noxious use" qualification for avoiding a finding of a taking, Scalia concedes that

> the distinction between "harm-preventing" and "benefit-conferring" regulation is often in the eye of the beholder. It is quite possible, for example, to describe in *either* fashion the ecological, economic, and aesthetic concerns that inspired the South Carolina legislature in the present case. One could say that imposing a servitude on Lucas's land is necessary in order to prevent his use of it from "harming" South Carolina's ecological resources; or, instead, in order to achieve the "benefits" of an ecological preserve.

To back up this last, he cites two cases, one from New Hampshire and one from Connecticut, in which landowners were barred from filling in coastal marshlands in order to preserve the integrity and functioning of the shoreline marine environment. In the Connecticut case, the benefits of nonfilling were stressed, so the court ruled that the law essentially took the marsh for a coastal park, and the town had to pay compensation; in the New Hampshire case, the harms of filling were stressed so the landowner got nothing.

> A given restraint will be seen as mitigating "harm" to the adjacent parcels or securing a "benefit" for them, depending upon the observer's evaluation of the relative importance of the use that the restraint favors.... Whether Lucas's construction of single-family

residences on his parcels should be described as bringing "harm" to South Carolina's adjacent ecological resources thus depends principally upon whether the describer believes that the State's use interest in nurturing those resources is so important that *any* competing adjacent use must yield.

When it is understood that "prevention of harmful use" was merely our early formulation of the police power justification necessary to sustain (without compensation) *any* regulatory diminution in value; and that the distinction between regulation that "prevents harmful use" and that which "confers benefits" is difficult, if not impossible, to discern on an objective, value-free basis; it becomes self-evident that noxious-use logic cannot serve as a touchstone to distinguish regulatory "takings"—which require compensation—from regulatory deprivations that do not require compensation.

This gives Scalia his conclusion—with some interesting distinctions.

Where the State seeks to sustain regulation that deprives land of all economically beneficial use, we think it may resist compensation only if the logically antecedent inquiry into the nature of the owner's estate shows that the proscribed use interests were not part of his title to begin with. This accords, we think, with our "takings" jurisprudence, which has traditionally been guided by the understandings of our citizens regarding the content of, and the State's power over, the "bundle of rights" that they acquire when they obtain title to property. It seems to us that the property owner necessarily expects the uses of his property to be restricted, from time to time, by various measures newly enacted by the State in legitimate exercise of its police powers; "[a]s long recognized, some values are enjoyed under an implied limitation and must yield to the police power."[5] ... And in the case of personal property, by reason of the State's traditionally high degree of control over commercial dealings, he ought to be aware of the possibility that new regulation might even render his property economically worthless,... *In the case of land, however, we think the notion pressed by the Council that title is somehow held subject to the "implied limitation" that the State may subsequently eliminate all economically valuable use is inconsistent with the historical compact recorded in the Takings Clause that has become part of our constitutional culture* [italics ours].[6]

It is certain that land ownership does not carry with it the right to engage *all* enterprises profitable to the owner, Scalia continues. Common law principles forbid, for instance, modifications to your property that will hurt your neighbor. But if such principles are not applicable, deprivation of normal rights of use must be compensated:

> Any limitation so severe cannot be newly legislated or decreed (without compensation), but must inhere in the title itself, in the restrictions that background principles of the State's law of property and nuisance already place upon land ownership.... In light of our traditional resort to "existing rules or understandings that stem from an independent source such as state law" to define the range of interests that qualify for protection as "property" under the Fifth (and Fourteenth) amendments.... This recognition that the Takings Clause does not require compensation when an owner is barred from putting land to a use that is proscribed by those "existing rules or understandings" is surely unexceptional. When, however, a regulation that declares "off-limits" all economically productive or beneficial uses of land goes beyond what the relevant background principles would dictate, compensation must be paid to sustain it.

Do such principles support the state's action in forbidding the houses?

Justice Scalia foresees an answer, but it is not the Court's matter to decide at this time:

> It seems unlikely that common-law principles would have prevented the erection of any habitable or productive improvements on petitioner's land.... The question, however, is one of state law to be dealt with on remand. We emphasize that to win its case South Carolina must do more than proffer the legislature's declaration that the uses Lucas desires are inconsistent with the public interest, or the conclusory assertion that they violate a common-law maxim.... As we have said, a "State, by *ipse dixit*, may not transform private property into public property without compensation...."[7] Instead, as it would be required to do it if sought to restrain Lucas in a common-law action for public nuisance, South Carolina must identify background principles of nuisance and property law that prohibit the uses he now intends in the circumstances in which the property is presently found. Only on this showing can the State fairly claim that, in proscribing all such beneficial uses, the Beachfront Management Act is taking nothing.

> The judgment is reversed and the cause remanded for proceedings not inconsistent with this opinion.

Judgement Against the Environment?

Is *Lucas* the environmental disaster its critics have claimed it to be? There is certainly novelty in the majority's interpretation, as an enraged Justice Blackmun pointed out in his dissent:

The South Carolina Supreme Court found that the Beach Management Act did not take petitioner's property without compensation. The decision rested on two premises that until today were unassailable—that the State has the power to prevent any use of property it finds to be harmful to its citizens, and that a state statute is entitled to a presumption of constitutionality.

Citing numerous cases to the point, Blackmun continues:

> If the state legislature is correct that the prohibition on building in front of the setback line prevents serious harm, then, under this Court's prior cases, the Act is constitutional. "Long ago it was recognized that all property in this country is held under the implied obligation that the owner's use of it shall not be injurious to the community, and the Takings Clause did not transform that principle to one that requires compensation whenever the State asserts its power to enforce it." *Keystone Bituminous Coal Assn. v. DeBenedictis.*...The Court consistently has upheld regulations imposed to arrest a significant threat to the common welfare, whatever their economic effect on the owner.[8]

More case citations follow. Justice Blackmun also points out, as did other justices, that the case came to the Court at an odd moment, since the Beachfront Act had already been amended, and the petitioner's problems may very well have been solved before the case was heard. There was some puzzlement as to why the majority of the Court wanted so much to hear it, to decide it, and to make such sweeping statements about what it meant, when the whole matter might have been quietly disposed of in South Carolina.[9]

Lucas seems to set aside all zoning or environment protection laws as unconstitutional; only subsequent decisions will tell. On the other hand, the decision was narrow, and South Carolina still gets to decide exactly *how much* damage was done to Lucas. But they probably cannot assess the damage at zero and remain "not inconsistent with this opinion"; if *Lucas* stands, environmental protection may have a hard time in the courts for some time to come.

RICHARD EPSTEIN'S SOCIAL CONTRACT

A Supreme Court decision stands solely on the basis of the current justices' reading of the U.S. Constitution and on the precedents of the Court. But judges have been known to take notice of facts not presented to the Court, and of legal and political theory that just happens to be in the legal and political air. Justice Scalia cites many precedents, but arguably Justice Blackmun cites just as many on the other side, and the principles enunciated by the dissent are perhaps clearer than those articulated by the majority. Could theory play a role in this case, as much as precedent and the plain words of the Constitution? Justice Scalia finds himself taking notice of one such theory, in his discussion of when regulation goes "too far" and becomes a "taking," when he cites Richard Epstein's "Takings: Descent and Resurrection," published in the *Supreme Court Review*.[10] With precedent so divided, there is good reason to think that this theory, not Court practice alone, may govern the result. For that reason, we shall take a look at Richard Epstein's peculiar theory. In the third and final section of this chapter, we will survey some of the consequences, intended and otherwise, of this teaching.

Property Rights: The Claim

Richard Epstein published *Takings: Private Property and the Power of Eminent Domain* in 1985, two years before the *Supreme Court Review* article, thereby launching the current phase of the takings debate. In it Epstein argues that property entitlements—rights to private property and exclusive use thereof—are absolute, not to be infringed in any way or for any purpose by governments, save for the provision that government may "take" a property for public use on payment of just compensation.

Epstein derives this assertion from a kind of *original position*, a scenario of the origins of society that one can compare with those of other social contract theorists—Hobbes, Locke, Rousseau, and John Rawls. Epstein's scenario is easy to understand, a trait it shares with most utopian projections. We begin with property owners, who own their property absolutely and by natural right[11] (unsupported by theological warranty), but who need collective mechanisms to accomplish certain purposes. First, they need the police power of the state both to protect them against those who would harm property and person and to collect the funds to do so. Second, they need the policy and execution powers of the state to increase the amount of property available to all the people.

By this last, the state has one (and only one) function in the economy. It is permitted to use its collective force to increase the entirety of the common wealth, to enlarge the general pie shared by the citizens (for instance, by mounting a military effort to subdue and strip a neighboring territory). For this purpose, Epstein concedes that there have to be coerced *exchanges* (taxes and other confiscations) between the state and its citizens, because citizens will not volunteer the resources that the state needs in order to do its work. But there must be no redistribution of that wealth built into the process. "The implicit normative limit upon the use of political power is that it should preserve the relative entitlements among the members of the group, both in the formation of the social order and in its ongoing operation."[12] Each citizen from whom resources have been taken for this purpose must receive in turn an amount of the enlarged commonwealth proportional to that which was taken. "Finally, the public use requirement conditions the use of the coercive power by demanding that any surplus generated by the action . . . is divided among individuals in accordance with the size of their original contributions. Each gain from public action therefore is uniquely assigned to some individual, so that none is left to the state, transcending its citizens."[13] That is the point, of course: By no action of taking private property may the state empower itself.

Epstein draws out the consequences of this understanding of the right of private property:

> In essence the entire system of governance presupposes that in a state of nature there are two, and only two, failures of the system of private rights. The first is the inability to control private aggression, to which the police power is the proper response. The second is that voluntary transactions cannot generate the centralized power needed to combat private aggression. There are transaction costs, holdout, and free-rider problems that are almost insuperable when the conduct of a large number of individuals must be organized. To this problem, the proper response is the power to force exchanges upon payment for public use.[14]

The antidote to the coercion is this very provision, that any surplus generated by the exchanges is returned to private ownership in proportion to the means taken. His conclusion, he asserts, follows John Locke's account of the essentially limited nature of government. The eminent domain solution shows how a government can be organized to overcome the twin problems of aggression and provision of public goods. As these two problems are the only ones that call forth the state, so they define the limits to which the state may direct its monopoly of force. The theory that justifies the formation of the state also demarcates the proper ends it serves.[15] According to Epstein (and his reading of Locke), by the nature of our Constitution, no matter what the circumstances, and no matter how overwhelming the public desire to do so, the people acting in concert cannot adopt any common purposes for themselves and their association beyond those he has described.

Epstein characterizes this theory of the functions and limits of the political association as "simple." Indeed it is. But what possible justification can there be for announcing that one and only one set of "natural" rights and public interests are to be held as absolute and honored by all? Can Epstein think that "nature" somehow guarantees the absolute rights of property owners to hold and to do what they like with their land, and that the community can do no other than devote its resources to the protection of that right from "private aggression"—burglars and trespassers—and to the effort to enlarge the pie the property owners share? Why so?

Property Rights: The Tradition

Epstein himself cites two authorities for his views: the seventeenth-century political philosopher John Locke and the eighteenth-century jurist Sir William Blackstone, the great codifier of the English law.

Locke. Locke's views of the origins of the right of property, found in the famous "Second Treatise,"[16] are notoriously fuzzy. He locates the beginning of property in God's creation and ownership of the world, as would any writer of his time; God then granted to humanity the right and duty to "own" the world in God's place. Humans lived for some time in a "state of nature," which Locke seems to have thought to be an actual historical state (not unlike the state of the Native Americans as the Europeans found them), in which all property was held in common—not owned by communities, but available to anyone on the basis of open access. Whence came individual, or private, property?

Here Locke departs strongly from his immediate predecessors.[17] Robert Filmer (*Patriarcha*, 1680), speaking for Tories and tradition, had argued that God granted the world not to people generally but to Adam, father of us all, and thereby to patriarchal communities modeled on the family, which in turn was modeled on God's relation to humankind; the community's tradition alone guaranteed whatever rights an individual might have in property. Thomas Hobbes (*Leviathan*, 1651) presupposed a lawless, war-torn state of nature, from which humans emerged only by handing over all natural rights—liberty first, as well as any inchoate rights to property—to a central government, a monarch, who in turn would allot private property as best served the interest of the state and guarantee the protection of property holders in his or her jurisdiction. For both writers, as for all classic conservatism since, there really are no individual rights retained into civilized society, *save as* the body politic, or the monarch, decides to protect certain individual interests as "rights" for the common good.

Locke wants above all to protect the individual right against this claim: "I shall endeavor to show, how men might come to have property in several parts of that which God gave to mankind in common, and that without any express compact of all the commoners."[18] So he starts with what is most personal and least common:

> Though the Earth, and all inferior Creatures be common to all Men, yet every Man has a Property in his own Person. This no Body has any Right to but himself. The Labour of his Body, and the Work of

his Hands, we may say, are properly his. Whatsoever then he removes out of the State that Nature hath provided, and left it in, he hath mixed his Labour with, and joyned to it something that is his own, and thereby makes it his Property.... For this Labour being the unquestionable Property of the Labourer, no Man but he can have a right to what that is once joyned to, at least where there is enough, and as good left in common for others.[19]

A difficulty arises immediately. Locke earlier argued eloquently that we are not our own, but are the property of God. Is a separate gift of self required for property in oneself?

In any case, it follows that the acorns I gather, the apples I pick, even the ore I dig, from the common wild, is now mine by right. "Thus this Law of reason makes the Deer, that Indian's who hath killed it; 'tis allowed to be his goods who hath bestowed his Labour upon it, though before, it was the common right of every one."[20] And from this foundation follows the individual's right to assign or transfer the labor of one's body, or that property acquired by labor; from this consequence in turn follows the primacy of contract and consent in establishing a government.

Filmer was not the only opponent to think Locke had things wrong; both Hugo Grotius (*De Jure Belli ac Pacis*, 1625) and Samuel Pufendorf (*De Jure Naturae*, 1672), the greatest of Locke's predecessors, asserted that the rights of private property could only come about by common consent. After all, by what warrant does the individual claim as "his" the items he has taken from the woods? Granted, there are good reasons for not challenging the Indian for the deer that is on his shoulder, as there is good reason for not challenging the wolf for the bone in his mouth. But the "right of property" is not among them.

Indeed, how did we decide that those woods were held "in common"? As Robin Hood discovered, the deer with which you have mixed your labor, killed and taken from the woods, does not become your property but lands you in jail should those woods turn out to belong to someone else. To make sense of land or goods held *in common*, we must distinguish that state from land or goods privately owned; the distinction precedes the designation. The Indian had no right to go hunting, and hence no right to his kill, except in woods designated as open to his hunting. So Locke presupposes the notion of private property, making his predecessors right. That is, until the body politic has designated that "wilderness" as there for the taking, there is no common property in which Locke's Indian may confidently go hunting. Incidentally, the tribally defended hunting grounds of the Native American were nowhere near as "common" as Locke believed, but he had no way of knowing that.

As if to emphasize that the right of private property is still subject to collective good, Locke goes on to restrict ownership to appropriate use:

"The same Law of Nature, that does by this means give us Property, does also bound that Property, too. *God has given us all things richly*, I Tim. vi.17, is the Voice of Reason confirmed by Inspiration. But how far has he given it us? To enjoy. As much as any one can make use of to any advantage of life before it spoils; so much he may by his labour fix a Property in. Whatever is beyond this, is more than his share, and belongs to others."[21] There is no suggestion here that each man is to judge his own cause as far as acquisition goes; Locke's powerful opposition to such situations elsewhere may testify that he intends the body politic to determine what shall count as "too much" for appropriate private use.

So Locke has left us with very little to ground Epstein's claims about beachfront properties. Even if property in self and labor can be shown (not clear) and can ground property in anything else (even less clear), it is still very unlikely that mixing my labor, or even mixing my hopes and dreams, with a piece of land will give me the right to develop it against the collective wisdom that it ought, for the public safety, to be left as it was—or the right to demand full payment from the public for the worth that it *would* have had if I *had* been allowed to develop it. In all these appeals to law and the wisdom of the Constitution, can Blackstone do any better?

Blackstone. Certainly part of the same tradition, Blackstone's *Commentaries*, first published in 1765, based English law squarely on the rights of person, liberty, and especially of property: "There is nothing which so generally strikes the imagination, and engages the affections of mankind, as the right of property; or that sole and despotic dominion which one man claims and exercises over the external things of the world, in total exclusion of the right of any other individual in the universe."[22]

As to the origins of rights, Blackstone is much more specific than Locke or Epstein: "In the beginning of the world, we are informed by holy writ, the all-bountiful Creator gave to man 'dominion over all the earth; and over the fish of the sea, and over the fowl of the air, and over every living thing that moveth upon the earth.' This is the only true and solid foundation of man's dominion over external things, whatever airy metaphysical notions may have been started by fanciful writers upon this subject."[23] The same bountiful Creator taught us to respect private property, that owned by individuals. "The notion of property is universal, and is suggested to the mind of man by reason and nature, prior to all positive institutions and civilized refinements. If the laws of the land were suspended, we should be under the same moral and natural obligation to refrain from invading each other's property as from attacking and assaulting each other's persons."[24]

The right to acquire individual property, taken from this common resource for all humankind, he derives in the traditional manner. At first property was in the use of a resource only; then, as communities became more crowded and disputes broke out, in the substance of the thing itself. The "improvement" of any resource by the use of one's own "bodily labour, bestowed upon any subject which before lay in common to all men, is universally allowed to give the fairest and most reasonable title to an exclusive property therein."[25] Where real property lies in the common holdings, for example, occupancy and use will establish property. (Even so, in a footnote, Blackstone rejects John Locke's claim that "mixing one's labour" with some resource is sufficient by itself to establish private property, for the reasons noted.[26])

Blackstone places the right of personal property as one of the three *absolute* rights, "inherent in every Englishman," alongside personal security and personal liberty.[27] That right "consists in the free use, enjoyment, and disposal of all his acquisitions, without any control or diminution, save only by the laws of the land."[28] Those laws forbid even the King of England to seize private land by extralegal means. On the community's seizure of private property for public purposes, say for a public road, Blackstone asserts that "the good of the community" cannot empower the community to build the road "without consent of the owner of the land." Only the legislature (as opposed to a local tribunal) can force the property owner to relinquish the land, and then with limitations:

> Not by absolutely stripping the subject of his property in an arbitrary manner; but by giving him a full indemnification and equivalent for the injury thereby sustained. The public is now considered as an individual, treating with an individual for an exchange. All that the legislature does is to oblige the owner to alienate his possessions for a reasonable price; and even this is an exertion of power, which the legislature indulges with caution and which nothing but the legislature can perform.[29]

Blackstone goes right on to extend the principle to other forms of property owned. With regard to taxation, for example, he insists that "no subject of England can be constrained to pay any aids or taxes, even for the defence of the realm or the support of government, but such as are imposed by his own consent, or that of his representatives in parliament."[30] Consent, then, makes the taking of private property legal; only with respect to the one case of the actual seizure of a piece of land does Blackstone assert the right of compensation. (Neither then nor now could a citizen successfully claim the right to be compensated for money seized for taxes.)

So Blackstone also fails to give Epstein much comfort. First, his rights derive entirely from Scriptural bases that Epstein emphatically denies. Second, while the right of individual property itself is surely protected, the legislature's right to limit the use of that property by the law of the land is unquestioned.

These two limitations are part of the same insight. Blackstone, Locke, and their contemporaries knew perfectly well that "rights" do not just appear on the earth like so many mushrooms after rain. Either the right to hold property comes from an authority strong enough to defy all the powers of the earth—God—or that right exists only at the pleasure of all those powers. There is no *tertium quid* to which we might appeal. If God made the grant, then, in a line of reasoning taken directly from Aristotle, Thomas Aquinas, and Richard Hooker, Natural Law shows us its extent and its limits. For God does nothing without clear reason: He granted to humanity not only the right to use the product of the earth, but also the individual right to hold some small part of it to the exclusion of other individuals, in order to insure the fulfillment of human nature; for the free and responsible use of privately held property is necessary to that fulfillment. The granting power also determines the limitation of the grant: Because God has no desire whatsoever to promote human selfishness or isolation, God grants the privacy of property only subject to community determinations of the common good.

But with God excluded from the story, only human guarantees allow us to assert the right of property—the strongest human in the neighborhood, who allows me to continue to use land that I call "mine" because it suits his interests at present, or the collective human that I call "government." Again, there is no third entity. We acknowledge the right of the government to establish and defend our interests as "rights" insofar as such designation serves the common good, or we assert that there is no right at all—only the fact that, being strong enough to defend what I call mine, I actually hold it and use it, and that no one has done anything about it yet. Being "strong enough" may include being clever enough to deceive my neighbors and other would-be invaders into thinking that some strong big brother will defend it for me, or rich and influential enough to persuade the legislative and executive branches of a democratic government to make laws in my favor, and further to appoint judges who will defend that right, should it come up in court.

So property rights without God really do rest on uncertainty—while a friendly administration is in, I do what I like with my property, and when the unfriendlies take over, they stop me. That is exactly the sort of uncertainty that Locke and Blackstone tried to end, which is why they make such poor grounds for Epstein's claims.

What makes private property a firm and defensible Constitutional right? The Constitution alone, and the people of the United States who have accepted it in the past and continue with it for the present (it can, of course, be changed). And what makes it superior to the law of the land? Nothing whatsoever. Legislation to protect land, water, and air from human inhabitants who might degrade it is the quintessential activity of the police power of the state, acting to restrain private activities for the common good in the long run. On no theory of law ever hallowed by our tradition or accepted by this nation is there a right to damage land for your own profit or hold the land hostage until the state pays you its full value. Epstein and, to the extent that he relies on Epstein, Scalia, are making things up.

RON ARNOLD'S AGENDA

Law and politics may be in fantasyland when they begin their reasoning from some absolute right of private land or (as we shall see) private *rights* to public land. But fantasyland is not an unpleasant place to live, and surely if someone can make money by keeping people there, the hotels will go up immediately.

Antienvironmentalism

The latest antienvironmentalism—the backlash supposedly triggered by the burdensome environmental regulations of the last two decades— works at building such hotels. The interests behind this new movement are themselves old, and well known: property owners who object to environmental restrictions that limit the uses of their property and reduce its value in sale; industries (timber and extraction) that have depended on the virtually unrestricted use of natural resources for profit; recreational and other users of natural areas (for instance, the operators of off-road recreational vehicles) who are prohibited from certain activities deemed to destroy the environment. But they have never before made common cause, and they have never been activists or collective interventionists. All that has changed.

Antienvironmentalist activism may have had its start in a series of articles written in 1979 for *Logging Management* by Ron Arnold, in which he called for an activist alliance to oppose the environmental movement in all its forms.[31] It was organized by Alan Gottlieb of the state of Washington, who had made his fortune as a direct-mail fundraiser for conservative politicians and causes (one of his creations was the Citizens Committee for the Right to Keep and Bear Arms). After a year in prison for tax evasion in 1984, Gottlieb was ready for a new right-wing cause to keep his mailing list together and came up with the Center for the Defense of Free Enterprise (CDFE). Joining him as executive vice president, Ron Arnold promoted his antienvironmentalist crusade as the "Wise Use Movement," the phrase *wise use* borrowed without permission from Gifford Pinchot, Teddy Roosevelt's chief of the U.S. Forest Service. Gottlieb and Arnold were in turn joined by Charles Cushman, the executive director of the National Inholders Association (an *inholder* owns a plot of private land in the middle of a federal park or other reservation). Together with other like-minded associations, the CDFE battles environmental regulation, seeks concessions for private industry on public land, and above all carries on ideological campaigns against any efforts to preserve the environment.

Wise Use Movement

The constellation of allies in the Wise Use movement is instructive. It ranges from the Wilderness Impact Research Foundation—founded in 1986 by Grant Gerber, a Nevada attorney, as a Christian organization dedicated to the defeat of "pagan" environmental movements—to the Blue Ribbon Coalition of Idaho, an alliance of 200 dirt-bike and snowmobile clubs that want public lands opened up for their sport. Their approach to the woods is summed up by Henry Yake, a past president of the Blue Ribbon Coalition, as cited by Thomas Lewis in a 1992 exposé in *National Wildlife*: "Wilderness has no economic value."[32] Legal action is being explored by the Mountain States Legal Foundation, led by William Perry Pendley—a holdover from the 1970s Sagebrush Rebellion, which tried to get all federal lands transferred to states or private parties. Charles Cushman heads the Multiple Use Land Alliance, dedicated to opening up federal lands for mining and lumbering. The People for the West (PFW), one of the largest of these groups, recruits most of its membership from the rural Western states, capitalizing on unemployment (actual or feared) and resentment of central government "interference" in individual lives. All in all, there are between 400 and 500 organizations in the Wise Use movement, and they tend to be angry and apocalyptic, casting their war as a cosmic struggle of Good against Evil.[33]

The sponsors of the Wise Use movement, who supply the money for literature, mailings, and the many conferences, are also worthy of note. One of the more interesting participants is the Reverend Sun Myung Moon's Unification Church, connected to Wise Use through the American Freedom Coalition (AFC), which sponsors the conferences. The AFC was organized in 1987 by Colonel Bo Hi Pak, a ranking associate of the Reverend Moon for United States activities, and the fundamentalist Gary Jarmin as the basis for a third political party through which Moon's political agenda might be funneled. Arnold served as president of the Washington State AFC in 1989 and 1990 and a registered agent for Moon in 1989. A Washington State AFC director in 1989, Gottlieb owns the office building where that organization has its headquarters.[34]

The Unification Church is not the only source of money. The Western States Public Lands Coalition (WSPLC), an association of mining companies set up in 1988, was incorporated to establish "a permanent coalition between industry and local government officials in the western U. S. to protect their mutual interests, ensuring that timber, grazing, ranching, oil and gas, and mining activities continue on public lands."[35] That "continuation" would be of the 1872 Mining Law, which gives mining companies right over all other uses on public lands and demands no royalties of them—an enormously profitable deal. Realizing that political allies were essential to keep the law so solidly in their interests, the WSPLC spun off the PFW in the next year. The "grassroots" following of the PFW was then collected by an extensive and expensive mailing campaign, funded by $1.7 million from the mining industry—"peanuts," according to Jim Jensen of the Montana Environmental Information Center, "by comparison to what they should be paying and will be paying [for use of the land] when the law changes."[36] A list of the directors of the WSPLC shows corporate executives of ten mining companies, with corporate contributions yearly of well over $350,000. That is a tidy war chest for spreading a message.

And spread it they do, by all the traditional means. for instance, "An op-ed article about PFW in a Santa Fe newspaper, *The New Mexican*, appeared to be a heartfelt piece by local Pecos PFW organizer Hugh Ley. But on investigation it turned out to be a press release from Pueblo headquarters."[37] What is traditional is the cloaking of right-wing causes in grassroots garb, funded by the major corporations of affected industries, that push their agendas. What is new in all this is the antienvironmental message. We find other examples of this technique listed in the *National Wildlife* article. For example, the "Information Council on the Environment (ICE)" argued that the average temperature in Minnesota was falling and that therefore "global warming" was not to be feared. When people learned that ICE was created and funded by coal and utility companies and that the average temperature in Minnesota was rising, ICE "melted away." Then there is the Marine Preservation Association, 15 oil companies dedicated to "promote the welfare and interests of the petroleum and energy industries"; the National Wetlands Coalition, sponsored by oil and gas companies and developers, whose purpose is to remove restrictions on wetlands use; the Environmental Conservation Association with the same agenda; the Endangered Species Reform Coalition, sponsored by utility companies and others in an effort to weaken the Endangered Species Act—and the list continues.[38] If you received a mailing from one of those organizations, featuring only the organization's name and a typical logo such as ducks flying over marshes, would you assume that its agenda *opposed* environmental protection?

Wise Use got its start in Reno, Nevada, when about 200 organizations came together in conference in August of 1988 to establish a plan of action. The papers from that conference were published by the Free Enterprise Press in 1989 as *The Wise Use Agenda*. Items from that agenda include positions on issues we have seen before in this book: immediate petroleum development, for instance, in the Arctic National Wildlife Refuge; the cutting of all old growth on national forest land;

rewriting of the Endangered Species Act to remove protection for "non-adaptive" species—and, something new, "civil penalties against anyone who legally challenges 'economic action or development on federal lands.'"[39] Because the WSPLC is a nonprofit 501(c) (6) tax-exempt corporation, entitling the organization to lobby for favorable legislation, the entire agenda is being taken to the Congress for enactment.

Even so, the major campaign for several years has been directed at the Constitution and the Supreme Court. Above all, what Wise Use has wanted is a ruling that any government regulation that reduces the value of property constitutes a "taking" and requires compensation. Since the value of any property is arguably reduced if the uses to which it may be put are reduced, and since every environmental regulation does that, such a ruling would require taxpayers to *pay* every property owner affected by a federal environmental law for him or her to obey. The opinion in *Lucas*, of course, does exactly that. The main court precedents fall against the ruling (see, for example, *Hudson Water Company* v. *McCarter*, 1907). Municipal zoning regulations have always been upheld as entirely legal. If *Lucas* stands and is extended, however, we may end up fighting even for such zoning. With the present composition of the Court, nothing seems safe.

CONCLUSION

Lucas is, as we have seen, unsupported by theory or tradition, and such decisions tend to be evanescent. "Wise Use," a conglomeration of cynical attempts to deceive the nation into permitting some very rich mining and lumbering interests to continue making vast profits at the expense of the taxpayer, seems a good candidate for exposure and dismissal. But political moods and swings can never be discounted when the environment is in question. If on the strength of this decision, Lucas builds his beach houses on one of the tiny fragments of salt marsh remaining on the East Coast, that marsh is gone for good, and later decisions reversing *Lucas* can do nothing to restore it. Where the environment is concerned, the most abstract theory turns not only to practice, but to irreversible practice, all too quickly. (See the Epilogue for further discussion.) Americans have been slow to recognize a duty to inform themselves on very abstract matters of political theory, law, and philosophy; yet as this case shows, there is no limiting where theory will lead us.

QUESTIONS FOR DISCUSSION AND REFLECTION

+ Where did our "right of private property" originate? What was the original purpose of such sentiments as "A man's home is his castle"?

+ Considering the problems arising from it, should private property in land be abolished?

+ Is there any formula for adjudicating the rights of the public and the private property owner when there is such egregious conflict as found in *Lucas*?

Notes

1. *Lucas v. South Carolina Coastal Council* No.91-453 (U.S. June 29, 1992) 22 *Environmental Law Reporter* 21104. Unless otherwise indicated, this section will be drawn in its entirety from that case.

2. That last phrase, to which emphasis is added by Scalia, is found in several cases: *Keystone Bituminous Coal Assn. v. DeBenedictis* (480 U.S. 470, 495 [1987]) uses it, citing *Hodel v. Virginia Surface Mining & Reclamation Assn., Inc* (452 U.S. 264, 295-296 [1981]), which in turn takes it from *Agins v. Tiburon* (447 U.S. 255, 260 [1980]).

3. *San Diego Gas & Electric Co. v. San Diego*, 450 U.S. at 652 (Brennan, J., dissenting), cited in *Lucas* at ELR 21108.

4. 123 U.S. 623 (1887).

5. J. Holmes in *Mahon*, op.cit. at 413.

6. *Lucas*, 22ELR 21111.

7. *Webb's Fabulous Pharmacies, Inc. v. Beckwith*, 449 U.S. 155, 164 (1980).

8. *Lucas v. South Carolina Coastal Council* (Blackmun, J., dissenting).

9. *Id.*; Kennedy, J., concurring, *inter alia*.

10. Richard Epstein, "Takings: Descent and Resurrection," 1987 *Sup. Ct. Rev.* 1, 4.

11. Epstein, "Takings" pp. 5–6. In his words,

> The political tradition in which I operate, and to which the takings clause itself is bound, rests upon a theory of "natural rights." That theory does not presuppose the divine origin of personal rights and is consistent, I believe, with both libertarian and utilitarian justifications of individual rights, which, properly understood, tend to converge in most important cases. Whatever their differences, at the core all theories of natural rights reject the idea that private property and personal liberty are solely creations of the state, which itself is only other people given extraordinary powers. Quite the opposite, a natural rights theory asserts that the end of the state is to protect liberty and property, as these conceptions are understood independent of and prior to the formation of the state. No rights are justified in a normative way simply because the state chooses to protect them, as a matter of grace.... At each critical juncture, therefore, independent rules, typically the rules of acquisition, protection, and disposition, specify how property is acquired and what rights its acquisition entails. None of these rules rests entitlements on the state, which only enforces the rights and obligations generated by theories of private entitlement.

12. Richard Epstein, *Takings* (Cambridge: Harvard University Press, 1985): p. 4.

13. Epstein, *Takings*, p. 5.

14. Ibid.

15. Ibid.

16. John Locke, *Two Treatises of Government*, ed. Peter Laslett (New York: Cambridge Press, 1963).

17. The discussion of Locke and his predecessors is abbreviated from Peter Laslett's "Introduction" to Locke, *Two Treatises*.

18. Locke, *Two Treatises*, Second Treatise, Chapter V (25): p. 327.

19. Ibid., Chapter V (27): pp. 328–329.

20. Ibid., Chapter V (30): p. 331.

21. Ibid., Chapter V (31): p. 332.

22. Sir William Blackstone, *Commentaries on the Laws of England: Volume 2: Of the Rights of Things*, ed. Chitty et al. (Philadelphia: Lippincott, 1856): Chapter 1, p. 1, par. 2.

23. Ibid., par. 3.

24. Ibid., p. 7, n. 3.

25. Ibid., p. 7, par. 5.

26. Ibid., p. 5; note 1; commenting on Locke, *On Government*, Chapter 5.

27. This privileged placement does not mean that the law will not take property from its owner: There are a variety of public crimes, including "Popish recusancy," conviction for which entails forfeiture of property to the Crown, or which carry with them "corruption of blood," making it impossible to pass property on to others. Ibid., pp. 203, 212.

28. Sir William Blackstone, *Commentaries on the Laws of England: Volume 1*, ed. Chitty, et al. (Philadelphia: Lippincott, 1856): p. 100.

29. Ibid., pp. 100–101.

30. Ibid.

31. Kate O'Callaghan, "Whose Agenda for America?" *Audubon* (Sept./Oct. 1992): pp. 80–91.

32. Thomas A. Lewis, "Cloaked in a Wise Disguise," *National Wildlife* (Oct./Nov. 1992): pp. 4–9.

33. Ibid., p. 7.

34. O'Callaghan, "Whose Agenda for America?" p. 87.

35. Ibid.

36. Ibid., p. 88.

37. Ibid., p. 89.

38. Thomas A. Lewis, "You Can't Judge a Group by Its Cover," *National Wildlife* (Oct./Nov. 1992): p. 9.

39. O'Callaghan, "Whose Agenda for America?" p. 90.

Suggestions for Further Reading:

Epstein, Richard. *Takings*. Cambridge, MA: Harvard University Press, 1985.

Locke, John. *Two Treatises of Government*. Introduced and edited by Peter Laslett. New York: Cambridge Press, 1963.

Toward the Millennium

It is 1996. In four years we will begin the third millennium of our times, and as we write, the environment is in graver danger than it has been for a long while—since 1970, and the first Earth Day. These times test whether the general interest in the protection of the natural environment can be treated as just another political interest, subject to trends, swings, and trade-offs. Since the first edition of *Watersheds* came out a few years ago, the political process has worked the way it should, by all political science textbook accounts: After a trendy swing toward environmental protection in the 1970s and 1980s—including an excellent book on the environment by a future vice president of the United States—the pendulum took an equally trendy swing in the other direction, against all government regulation in general and environmental protection in particular. It's like labor versus management: When the Democrats are in power, things go labor's way, and then when the pendulum swings back and the Republicans get in again, things go management's way for awhile. And then, things can turn back. It's all very American, all OK, according to the books. But every environmental law we have has been gutted or is about to be—if the current Congressional majority has their way. What on earth—or off it—will the next millennium be like if this trend continues?

The problem, of course, is that the natural environment that sustains us does not follow these pendulum swings. When you cut down during one administration the great forests of the northwestern United States, including trees dating from the beginning of the millennium just ending, you cannot put them back in the next. You need another millennium for that, and none of us are sure we have that time. Oil pumped, shipped, spilled, burned, and wasted in one administration cannot be replaced in the next; four or five of these millennia are needed to replace the oil, and the damage that the spills, fumes, and wastage may have caused may never be repaired. If fishers want to fish, and conservationists want to conserve, you cannot split the difference year after year; soon the fish are so few, and so displaced by other species, that they cannot recover even if you stop the fishing altogether. The political notion of "compromise" simply does not apply when irreversible changes to the world are in question. We need not the normal, Madisonian, workings of faction and the political process, but a universal education in environmental value that can sustain an effort at environmental protection through adverse administrations through the next century, indeed through the whole of the coming millennium.

In *Watersheds,* the epilogue signaled a warning to watch out for threats from odd quarters—quarters that we felt were sufficiently marginal to be worth only a passing mention, to require only the ritual planting of a red flag, to remind our readers to view these things with appropriate alarm. Among these threats were Earth First!, an unlovable but inconsequential group of misguided environmentalists who occasionally engaged in dramatic action to protect natural values and who occasionally defended (but rarely engaged in) violence as a tool of political action. We have not heard from these activists lately; probably, as foreseen, they have disappeared. Another threat was *ecotage*, the destruction of the environment for political purposes; we cited the firing of the Kuwaiti wells by Saddam Hussein at the end of the Gulf War in 1991 as an example. The wells were extinguished in six months, oil production is now normal, and no such threat has materialized since. But one set of threats, which we took to be so transparently cynical and greedy as to lack any staying power in America, we have had to bring to chapter status—see Chapter 10. "Wise Use" has taken root and unwisely been allowed to grow; that lack of wisdom deserves a final word.

It is commonplace that corruption by money is a constant danger in the U.S. political system. Money buys airtime, publishes and distributes political advertisements, and through its control of court processes and access to legal help, can make it very difficult to fight lies with truth. So we make sporadic efforts at "campaign reform," trying to limit the amount of money that flows into the political process. These efforts are not generally effective: In the effort to balance the twin values of individual freedom (to support anyone or any cause with all available resources) and the common good (which would restrict that freedom in order to present the public with an informed and balanced account of political issues), freedom generally wins. The democratic system assumes that wealthy parties will pour money into efforts to persuade the public to support legislation favorable to their economic interests, and then hopes that the voters will have enough sense to resist them. An educated public is expected to have the type of discernment possessed by the body's immune system when it is working properly: Knowing where the money to fund the campaign is coming from, we selectively discount its messages. As a people, we accept the danger of corruption rather than restrict freedom of communication.

That all-American approach to political causes is fatally flawed in the environmental area. For causes draw their support by tapping deep veins of beloved and traditional values in the American political tradition, while environmentalism has only unpleasant nontraditional positions to defend. So the "Wise Use" campaign—funded entirely by mining, grazing, and lumbering interests—appeals to individual liberty, Western individualism, and resistance to any form of regulation (all traditional values), while the environmentalists have nothing to offer but restraint, prudence, limit, and forbearance. As Plato pointed out, in any trial where the jury are small children, the pastry-cook will defeat the physician every time.

The fact that unrestricted exploitation of environmental resources will surely place terrible limits on the life of everyone within a few decades cannot come to light without an educational campaign of unequaled power—one that can make long-term consequences and interests as vivid as tomorrow, and can place the value of the natural environment in strong contrast to the effects of exploitation. That campaign must trace the origin of the funds for the antienvironment movement and put in easily understandable terms the political arrangements by which certain economic interests (very few of them American!) strip Western resources at no cost to themselves and at infinite cost to the taxpayer. We have no such campaign; we cannot afford one. What we have is the policy of unlimited exploitation, at taxpayer's expense, kept in place by legislators whose independence from those economic interests is in grave doubt.

As we write, the latest polls suggest that the level of willingness to protect the environment remains high among the American people. The legislatures, listening to different drummers, are not aware of this fact or choose to ignore it. Sometime before the millennium, we must return to the American people the ability to communicate their real opinions and make them heard in the centers of power; there is no other way to save their inheritance in nature.

Bibliography

Chapter 1 Dirty Bombs: The Legacy of War

Ackland, Len. "A Dump Called Rocky Flats," *Bulletin of Atomic Scientists* (Nov./Dec. 1994).

Ahearne, John F. "Fixing the Nation's Nuclear Weapons Plants," *Technology Review* (July 1989): p. 24–35.

——."The Future of Nuclear Power," *American Scientist* (Jan./Feb. 1993).

Albright, David. "Chernobyl and the U.S. Nuclear Industry," *Bulletin of the Atomic Scientists* (November 1986): pp. 38–40.

American Medical Association. "Health Evaluation of Energy-Generating Sources." AMA Council of Scientific Affairs (10 November 1978).

Bailey, Steve. "Saying So Long to Uncle Sam: Veteran Cold War Contractor E G & G Marches into the Commercial Market After Turning Its Back on the Energy Department." *Boston Globe* (11 September 1994): Business Section, p. AB5.

Barringer, Felicity. "Chernobyl: Five Years Later, the Danger Persists." *The New York Times Magazine* (14 April 1991): pp. 28–39, 74.

Bloomfield, Lincoln P. "Nuclear Crisis and Human Frailty." *Bulletin for the Atomic Scientists* (October 1985): pp. 26 ff.

Burdick, Alan. "The Last Cold War Monument: Designing the `Keep-Out' Sign for a Nuclear Waste Site." *Harpers Magazine* (August 1992): pp. 62–67.

Cushman, John H., Jr., "U.S. Pays More Than Industry for Atomic Cleanup." *New York Times* (30 November 1993): p. A30.

D'Anastasio, Mark, with Miller, Frederic, Heard, Joyce, Javetski, Bill, and Holstein, William. "The Soviets End Their Silence—But the Damage Keeps Mounting." *Business Week* (19 May 1986): pp. 44–46.

Dickman, Stephen. "IAEA's Verdict on Chernobyl." *Nature Magazine* (26 May 1988): p. 285.

"DOE Picks up Court Cost Tab for Rockwell." *Denver Post* (20 September 1993).

Dold, Catherine. "From the Twentieth Century, with Love." *Discover* (October 1992): pp. 22–23.

Editorial. "Let's Hear the Rocky Flats Jurors." *New York Times* (1 November 1993).

Edwards, Mike. "Chernobyl: One Year After." *National Geographic* (April 1987): pp. 632–653.

Ehrlich, Paul, et al. *Ecoscience: Population, Resources, Environment.* San Francisco: Freeman, 1977.

Fialka, John J., and Cohen, Roger. "Chernobyl Fallout: Nuclear-Plant Projects in Nations Like Brazil Falter After Accident." *Wall Street Journal.*" (5 June 1986): p. A1.

Flavin, Christopher. "Nuclear Power's Burdened Future." *Bulletin of the Atomic Scientists* (July/Aug. 1987): pp. 26–31.

———. *Reassessing Nuclear Power: The Fallout from Chernobyl.* Worldwatch Paper No. 75. Washington, DC: Worldwatch Institute, 1981.

———. "Reassessing Nuclear Power." In *State of the World 1987.* Washington, DC: Worldwatch Institute, 1987.

Grossman, Karl. "Environmental Racism." In *People, Penguins and Plastic Trees.* Belmont, CA: Wadsworth, 1995.

Jagger, John. *The Nuclear Lion: What Every Citizen Should Know About Nuclear Power and Nuclear War.* New York: Plenum Press, 1991.

Kerwin, Katie. "Rocky Flats Contractor Gets Second Bad Review." *Rocky Mountain News* (3 April 1994).

Kidder, Rushworth. "Ethics: A Matter of Survival." *Futurist* (Mar.-Apr. 1992): pp. 10–12.

Kolata, Gina. "A Cancer Legacy from Chernobyl." *New York Times* (3 September 1992): p. A9.

Lawler, Anthony. "As O'Leary Struggles to Preserve Energy Department." *Science* (19 May 1995): p. 965.

Lenssen, Nicholas. *Nuclear Waste: The Problem That Won't Go Away.* Worldwatch Paper No. 106, Washington, DC: Worldwatch Institute, 1991.

Levin, S. K. "Who'll Pay for a U.S. Chernobyl?" *The Nation* (14 June 1986): pp. 815–818.

Lilienthal, David E. *Atomic Energy: A New Start.* New York: Harper & Row, 1980.

Lockwood, Robert P. "More Heat at Chernobyl." *TIME* (9 May 1988): p. 59.

Lowrance, William. *Of Acceptable Risk: Science and the Determination of Safety.* Los Altos, CA: William Kaufmann, 1976.

Makhijani, Arjun. "Always the Target?" *Bulletin of Atomic Scientists* (May/June 1995): p. 23.

Medvedev, Grigori. *The Truth About Chernobyl.* Translated by Evelyn Rossiter. New York: Basic Books, 1991. Originally published in 1989.

Mortimer, Nigel. "Nuclear Power and Carbon Dioxide: The Fallacy of the Nuclear Industry's New Propaganda." *The Ecologist,* vol. 21, no. 3 (May/June 1991): pp. 129–133.

Munson, Richard. *The Power Maker.* Emmaus, PA: Rodale Press, 1985.

Murphy, Pamela. "Coming Clean." *The National Voter* (4 March 1994): p. 14.

Myers, Nancy. "Coping with Chernobyl." *Bulletin of the Atomic Scientists* (September 1992): pp. 8–9.

Nader, Ralph, and Abbotts, John. *The Menace of Atomic Energy.* New York: Norton, 1977.

Patterson, Walter C. "Chernobyl–The Official Story." *Bulletin of the Atomic Scientists* (November 1986): pp. 34–36.

Powers, Thomas. "Chernobyl as a Paradigm of a Faustian Bargain." *Discover* (June 1986): pp. 33-35.

Raloff, Janet. "Source Terms: The New Reactor Safety Debate." *Science News,* vol. 127: pp. 250–253.

Rippon, Simon, et al. "The Chernobyl Accident." *Nuclear News* (June 1986): pp. 87–94.

Rothstein, Linda. "Nothing Clean About the Clean-Up." *Bulletin of the Atomic Scientists* (May/June 1995).

Schemann, Serge. "Soviet, Reporting Atom Plant 'Disaster,' Seeks Help Abroad to Fight Reactor Fire." *New York Times* (30 April 1986): p. A1. Supplemental articles by Harold M. Schmeck Jr., Philip M. Boffey, John Tagliabue, Michael Kaufman, Philip Taubman, Steve Lohr, Matthew Wald, Irvin Molotsky, Lee Daniels, and Theodore Shabad, same issue, A1 and continuing on pages A10, A11, and A12.

Schemann, Serge. "Chernobyl and the Europeans: Radiation and Doubts Linger." *New York Times* (12 June 1988): p. A1.

———."Chernobyl Fallout: An Apocalyptic Tale of Fear and Power." *New York Times* (26 July 1986).

———."Soviet Ratifies Nuclear Accident Conventions," *New York Times* (16 November 1986): p. A 19.

Schneider, Keith. "U.S. Takes Blame in Atom Plant Abuses." *New York Times* (2 November 1993): p. A12.

Schneider, Keith. "Wasting Away." *The New York Times Magazine* (30 August 1992): p. 45.

Schulman, Seth. *The Threat at Home: Confronting the Toxic Legacy of the U.S. Military.* Boston: Beacon Press, 1992.

Serrill, Michael. "Anatomy of a Catastrophe." *TIME* (1 September 1986).

Shenon, Philip. "Atomic Cleanup Is Seen Costing U.S. $92 Billion; Some Say Energy Department Still Underestimates." *New York Times* (5 January 1989): p. A16.

Starr, Barbara, and Hoppe, Richard. "Battling the Backlash Against Nuclear Energy." *Business Week* (19 May 1986): p. 46.

Thompson, Gordon. "What Happened at Reactor Four." *Bulletin of the Atomic Scientists* (Aug./Sept. 1986): pp. 26–31.

United States Department of Energy, Office of Environmental Management. *Closing the Circle on the Splitting of the Atom.* January 1995.

Wald, Matthew L. "At an Atomic Waste Site, the Only Sure Thing Is Peril." *New York Times* (21 June 1993): p. A1.

———."Bomb Plant Draws More Fire." *New York Times* (2 November 1993): p. A18.

———."Hazards at Nuclear Plant Fester Eight Years After Warnings: Little Has Been Done to Ease Fears of Catatrosphic Explosions." *New York Times* (24 December 1992): p. A 11.

———."Justice Department Called Too Lenient in Bomb Plant Case." *New York Times* (5 January 1993).

———."Manager of No. 1 Nuclear Site Is Rebuked by U.S." *New York Times* (9 December 1993).

———."New Disclosure over Bomb Plant." *New York Times* (22 November 1992).

———."Uranium Leak at Tennessee Laboratory Brings Fears of an Accidental Chain Reaction." *New York Times* (25 November 1994): p. A 18.

———."Uranium Rusting in Storage Pools Is Troubling U.S." *New York Times* (8 December 1993): p. A1.

———."Worker Peril Seen in Waste Clean-up." *New York Times* (10 March 1993).

Weaver, Kenneth F. "The Promise and Peril of Nuclear Energy." *National Geographic,* vol. 155, no. 4 (April 1979): p.459–493

Weinberg, Alvin M. "A Nuclear Power Advocate Reflects on Chernobyl." *Bulletin of the Atomic Scientists* (Aug./Sept. 1986): pp. 57–60.

World Resources Institute. *Information Please Environmental Almanac 1993.* New York: Houghton Mifflin, 1993.

Wyden, Peter. *Day One Before Hiroshima and After.* New York: Simon & Schuster, 1984.

Wynne, Brian. "Sheepfarming After Chernobyl." *Environment,* vol. 31, no. 2: pp. 11–15, 33.

Chapter 2 Too Much of a Good Thing:
The Population Problem

Abernethy, Virginia. "Second Opinion: Optimism and Overpopulation." *Atlantic Monthly* (December 1994).

Begley, Sharon. "Can More = Better?" *Newsweek* (12 September 1994).

Bray, Francesca. "Agriculture for Developing Nations." *Scientific American* (July 1994): pp. 30–37.

Brown, Lester. "Averting a Global Food Crisis." *Technology Review* (Nov./Dec. 1995): pp. 44–53.

Bruntland, Gro Harlem. "Empowering Women." Edited version of the address to the U.N. Cairo Conference on Women's Environment, December 1994.

Cen, Lincoln C., Fitzgerald, Winifred, and Bates, Lisa. "Women, Politics and Global Management." *Environment* (Jan./Feb. 1995).

Cohen, Joel E. "Population Growth and Earth's Human Carrying Capacity." *Science* (21 July 1995): p.341.

Connelly, Matthew, and Kennedy, Paul. "Must It Be the Rest Against the West?" *Atlantic Monthly* (December 1994.): pp. 61–91.

Crossette, Barbara. "U.S. Aid Cutbacks Endangering Population Programs, UN Agencies Say." *New York Times* (16 February 1996): p. A14.

Donahue, Brian. "Putting Population in Perspective." *Friends of the Earth* (Sept./Oct. 1994): p. 7.

Easterbrook, Greg. *A Moment on Earth*. New York: Viking, 1995.

Editorial. "Birthrates and Earth's Fate." *Boston Sunday Globe* (10 July 1994).

Ehrlich, Paul. *The Population Bomb*. New York: Ballantine Books, 1971.

Ehrlich, Paul R., and Ehrlich, Anne H. *The Population Explosion*. New York: Simon & Schuster, 1990.

Ehrlich, Paul R., and Ehrlich, Anne H. *Healing the Planet*. New York: Addison-Wesley, 1991.

Feeney, Griffith. "Fertility Decline in East Asia." *Science* (2 December 1994): p. 1518.

Hill, Bobbie, et al. "A Beijing Diary." *National Voter* (Dec./Jan. 1996): p. 11.

"How Much for How Many?" *Environmental Action* (Summer 1994).

Kaplan, Robert D. "The Coming Anarchy." *Atlantic Monthly* (February 1994): pp. 44–76.

Keller, Bill. "Zimbabwe Taking a Lead in Promoting Birth Control." *New York Times* (4 September 1994). From *Managing Planet Earth: Readings from Scientific American Magazine*. New York: Freeman, 1970.

Keyfitz, Nathan. "The Growing Human Population." *Scientific American* (September 1989.

LeGuenno, Bernard. "Emerging Viruses." *Scientific American* (October 1995): p. 56.

Limbaugh, Rush. *See I Told You So*. New York: Pocket Books, 1993.

McKinley, James C., Jr., "Anguish of Rwanda Echoed in a Baby's Cry." *New York Times* (21 February 1996): p. A1.

Mitchell, George, Jr., *World on Fire*. New York: Scribner, 1991.

"Our Earth, Ourselves: Population, Consumption and the Planet." *The Amicus Journal* (Winter 1994).

Planning the Global Family. Worldwatch Paper No. 80. Washington, DC: Worldwatch Institute, December 1987.

Population Institute. "Overpopulation Is Escalating Poverty." *Popline* (Mar./Apr. 1995).

Robey, Bryant, et. al., "The Fertility Decline in Developing Countries." *Scientific American* (December 1993): p. 60.

Sen, Gita. "The World Programme of Action: A New Paradigm for Population Policy." *Environment* (Jan./Feb. 1995): p. 10.

Tyler, Patrick E. "Hilary Clinton in China, Details Abuse of Women." *New York Times* (6 September 1996): p. A1.

World Population Data Sheet. Washington, DC: Population Reference Bureau, 1995.

Worldwatch Institute. *State of the World 1995*. New York: Norton 1995.

Chapter 3 Poisons and Public Accountability: Bhopal and Responsible Care

Abelson, P. H. "Chemicals from Waste Dumps." *Science* (26 July 1985): p. 335.
———."Treatment of Hazardous Waste." *Science* (1 August 1986): p. 509.

Anderson, Warren M. (Former Chairman, Union Carbide Corporation). "Bhopal: What We Learned" [UCC Document #158]. Distributed by Union Carbide Corporation, Danbury, Connecticut 06817-0001.

Beauchamp, Tom. "Love Canal." In *Case Studies in Business, Society, and Ethics.* Englewood Cliffs, N.J: Prentice-Hall, 1983.

Blumenthal, Ralph. "Fight to Curb `Love Canals.'" *New York Times* (30 June 1980): pp. B1, 11.

Brown, Michael. "Laying Waste: The Poisoning of America by Toxic Chemicals." New York: Parthenon, 1980.

Brown, Michael H. "A Toxic Ghost Town Harbinger of America's Toxic Waste Crisis." *The Atlantic,* vol. 263, no. 1 (July 1989).

Canadian Chemical Producers Association (Ottawa). "Responsible Care." In "Declaring Commitment," Speeches in Responsible Care. 1993.

Carson, Rachel. *Silent Spring.* Boston: Houghton-Mifflin, 1962.

Cathcart, Christopher. "CAER Means Educating Communities." *CMA NEWS* (April 1985).

Cavanaugh, Gerard F., and McGovern, Arthur F. *Ethical Dilemmas in the Modern Corporation.* Englewood Cliffs, N.J: Prentice-Hall, 1988.

Chemical and Engineering News (29 May 1995): Whole issue on Responsible Care.

Chemical Manufacturers' Association. *Bhopal: The Industry Stands Together, Communicates, Prepares Action Plan.* Special Report, 1985.

————. *Responsible Care: A Public Commitment.* Available from Chemical Manufacturers' Association, Washington, DC.

ChemicalWeek (6 and 13 July 1994). Special Double Issue on Responsible Care.

"Clean Up Old Hazardous Waste Dumps to Allay Public Fear, Simeral Urges." *CMA News* (Summer 1983): pp. 6–8.

Cook, J. "Risky Business." *Forbes* (2 December 1985).

Cox, Hank. "Love Canal Special Supplement." *Regulatory Action Network: Washington Watch* (September 1980).

De Grazia, Alfred. *A Cloud over Bhopal.* Bombay, India: Kalos Foundation, 1985. (Kalos Foundation for the India-America Committee for the Bhopal Victims, 55 Mamta-A, Appasaheb Marathe Marg, Prabhadevi, Bombay 400 025 India.)

Ehrlich, Paul, et al. *Ecoscience: Population, Resources, Environment.* San Francisco: Freeman, 1977.

Epstein, Samuel. *Hazardous Waste in America.* San Francisco: Sierra Club, 1982.

Fazal, Anwar. Foreword to *The Bhopal Syndrome: Pesticides, Environment and Health,* by David Weir. San Francisco: Sierra Club Books, 1987.

Gibbs, Lois Marie. *Love Canal: My Story.* Albany: State University of New York Press, 1982.

Griffin, M. "The Legacy of Love Canal." *Sierra* (Jan./Feb. 1988) pp. 26-27.

Hammer, J. "The Big Haul in Toxic Waste." *Newsweek,* vol. 112 (3 October 1988): pp. 38–39.

Hazarika, Sanjoy. "Settlement Slow in India Gas Disaster Claim." *New York Times* (25 March 1993).

Hevesi, Dennis. "Chronology of Events: Love Canal." *New York Times* (28 September 1988): p. B 1.

Hirschhorn, J. S. "Cutting Production of Hazardous Waste." *Technology Review* (April 1988): pp. 52–61.

"India's Tragedy: A Warning Heard Round the World." *U.S. News and World Report* (17 December 1984): p. 2.

Kadlecek, M. "Love Canal—Ten Years Later." *The Conservationist,* vol. 43 (Nov./Dec. 1988): pp. 40–43.

Kalelkar, Ashok S. "Investigation of Large-Magnitude Incidents: Bhopal as a Case Study." Presented at The Institution of Chemical Engineers Conference on Preventing Major Chemical Accidents, London, England, May 1988.

Klinkenborg, Verlyn. "Back to Love Canal." *Harpers* (March 1991).

Kurzman, Dan. *A Killing Wind: Inside Union Carbide and the Bhopal Catastrophe.* New York: McGraw-Hill, 1987.

Lavoise, Denise. "Bhopal Still Haunts Former Carbide Chief." *Hartford Courant* (5 April 1992): pp. D1, D7.

Leonard, B. "Cleaning Up." *Forbes* (1 June 1987): pp. 52–53.

Levine, Adeline Gordon. *Love Canal: Science, Politics, and People.* Lexington, MA: Lexington Books, 1982.

Marbach, W. D. "What to Do with Our Waste." *Newsweek* (27 July 1987): pp. 51–52.

Mehta, Pushpa S., et al. "Bhopal Tragedy's Health Effects: A Review of Methyl Isocyanate Toxicity." *Journal of the American Medical Association,* vol. 264, no. 21 (5 December 1990): p. 2781.

Mukerjee, Madhusree, "Persistently Toxic: The Union Carbide Accident in Bhopal Continues to Harm." *Scientific American* (June 1995): pp. 16–18.

Nader, Ralph, Brownstein, Ronald and Richard, John, eds. *Who's Poisoning America? Corporate Polluters and Their Victims in the Chemical Age.* San Francisco: Sierra Club Books, 1981.

Niagara Falls, New York, Deed of Love Canal Property Transfer (28 April 1953).

Pomice, E. "Cleaning up After Industry's Slobs." *Forbes,* vol. 139 (20 April 1987): p. 90.

Postel, Sandra. *Defusing the Toxics Threat: Controlling Pesticides and Industrial Waste.* Worldwatch Paper No. 79. Washington, DC: Worldwatch Institute, September 1987.

Raloff, J. "Biggest Benzene Risks Hide Close to Home." *Science News,* vol. 136 (14 October 1989): p. 245.

———."Unexpected Leakage." *Science News,* vol. 135 (18 March 1989): p. 164.

———."EPA Limits Industrial Benzene Emissions." *Science News,* vol. 136 (9 September 1989): p. 165.

Rayport, Jeffrey F., and Lodge, George C. "Responsible Care." Harvard Business School Case Study #N9-391-135: 15 January 1991.

Regenstein, Lewis. *America the Poisoned.* Washington, DC: Acropolis Books, 1982.

Rennie, John. "Trojan Horse: Did a Protective Peptide Exacerbate Bhopal Injuries?" *Scientific American* (March 1992): p. 27.

Revkin, A. C. "Trapping Toxics in the Trenches." *Discover,* vol. 9 (November 1988): p. 10.

Salholz. "The Next Love Canal?" *Newsweek* (7 August 1989): p. 28.

Schmitt, Eric. "Axelrod Says 220 Love Canal Families Can Return." *New York Times* (9 September 1988): p. B1.

Schneider, Keith. "U.S. Said to Lack Data on Threat Posed by Hazardous Waste Sites." *New York Times* (22 October 1991): C4.

Shabecoff, Philip. "Government Says Abandoned Love Canal Homes Are Safe Now," *New York Times* (15 May 1990): p. B1.

Underwood, Anne. "The Return to Love Canal." *Newsweek* (30 July 1990).

Union Carbide Corporation. *Bhopal Methyl Isocyanate Incident Investigation Team Report*. Danbury, CT: March 1985.

———. "Union Carbide Corporation Bhopal Fact Sheet." Available from Union Carbide Corporation, Corporate Communications Department, Section C-2, Danbury, CT 06817-0001.

Verhouek, Sam Howe. "After Ten Years, the Trauma of Love Canal Continues." *New York Times* (5 August 1988): p. B1.

———. "At Love Canal, Land Rush on a Burial Ground." *New York Times* (26 July 1990): p. A1.

———. "New Findings Delay Resettling of Love Canal." *New York Times* (7 March 1989): p. B5.

Vianna, Nicholas. Report to the New York State Department of Health. Reported in *Science* (19 June 1981): p. 19.

Weir, David. *The Bhopal Syndrome: Pesticides, Environment and Health*. San Francisco: Sierra Club Books, 1987.

Whalan, Robert. *Love Canal: A Public Health Time Bomb*. Report of the New York Department of Health, 1978.

Whelan, Elizabeth. *Toxic Terror: The Truth About the Cancer Scare*. Ottawa, IL: Jameson Books, 1985.

Whitney, Gary. "Hooker Chemical and Plastics." In *Case Studies in Business Ethics*. Edited by Thomas Donaldson. Englewood Cliffs, NJ: Prentice-Hall, 1984.

Winerip, Michael. "Home Bargains in Niagara Falls: Forget the Toxics." *New York Times* (29 May 1990): p. B1.

Zuesse, Eric. "Love Canal: The Truth Seeps Out." *Reason* (February 1981).

Chapter 4 Diversity and the Trees:
The Tropical Rainforest.

Ackerman, Diane. "A Reporter at Large: Golden Monkeys." *The New Yorker* (24 June 1991): p.36.

Brooke, James. "Brazilian Sequel: A Jailbreak, a Bitter Widow." *New York Times* (17 February 1993).

———. "Plan to Develop Amazon a Failure." *New York Times* (12 November 1991).

Christian, Shirley. "There's a Bonanza in Nature for Costa Rica, but Its Forests Too Are Besieged." *New York Times* (29 May 1992): p. A6.

Dold, Catherine. "Tropical Forests Found More Valuable for Medicine than Other Uses." *New York Times* (28 April 1992).

Eckholm, Erik. "Secrets of the Rain Forest." *The New York Times Magazine* (17 November 1988): p. 20.

Environmental Defense Fund. "Brazil Creates Rainforest Reserve for Yanomamis." *EDF Letter* (April 1992).

Linden, Eugene. "Lost Tribes, Lost Knowledge." *TIME* (23 September 1991): p. 46.

————."Playing with Fire." *TIME* (18 September 1989).

Myers, Norman. *The Primary Source.* New York: Norton, 1984.

————. *The Sinking Ark.* Oxford, England: Pergamon Press, 1979.

Perlez, Jane. "Whose Forest Is It, the Peasants' or the Lemurs'?" *New York Times* (7 September 1991): p. 2.

Preston, Richard. "A Reporter at Large: Crisis in The Hot Zone." *The New Yorker* (26 October 1992): p. 58.

Revkin, Andrew. *The Burning Season.* Boston: Houghton Mifflin, 1990.

Ryan, John C. *Life Support: Conserving Biological Diversity.* Worldwatch Paper No. 108. Washington, DC: Worldwatch Institute, 1992.

Sesser, Stan. "A Reporter at Large: Logging the Rain Forest." *The New Yorker* (27 May 1991).

Shoumatoff, Alex. *The World Is Burning.* Boston: Little, Brown, 1990.

Tolan, Sandy, and Postero, Nancy. "Accidents of History." *The New York Times Magazine* (23 February 1992).

Wilson, Edward O. *The Diversity of Life.* Cambridge, MA: Harvard University Press, 1992.

Chapter 5 To Reclaim a Legacy: The Tallest Trees in America

Adams, Brock. "A Comprehensive Forest Management Plan: Wood and Work for Washington." *S. 1536,* United States Senate, July 1991.

Adler, Jerry. "Top Talon." *National Wildlife,* vol. 30, no. 2 (Feb./Mar. 1992): pp. 50–59.

Alm, Andy. "Log Fight Comes to Headwaters." *Econews* (July 1991): p. 1.

————."Who's Messing with the Forests?" *Econews* (December 1991): p. 1.

Baden, John. "Spare That Tree!" *Forbes* (9 December 1991): pp. 229-234.

Bagley, Constance E. "Pacific Lumber Company: Case Presentation." Unpublished paper, June 1991.

Barrett, William. "Aluminum Cow." *Forbes* (6 January 1992): p. 275.

Boland, John. Editorial. *Wall Street Journal* (10 February 1988).

Booth, William. "New Thinking on Old Growth." *Science* (14 April 1989): p. 141.

Botte, Gisela, and Cray, Dan. "Is Your Pension Safe?" *TIME* (3 June 1991): p. 43.

Bowden, Charles. "Government First, Earth Last." *E: The Environmental Magazine,* vol. 3, no. 1 (Jan./Feb. 1992): pp. 56–57.

Brown, George, and Stark, Pete. "The Last Stand: Only Clinton Can Save a Priceless Redwood Grove." Op.-Ed, *New York Times* (1 December 1995).

Calkins, Laurel Brubaker. "The Case Against Hurwitz." *Houston Press* (25 April–1 May 1996): pp. 17ff.

Castro, Janice, et al. "A Sizzler Finally Fizzles." *TIME* (22 April 1991).

Caufield, Catherine. "The Ancient Forest." *The New Yorker* (14 May 1990): p. 46.

Corn, M. Lynne. "Spotted Owls and Old Growth Forests." *CRS Issue Brief.* Updated August 19, 1991. Environment and Natural Resources Policy Division, Congressional Research Service, Library of Congress.

Cushman, John Jr. "Court Fight over Timber Starts Immediately After Law Is Changed." *New York Times* (28 August 1995): p. A13.

Durbin, Kathie. "From Owls to Eternity." *E: The Environmental Magazine*, vol. 3, no. 2 (Mar./Apr. 1992): p. 30–37.

———."The Timber Salvage Scam: Tired of Those Pesky Environmental Laws? Call Congress for Quick Relief." *The Amicus Journal* (Fall 1995)

Editorial. "Owlmageddon," *The Economist*. (4 May 1991): p. 27.

Editorial. "Scientist on a Hot Seat." *National Wildlife*, vol. 29, no. 1 (December 1990): p. 28.

Egan, Timothy. "Economic Forces That Knock Down the Oldest Forests." *New York Times*, News of the Week in Review (8 October 1989).

———."Forest Supervisors Say Politicians Are Asking Them to Cut Too Much." *New York Times* (16 September 1991).

———."Hearings on the Spotted Owl Begin." *New York Times* (9 January 1992).

———."Oregon Failing Forecasters: Thrives as It Protects Owls." *New York Times* (11 October 1994): p. A1.

———."Trees That Yield a Drug for Cancer Are Wasted." *New York Times* (29 January 1992): pp. A1, A12.

EPIC. "Endangered Species Act/Headwaters Forest Alert: Owl Creek Victory Triggers Pacific Lunber's Plans for Revenge Cut." March 29, 1994, from Environmental Protection Information Center, P.O. Box 397, Garberville, CA 95542.

Farrell, James. *National Wildlife*, vol. 29, no. 1 (December 1990): p. 28.

Findley, Rowe. "Will We Save Our Own?" *National Geographic* (September 1990): pp. 106–134.

Foreman, David, and Haywood, B., eds. *Ecodefense: A Field Guide to Monkey-wrenching*, 2nd ed. Tucson, AZ: Ned Ludd Books, 1987.

Friedman, Milton. "The Social Responsibility of Business Is to Increase Its Profit." *The New York Times Magazine* (13 September 1970).

Fritsch, Jane. "Friend of Timber Industry Wields Power in Senate." *New York Times* (10 August 1995): p. B6.

Glick, Daniel. "Having Owls and Jobs Too: A Booming Economy Debunks the 'Owl-vs.-Jobs' Premise." *National Wildlife*, vol. 33, no. 5 (Aug./Sept. 1995).

Gup, Ted. "Owl vs. Man." *TIME* (25 June 1990): pp. 56–62.

Hamach, Tim. "The Great Tree Robbery." *New York Times* (19 September 1991).

J.C. "Service to Whom?" *Greenpeace* (Jan./Feb. 1991): p. 6.

Johnson, K. Norman, et al. (The Scientific Panel on Late-Successional Forest Ecosystems, ISC). "Alternatives for Management of Late-Successional Forests of the Pacific Northwest: A Report to the Agriculture Committee and the Merchant Marine and Fisheries Committee of the United States House of Representatives." October 8, 1991.

Kelly, David, and Braasch, Gary. *Secrets of the Old Growth Forests*. Layton, UT: Gibbs Smith Publisher, 1988.

Keyser, Christine. "Compromise in Defense of Earth First! A Monkeywrencher Trial Ends, and No One's Happy." *Sierra* (Nov./Dec. 1991): pp. 45–47.

"Land Bureau Seeks to Sell Protected Timber." *New York Times* (12 September 1991).

Laycock, George. "Of Men and Mules: Old Time Logging Makes a Comeback." *Audubon* (Sep./Oct. 1991).

"Logging Limits Sought over Seven Million Acres." *New York Times* (10 January 1992).

Manes, Christopher. *Green Rage: Radical Environmentalism and the Unmaking of Civilization.* Boston: Little, Brown, 1990.

McCoy, Charles. "Cutting Costs: For Takeover Baron, Redwood Forests Are Just One More Deal." *Wall Street Journal* (6 August 1993).

McGourty, Kelly. "The Spotted Owl in the Media." Internship report for the Huxley College of Environmental Studies, Western Washington University (14 June 1991).

McKay, Tim. "Crimes Bedevil National Forests." *Econews* (December 1991): p. 5.

————."Two Birds in Hand May Keep Trees in the Bush: Marbled Murrelet Joins Spotted Owl." *Econews* (July 1991): p. 1.

McKay, Tim. (Northcoast Environmental Center), and Pace, Felice (Klamath Forest Alliance). "New Perspectives on Conservation and Preservation in the Klamath Siskiyou Region." Published paper. 1991.

McKibben, Bill. "What Good Is a Forest?" *Audubon* (May/June 1996): pp. 54ff.

McNeil, Donald G., Jr., et al. "The Withering Woods." Special section on the North Coast forests in "The News of the Week in Review." *New York Times* (3 November 1991).

Miller, G. Tyler, Jr. *Living in the Environment,* 9th ed. Belmont, CA: Wadsworth, 1990.

Mitchell, John G. "Sour Times in Sweet Home." Audubon (May 1991): pp. 86–97.

North Coast Redwood Interpretive Association. "Old Growth Redwood: Parks in Jeopardy." Published paper. 1991.

"Northwest Loggers Challenge Rules on Spotted Owl." *New York Times* (1 September 1991).

Pacific Lumber Company, Annual Reports, especially years 1981 through 1984.

Pollack, Andrew. "Lumbering in the Age of the Baby Tree." *New York Times,* Business Section (24 February 1991): p. 1.

Porterfield, Andrew. "Railroaded: The LBO Trend on Wall Street Is Playing Havoc with the Nation's Forests." *Common Cause Magazine* (Sept./Oct. 1989): pp. 21–23.

Rauber, Paul. "The August Cove." *Sierra* (Jan./Feb. 1992): p. 26.

Reinhardt, Forest L. "Champion International Corporation: Timber. Trade and the Northern Spotted Owl." Harvard Business School Case Study 9-792-017 (15 March 1993).

Reinhold, Robert. "Failure of S & L in California Could Save a Redwood Forest." *New York Times* (27 March 1991): pp. A1ff.

Schneider, Keith. "When the Bad Guy Is Seen as the One in the Green Hat." "News of the Week in Review." *New York Times* (16 February 1992).

Schneider, Paul. "When a Whistle Blows in the Forest..." *Audubon* (Jan./Feb. 1992): pp. 42–49.

Seed, J., Macy, J., Fleming, P. and Naess, Arne, eds. *Thinking Like a Mountain: Towards a Council of All Beings.* Philadelphia: New Society Publishers, 1988.

Shepard, Jack. *The Forest Killers.* New York: Weybright and Talley, 1975.

Sims, Grant. "Can We Save the Northwest's Salmon?" *National Wildlife* (Oct./Nov. 1994): pp. 42–48.

Skow, John. "Redwoods: The Last Stand." *TIME* (6 June 1994).

Taylor, Bron. "The Religion and Politics of Earth First!" *The Ecologist,* vol. 21, no. 6 (Nov./Dec. 1991): pp. 258–266.

Thornbury, D.L. *California's Redwood Wonderland: Humboldt County.* San Francisco: D.L. Thornbury at the Sunset Press, 1923.

Tisdale, Sallie. "Annals of Place: In the Northwest." *The New Yorker* (26 August 1991): pp. 37–62.

———."Save a Life, Kill a Tree." *New York Times* (26 October 1991).

———."The Pacific Northwest." *The New Yorker* (26 August 1991): p. 54.

United States Fish and Wildlife Service. "Economic Analysis of Designation of Critical Habitat for the Northern Spotted Owl." Washington, DC: August 1991.

United States Forest Service, Department of Agriculture; United States Bureau of Land Management, Department of the Interior. "Actions the Administration May Wish to Consider in Implementing a Conservation Strategy for the Northern Spotted Owl." May 1, 1990.

Velasquez, Manuel. "Ethics and the Spotted Owl Controversy." *Issues in Ethics* (Santa Clara Ethics Center), vol. 4, no. 1 (Winter/Spring 1991): pp.1, 6.

Wilcove, David S. "Of Owls and Ancient Forests." *Ancient Forests of the Pacific Northwest* (Washington, DC: Island Press, 1990).

Wilkerson, Hugh, and van der Zee, John. *Life in the Peace Zone: An American Company Town.* New York: Macmillan, 1971.

Williamson, Lonnie. "The Forest for the Trees." *Outdoor Life,* vol. 186, no. 5 (November 1990): pp. 54–58.

Wuerther, George. "Tree-Spiking and Moral Maturity." *Earth First!* (1 August 1985): p. 5, 7.

Chapter 6 Oil and Water

"Alaska Oil Spill Continues to Spread as Limited Shipping Resumes at Valdez." *Wall Street Journal* (29 March 1989): p. A3.

Barrett, Paul M. "Environmentalists Cautiously Praise $1 Billion Exxon Valdez Settlement." *Wall Street Journal* (14 March 1991): p. A4.

Bavaria, Joan. Editorial. "Business, Clean up Your Environmental Act! Withholding Investment Can Influence Corporate Actions." *Newsday* (7 September 1989).

Boyd, Gerald M. "Bush Sends Team to Assess Cleanup." *New York Times* (29 March 1989): p. B5.

Browne, Malcolm W. "Alaska Bans Herring Fishing in Oil-Fouled Sound." *New York Times* (4 April 1989): pp. A1, B8.

———."Arsenal of Lasers vs. an Angry, Oily Sea." *New York Times* (29 March 1989): p. B5.

————."Experts See Glass Beads as Low-Cost Tool for Oil-Spill Cleanup." *New York Times* (11 April 1992): p. 12.

————."In Alaskan Disaster, *Science* Seeking Lessons for Marine Life." *New York Times* (2 April 1989): p. A22.

————."In Once-Pristine Sound, Wildlife Reels Under Oil's Impact: Biologists Say Spill Could Set Records for Loss of Birds, Fish and Mammals." *New York Times,* "Science Times." (4 April 1989): pp. C1, C5.

————."Spill Could Pose a Threat for Years." *New York Times* (31 March 1989): p. A12.

"Captain Has History of Drinking and Driving." Special to the *New York Times* (28 March 1989): p. B7.

Chasis, Sarah. and Speer, Lisa. "How to Avoid Another Valdez." *New York Times* (20 May 1989): p. 27.

Cushman, John H., Jr. "Alaska Cleanup May Drag Into '90, U.S. Says." *New York Times* (11 May 1989): p. A27.

————."Coast Guard Studies Need for Improved Ship Traffic Control." *New York Times* (26 June 1989): p. 17.

————."Questions Unanswered in Tanker's Grounding." *New York Times* (2 July 1989): p. 18.

————."Sparks Fly at Alaska's Spill Inquiry." *New York Times* (20 May 1989): p. L9.

————."Spill Panel Considers Pilots' Timing." *New York Times* (30 June 1989): p. A10.

Davidson, Art. *In the Wake of the Exxon Valdez*. San Francisco: Sierra Club Books, 1990.

Deutsch, Claudia H. "The Giant with a Black Eye: An Oil Spill Puts Exxon on the Defensive When Everything Else Is Going Right." *New York Times,* Business Section (2 April 1989): p. 1.

Dionne, E. J., Jr. "Big Oil Spill Leaves Its Mark on Politics of Environment." *New York Times* (3 April 1989): pp. A1, A12.

Editorial. "Another Wake-up Call: Save Energy." *New York Times* (4 September 1990): p. A16.

Editorial. "The Consequences of Complacency." *Fairpress* (6 April 1989): p. A10.

Editorial. "Dolphins and Double Hulls." *New York Times* (14 April 1990).

Editorial. "Fight on, Exxon." *Wall Street Journal* (2 May 1991): p. A16.

Editorial. "Late and Lame on the Big Spill." *New York Times* (12 April 1989): p. A24.

Editorial. "Long Shadow of the Exxon Valdez." *New York Times* (21 September 1994).

Editorial. "On Oil Spills: Trust Turns into Anger." *New York Times* (28 June 1989): p. A22.

Editorial. "The True Cost of Energy." *New York Times* (19 August 1990): p. E18.

Egan, Timothy. "Elements of Tanker Disaster: Drinking, Fatigue, Complacency." *New York Times* (22 May 1989): p. B7.

————."Exxon Concedes It Can't Contain Most of Oil Spill; Admits Delay in Cleanup; Coast Guard Officer Is Said to Have Smelled Alcohol on Breath of the Captain." *New York Times* (30 March 1989): p. A1, A20.

————."Fisherman and State Take Charge of Cleaning Up Alaska Oil Spill: Defensive Steps Taken After Company Fails to Halt Spread of Slick." *New York Times* (29 March 1989): pp. A1, B5.

————."Fishermen Fear Spill Will Hurt into the 90's." *New York Times* (29 March 1989): p. B5.

————."High Winds Hamper Oil Spill Cleanup off Alaska." *New York Times* (28 March 1989): pp. A1, B7.

"Environmental Worry Up." *New York Times* (2 July 1989).

Feder, Barnaby J. "Group Sets Corporate Code on Environmental Conduct." *New York Times* (8 September 1989): pp. D1, D5.

Gold, Allan R. "Exxon to Pay up to $15 Million for Spill." *New York Times* (15 March 1991): pp. B1, B2.

————."Newport Spill Widens, but Harm May Be Limited." *New York Times* (26 June 1989): p. A1.

————."Pilot Says He Tried to Warn Tanker Headed for Reef." *New York Times* (27 June 1989): p. A12.

Golden, Tim. "Oil in Arthur Kill: Publicity and Peril for Urban Marsh." *New York Times* (18 January 1990): pp. B1, B4.

Graham, Frank, Jr. "Oilspeak, Common Sense, and Soft Science." *Audubon* (September 1989): pp. 102–111.

Gutfeld, Rose, and Sullivan, Allanna. "Exxon, Alyeska Sued by Wildlife Group." *Wall Street Journal* (18 August 1989): p. B12.

Hair, Jay D. (President, National Wildlife Federation). "Prince William Sound Oil Spill Disaster: Exxon's Responsibilities." Memorandum to Lawrence G. Rawl, Chairman, Exxon Corporation. May 11, 1989.

————."Statement." Exxon Corporation Annual Shareholders Meeting, May 18, 1989.

Holusha, John. "Chairman Defends Exxon's Effort to Clean Up Oil." *New York Times* (19 April 1989): p. A21.

Laycock, George. "The Baptism of Prince William Sound." *Audubon* (September 1989): pp. 74-91.

Lemonick, Michael D. "The Two Alaskas." *TIME* (17 April 1989): pp. 56–66.

Luoma, Jon R. "Terror and Triage at the Laundry." *Audubon* (September 1989): pp. 92–101.

Lyall, Sarah. "Oil Tanker Refloated off Wales: Spilled Cargo Makes 25-Mile-Long-Slick." *New York Times* (22 February 1996): p. A8.

Malcolm, Andrew H., Suro, Roberto, and Witkin, Richard. "How the Oil Spilled and Spread: Delay and Confusion off Alaska." *New York Times* (16 April 1989): pp. A1, A30.

Matsen, Brad. "Fishermen Battle Pain, Anger and Spilled Oil." *National Fisherman* (June 1989): pp. 2–4, 95.

Mauer, Richard. "Unlicensed Mate Was in Charge of Ship That Hit Reef, Exxon Says; Hull Seriously Damaged by Rocks Two Miles Apart." *New York Times* (27 March 1989): pp. A1, B12.

McCoy, Charles, and Sullivan, Allanna. "Exxon's Withdrawal of Valdez Pleas Will Maintain Pressure to Settle Case." *Wall Street Journal* (28 May 1991): pp. A3, A6.

McGinley, Laurie. "Valdez Decision Spreads Blame for Alaska Spill: Safety Board Cites Exxon, Skipper, His Third Mate, Coast Guard and Officials." *Wall Street Journal* (1 August 1990): pp. A1, A4.

———."$9.7 Million Land Damages Won in Valdez Case." *New York Times* (26 September 1994): p. A12.

Muscat, Paul, and Gilson, Michael. Letter to the Editor. "Oilfields Scar Arctic Wildlife Refuge Even Now." *New York Times* (4 April 1989).

"$9.7 Million Land Damages Won in Valdez Case." *New York Times* (26 September 1994): p. A12.

"Oilfield Practices Viewed as Threat to Land in Arctic." *New York Times* (5 March 1989): p. A1.

Revzin, Philip. "Years Temper Damage of Worst Oil Spill: Starkest Fears of 1978 Amoco Disaster Weren't Realized." *Wall Street Journal* (4 April 1989): p. A10.

Rierdon, Andi. "Connecticut Q & A." *New York Times* (11 December 1988).

Rothman, Andrea, et al. "Who's That Screaming at Exxon? Not the Environmentalists." *Business Week* (1 May 1989): p. 31.

Salpukas, Agis. "Spilled Oil May Not Be from Exxon Valdez." *New York Times* (1 December 1993): p. A2, D7.

Schmidt, William E. "The Afflicted Shetlands Pray, for Man and Beast." *New York Times* (11 January 1993).

———."Storm Batters Wrecked Tanker, Worsening Oil Spill in Shetlands." *New York Times* (12 January 1993): pp. A1, A9.

Schneider, Keith. "Dispute Erupts on Settlement in Valdez Spill." *New York Times* (16 October 1994): p. A22.

———."New Equipment Enables Alaska to Intensify Cleanup." *New York Times* (3 April 1989): p. A12.

———."Transfer of Remaining Oil from Tanker Moves Slowly: Salvage Is Risky, Offer of Help Rejected." *New York Times* (2 April 1989): p. A22.

———."Under Oil's Powerful Spell, Alaska Was off Guard: Enriched and Reassured, Industry and State Cut Disaster Preparations." *New York Times* (2 April 1989): pp. A1, A22.

Shabecoff, Philip. "Captain of Tanker Had Been Drinking, Blood Tests Show; Illegal Alcohol Level; Coast Guard Opens Effort to Bring Charge of Operating Ship While Intoxicated." *New York Times* (31 March 1989): pp. A1, A12.

———."House Panel Urges One-Year Ban on Oil Drilling off Much of U.S." *New York Times* (30 June 1989): pp. A1, A10.

———."Oil Industry Gets Warning on Image: Lujan Says Public Reaction to Alaska Spill Could Block Drilling in New Fields." *New York Times* (4 April 1989): p. B8.

———."The Rash of Tanker Spills Is Part Of a Pattern of Thousands a Year." *New York Times* (29 June 1989): p. A20.

Solomon, Caleb. "Exxon Attacks Scientific Views of Valdez Spill." *Wall Street Journal* (15 April 1993): p. B1.

———."The Hunt for Oil: Petroleum Industry Pins Future on Finding Large Overseas Fields." *Wall Street Journal* (25 August 1993): p. A1, A4.

Stevens, William D. (President, Exxon Company, U.S.A.). "Statement" before the National Ocean Policy Study of the Senate Committee on Commerce, Science and Transportation of the United States Senate.

Stevens, William K. "The Bay Was Lucky, Marine Scientists Say." *New York Times* (26 June 1989): p. A16.

———."Despite Gains, Dealing with Big Oil Spills Is Still a Struggle." *New York Times* (27 June 1989): Environment Section.

———."Size of Oil Spill May Be No Guide to Its Impact." *New York Times* (4 April 1989): p. C6.

Stevenson, Richard W. "Why Exxon's Woes Worry ARCO: Thriving ARCO May Be Hard-Hit if Congress Curbs Alaskan Exploration." *New York Times,* Business Section (14 May 1989): p. 1.

Sullivan, Allanna. "Exxon Discloses Oil-Spill Expenses over $1.25 Billion." *Wall Street Journal* (25 July 1989): p. 3A.

———."Valdez Talks Didn't Consider Natives' Claims." *Wall Street Journal* (13 June 1991): p. A6.

Sullivan, Allanna, and Bennett, Amanda. "Critics Fault Chief Executive of Exxon on Handling of Recent Alaskan Oil Spill." *Wall Street Journal* (31 March 1989).

"Tanker Spills off Hawaiian Coast." *New York Times* (4 March 1989): p. 6.

Wald, Matthew L. "Angry Shareholders Confront Exxon Chief over Alaska Spill." *New York Times* (19 May 1989): p. B1.

———."Cleanup Efforts Fail to Hold Delaware Oil." *New York Times* (26 June 1989): p. A16.

———."Cleanup of Oily Beaches Moves Slowly." *New York Times* (23 April 1989): p. A30.

———."Drilling Plans Point up Questions on Oil and Wilderness in Alaska: Industry Showcase or Environmental Disaster?" *New York Times* (23 April 1989): pp. A1, A30.

———."Exxon May Have Small Liability for Spill Claims." *New York Times* (28 March 1989): p. B7.

———."Liability Issue Stalls Bill on Oil Spills." *New York Times* (22 June 1990): p. A12.

———."Oil Spills Leaving Trail of Disturbing Questions." *New York Times* (27 June 1989): pp. A1, A12.

Wells, Ken. "For Exxon, Cleanup Costs May Be Just the Beginning." *Wall Street Journal* (14 April 1989): p. B1.

———."Ship Spews Oil After Collision off Indonesia." *Wall Street Journal* (22 January 1993): p. A7.

———."Oil Spill Drifts; Salmon Farms Are Threatened: Shetland Fishing Operations Face Millions of Dollars in Immediate Damages."*Wall Street Journal* (11 January 1993): p. A11.

———."Volunteers Battle Storm, Pollution, but Oil Spill's Wildlife Toll Mounts."*Wall Street Journal* (11 January 1993): p. A11.

Wells, Ken, and Chase, Marilyn. "Paradise Lost: Heartbreaking Scenes of Beauty Disfigured Follow Alaska Oil Spill." *Wall Street Journal* (31 March 1989): pp. A1, A4.

Wells, Ken, and McCoy, Charles. "Exxon Says Fast Containment of Oil Spill in Alaska Could Have Caused Explosion." *Wall Street Journal* (5 April 1989): p. A3.

———."Out of Control: How Unpreparedness Turned the Alaska Spill into Ecological Debacle." *Wall Street Journal* (3 April 1989): pp. A1, A4.

Wells, Ken, and Sullivan, Allanna. "Stuck in Alaska: Exxon's Army Scrubs Beaches, but Many Don't Stay Cleaned (As Oil Persists and Costs Top $1 Billion, Firm Agrees to Resume Job in Spring. Will the Goo Turn to Asphalt?)." *Wall Street Journal* (27 July 27 1989): pp. A1, A8.

Wieland, Anne Pacsu. "Legacy of an Oil Spill." *Swarthmore College Bulletin* (November 1991): pp. 10–15, 63.

Wolff, Craig. "Exxon Admits a Year of Breakdowns in S.I. Oil Spill." *New York Times* (10 January 1990): pp. A1, B3.

———."Leaking Exxon Pipe Ran Through Regulatory Limbo." *New York Times* (11 January 1990): pp. B1, B7.

Chapter 7 Wounded Air:
Global Climate Change

Allman, William F., and Wagner, Betsy. "Climate and the Rise of Man." *U.S. News and World Report* (8 June 1992): p. 60.

Ausubel, Jesse H. "A Second Look at the Impacts of Climate Change." *American Scientist* (May/June 1991): p. 21.

Bazzaz, Fakhri A., and Fajer, Eric D. "Plant Life in a CO2-Rich World." *Scientific American* (January 1992): p. 68.

Broecker, Wallace S. "Global Warming on Trial." *Natural History* (April 1992).

Economy, Elizabeth. "China's Power to Harm the Planet." *New York Times*, Op.-Ed. (10 September 1995).

Flavin, Christopher. *Slowing Global Warming: A Worldwide Strategy*. Worldwatch Paper No. 91, Washington DC: Worldwatch Institute, 1989.

"Giant Iceberg Breaks off Antarctica." *Science News* (29 April 1995): p. 271.

Houghton, J.T., et al. *Climate Change 1992: The Supplementary Report to the IPCC Scientific Assessment*. New York: Cambridge University Press, 1992.

Kerr, Richard A. "Clouds Keep Ocean Temperatures Down." *Science News* (11 May 1991): p. 303.

———."Hansen vs. the World on the Greenhouse Threat." *Science* (2 June 1989): p. 1041.

———."How to Fix the Clouds in Greenhouse Models." *Science* (6 January 1989): p. 28.

———."Greenhouse Report Foresees Growing Global Stress." *Science* (3 November 1995): p. 731.

———."It's Official: First Glimmer of Greenhouse Warming Seen." *Science* (8 December 1995): p. 1565.

———."Study Unveils Climate Cooling Caused by Pollutant Haze." *Science* (12 May 1995): p.802.

Lewis, Paul. "Danger of Floods Worries Islanders." *New York Times* (13 May 1992).

———."Island Nations Fear a Rise in the Sea." *New York Times* (17 February 1992).

Long, Larry. "Population by the Sea." *Population Today* (April 1990): p. 6.

Los Angeles Times Special Report. "Scientists Document Cooling Effect from Volcanoes." *Hartford Courant* (13 December 1992).

Lynch, Colum F. "Warm up to the Idea: Global Warming Is Here." *The Amicus Journal* (Spring 1996): p. 20.

Miller, Alan, and Mintzer, Irving. "Global Warming: No Nuclear Quick Fix." *Bulletin of the Atomic Scientists* (June 1990): p. 31.

Mitchell, George J. *World on Fire*, New York: Scribner (1991).

Monastersky, R. "Greenland Ice Shows Climate Flip-Flops." *Science News*, vol. 142 (26 September 1992): p.199.

———."Haze Clouds the Greenhouse." *Science News*, vol. 141 (11 April 1992).

———."Hot Year Prompts Greenhouse Concern." *Science News*, vol. 139 (19 January 1991): p.36.

———."A Moisture Problem Muddles Climate Work." *Science News*, vol. 141 (4 April 1992): p. 212.

———."Pinatubo and El Nino Fight Tug of War." *Science News* (18 January 1992).

———."Signs of Global Warming Found in Ice." *Science News*, vol. 141 (7 March 1992): p. 148.

———."Swamped by Climate Change?" *Science*, vol. 138: p. 184.

———."Warming Shouldn't Wither U.S. Farming." *Science News*, vol. 137: p. 308.

Mydans, Seth. "Along Thai Border, Malaria Outpaces New Drugs." *New York Times* (3 March 1996).

Oppenheimer, Michael, and Boyle, Robert. *Dead Heat*. New York: Basic Books, 1990.

Oppenheimer, Michael, and Gaffin, Stuart. Internal lecture for Environmental Defense Fund, Spring 1992.

Pendick, D. "Debate May Resume over Volcano-Climate Link." *Science News*, vol. 142 (14 November 1992): p. 324.

Raloff, J. "Tough Carbon Budget Could Slow Warming." *Science News* (2 December 1989): p. 359.

Scheuer, James H. "Bush's 'Whitewash Effect' on Warming." *New York Times*, Op.-Ed. (3 March 1990).

Schneider, Steven H. *Global Warming*, San Francisco: Sierra Club Books, 1989.

Sedjo, Roger A. "Forests: A Tool to Moderate Global Warming?" *Environment*, vol. 31, no. 1 (Jan./Feb. 1989): p. 14.

Shabecoff, Philip. "Team of Scientists Sees Substantial Warming of Earth." *New York Times* (6 April 1990).

———."Temperature for the World Rises Sharply in the 1980s." *New York Times* (29 March 1988).

Simons, Marlise. "Scientists Urging Gas Emission Cuts." *New York Times* (5 November 1990).

Stevens, William K. "Climate Talks Enter Harder Phase of Cutting Back Emissions." *New York Times* (11 April 1995): p. C4.

———."Clouds Are Yielding Clues to Changes in Climate." *New York Times* (24 April 1990): p. C1.

———."Estimates of Warming Gain More Precision and Warn of Disaster." *New York Times* (15 December 1992): pp. C1, C9.

———."Global Climate Changes Seen as Force in Human Evolution." *New York Times* (16 October 1990): p. C 1.

———."Global Warming Experts Call Human Role Likely." *New York Times* (10 September 1995): p. 1.

———."Global Warming Resumes in 1994, Climate Data Show." *New York Times* (27 January 1995): P. A1.

———."Ice Shelves Melting as Forecast, but Disaster Script Is in Doubt." *New York Times* (30 January 1996): p. C4.

———."In a Warming World, Who Comes Out Ahead?" *New York Times* (5 February 1991): p. C1.

———."In Rain and Temperature Data, New Signs of Global Warming." *New York Times* (26 September 1996): p. C4.

———."In the Ebb and Flow of Ancient Glaciers, Clues to a New Ice Age." *New York Times* (16 January 1990): p. C1.

———."'95 the Hottest Year on Record as the Global Trend Keeps Up." *New York Times* (4 January 196): P. A1.

———."Price of Global Warming? Debate Weighs Dollars and Cents." *New York Times* (10 October 1995): p. C4.

———."Scientists Say Earth's Warming Could Set off Wide Disruptions." *New York Times* (18 September 1995): p. A1.

———."Separate Studies Rank '90 as World's Warmest Year." *New York Times* (10 January 1991).

———."Study Supports Global Warming Prediction." *New York Times* (14 December 1989).

———."Volcano's Eruption in Philippines May Counteract Global Warming." *New York Times* (19 June 1991).

———."Warming of the Globe Could Build on Itself, Some Scientists Say." *New York Times* (19 February 1991): p. C4.

———."With Energy Tug of War, U.S. Is Missing Its Goal." *New York Times* (28 November 1995): p. A1.

Travis, J. "The Loitering El Nino: Greenhouse Guest?" *Science News,* vol. 149 (27 January 1996): p. 54.

Tyler, Patrick E. "China's Inevitable Dilemma: Coal Equals Growth." *New York Times* (29 November 1995): p. A1

World Resources Institute Report, 1987.

Wright, Karen. "Heating the Global Warming Debate." *The New York Times Magazine* (3 February 1991): p. 24.

Chapter 8 The Silence of the Birds: Rachel Carson and the Pesticides

Brooks, Paul. *The House of Life: Rachel Carson at Work.* Boston: Houghton Mifflin, 1972.

Carson, Rachel. *Silent Spring.* Greenwich, CT: Fawcett, 1962.

Downs, Robert B., *Upsetting the Balance of Nature.* London: Macmillan, 1970.

Freeman, Martha, ed. *Always, Rachel: The Letters of Rachel Carson and Dorothy Freeman.* Boston: Beacon Press, 1995.

Gartner, Carol B. *Rachel Carson.* New York: Frederick Ungar, 1983.

Graham, Frank, Jr., *Since Silent Spring.* Boston: Houghton Mifflin, 1970.

Hambidge, Gove. "The New Insect-Killers." *Harper's Magazine* (February 1945): pp. 264–268.

"Hormonal Sabotage," *Natural History* (March 1996).

Jezer, Marty. *Rachel Carson.* New York: Chelsea House, 1988.

Line, Leslie. "Old Nemesis, DDT, Reaches Remote Midway Albatrosses." *New York Times* (12 March 1996): p. B1.

McKay, Mary A. *Rachel Carson.* New York: Twayne, 1993.

Miller, G. Tyler, Jr. *Living in the Environment,* 9th ed. Belmont, CA: Wadsworth, 1996.

Powledge, Fred. "Toxic Shame." *Amicus Journal* (Winter 1991); pp. 38–44.

Raloff, J. "Pesticides May Challenge Human Immunity." *Science News,* vol. 149 (9 March 1996): p. 149.

———."The Pesticide Shuffle." *Science News,* vol. 149 (16 March 1996): pp. 174–175.

———."The Role of Chlorine—and Its Future." *Science News* (22 January 1994): p. 59.

Sterling, Philip. *Sea and Earth: The Life of Rachel Carson.* New York: Thomas Y. Crowell, 1970.

Webster, Donovan. "Heart of the Delta." *The New Yorker* (8 July 1991): pp. 46–66.

Weir, David. *The Bhopal Syndrome: Pesticides, Environment and Health.* San Francisco: Sierra Club Books, 1987.

Yoon, Carol Kaesuk. "Nibbled Plants Don't Just Sit There: They Launch Active Attacks." *New York Times* (23 June 1992): p. C1.

Chapter 9 Skunked:
The Death of the Great Fisheries

Chapelle, Howard I. *The American Fishing Schooners: 1825–1935.* New York: Norton, 1973.

Clayton, Mark. "Hunt for Jobs Intensifies as Fishing Industry Implodes." *Christian Science Monitor* (25 August 1994).

Connolly, James B. *The Book of Gloucester Fisherman.* New York: John Day, 1927.

Draft Statement for the Buyout Design Group, available from East Coast Fisheries Federation, Inc., Narragansett, RI.

Editorial. "A Modest Step to Save the Fish." *New York Times* (8 August 1995).

Fairlie, Simon, Hagler, Mike, and O'Riordan, Brian. "The Politics of Overfishing." *Ecologist* [special double issue], vol.25, nos. 2 and 3 (Mar./Apr. and May/June 1995): pp. 46–73.

Farnsworth, Clyde H. "Canada Acts to Cut Fishing by Foreigners: Will Seize Boats Outside Its Waters." *New York Times* (22 May 1994).

Food and Agriculture Organization of the United Nations (FAO). *Marine Fisheries and the Law of the Sea: A Decade of Change.* FAO Fisheries Circular No. 83 (Rome, Italy, 1993).

Garland, Joseph E. *Down to the Sea: The Fishing Schooners of Gloucester.* Boston: Godine, 1983.

Goode, G. Browne, et al. *The Fisheries and Fishery Industries of the United States,* 6 vols. Washington, DC: U.S. Commission of Fish and Fisheries, 1887.

Graham, Frank, Jr. "Defender of the Fishes." *Audubon* (Sept./Oct. 1994): pp. 96–99.

Greenpeace International. *It Can't Go on Forever: The Implications of the Global Grab for Declining Fish Stocks.* Amsterdam: Author, July 1993.

Grotius, Hugo. *Mare Liberum (The Freedon of the Seas).* Translated by R.V.D. Magoffin. New York: Oxford University Press, 1916. Originally published 1609.

Hagler, Mike. "Deforestation of the Deep: Fishing and the State of the Oceans." *Ecologist* [special double issue], vol. 2, nos. 2 and 3 (Mar./Apr. and May/June 1995): pp. 74–79.

Innis, Harold A. *The Cod Fisheries.* Toronto: University of Toronto Press, 1954.

"Introduction" and "Glossary." *Ecologist* [special double issue], vol. 25, nos. 2 and 3 (Mar./Apr/ and May/June 1995).

Kipling, Rudyard. *Captains Courageous.* New York: Century, 1896.

MacLeish, William H. *Oil and Water: The Struggle for Georges Bank.* Boston: Atlantic Monthly Press, 1985.

Massachusetts Offshore Groundfish Task Force. *New England Groundfish in Crisis—Again.* Boston: Executive Office of Environmental Affairs, 1990.

McGoodwin, James R. *Crisis in the World's Fisheries.* Stanford, CA: Stanford University Press, 1990.

National Marine Fisheries Service. *Our Living Oceans: Report on the Status of U.S. Living Marine Resources, 1993.* Silver Springs, MD: National Marine Fisheries Service, December 1993.

Nickerson, Colin. "Pirates Plunder Fisheries." *Boston Sunday Globe* (17 April 1994).

Northeast Fisheries Science Center. *Status of the Fishery Resources off the Northeastern United States for 1994.* Woods Hole, MA: NOAA Technical Memorandum NMFS-NE-108, 1995.

O'Hearne, Joseph C. *New England Fishing Schooners.* Milwaukee, WI: Kalmbach, 1947.

O'Malley, James D. "Preliminary Findings." In "Draft Statement on Buyout Design." Narrangansett, RI: East Coast Fisheries Federation, Inc., September 1994. Available from East Coast Fisheries Federation, Inc., P.O. Box 649, Narragansett, RI 02882; (401) 782-3440.

Parfit, Michael. "Diminishing Returns: Exploiting the Ocean's Bounty." *National Geographic,* vol. 188, no. 5 (November 1995): pp. 2–37.

Ross, Elizabeth. "Hard-Hit New England Fisherman Receive Financial Aid." *Christian Science Monitor* (23 March 1994).

Shapiro, Bill."The Most Dangerous Job in America." *Fortune* (31 May 1993).

Smith, M. Estellie. "Chaos, Consensus and Common Sense." *Ecologist* [special double issue], vol. 2, nos. 2 and 3 (Mar./Apr. and May/June 1995): pp. 8–85.

Warner, William W. *Distant Water: The Fate of the North Atlantic Fisherman.* Boston: Little, Brown, 1977.

Weber, Peter. *Abandoned Seas: Reversing the Decline of the Oceans.* Worldwatch Paper No. 116. Washington, DC: Worldwatch Institute, November, 1993.

———.*Net Loss: Fish, Jobs, and the Marine Environment.* Worldwatch Paper No. 120. Washington, DC: Worldwatch Institute, July 1994.

Chapter 10 Property Rights and Takings:
The Law and the Political Tradition

Blackstone, Sir William. *Commentaries on the Laws of England,* vols. 1 and 2, Edited by Chitty, et al. Philadelphia: Lippincott, 1856.

Epstein, Richard. "Takings: Descent and Resurrection." 1987 *Sup.Ct.Rev.* 1,4.

———.*Takings.* Cambridge, MA: Harvard University Press, 1985.

Lewis, Thomas A. "Cloaked in a Wise Disguise." *National Wildlife* (Oct./Nov. 1992): pp. 4–9.

———."You Can't Judge a Group by Its Cover." *National Wildlife* (Oct./Nov. 1992).

Locke, John. *Two Treatises of Government.* Introduced and edited by Peter Laslett. New York: Cambridge Press, 1963.

Lucas v. South Carolina Coastal Council No. 91-453 (U.S. June 29, 1992) 22 *Environmental Law Reporter* 21104.

O'Callaghan, Kate. "Whose Agenda for America?" *Audubon* (Sept./Oct. 1992): pp. 80–91.

Index